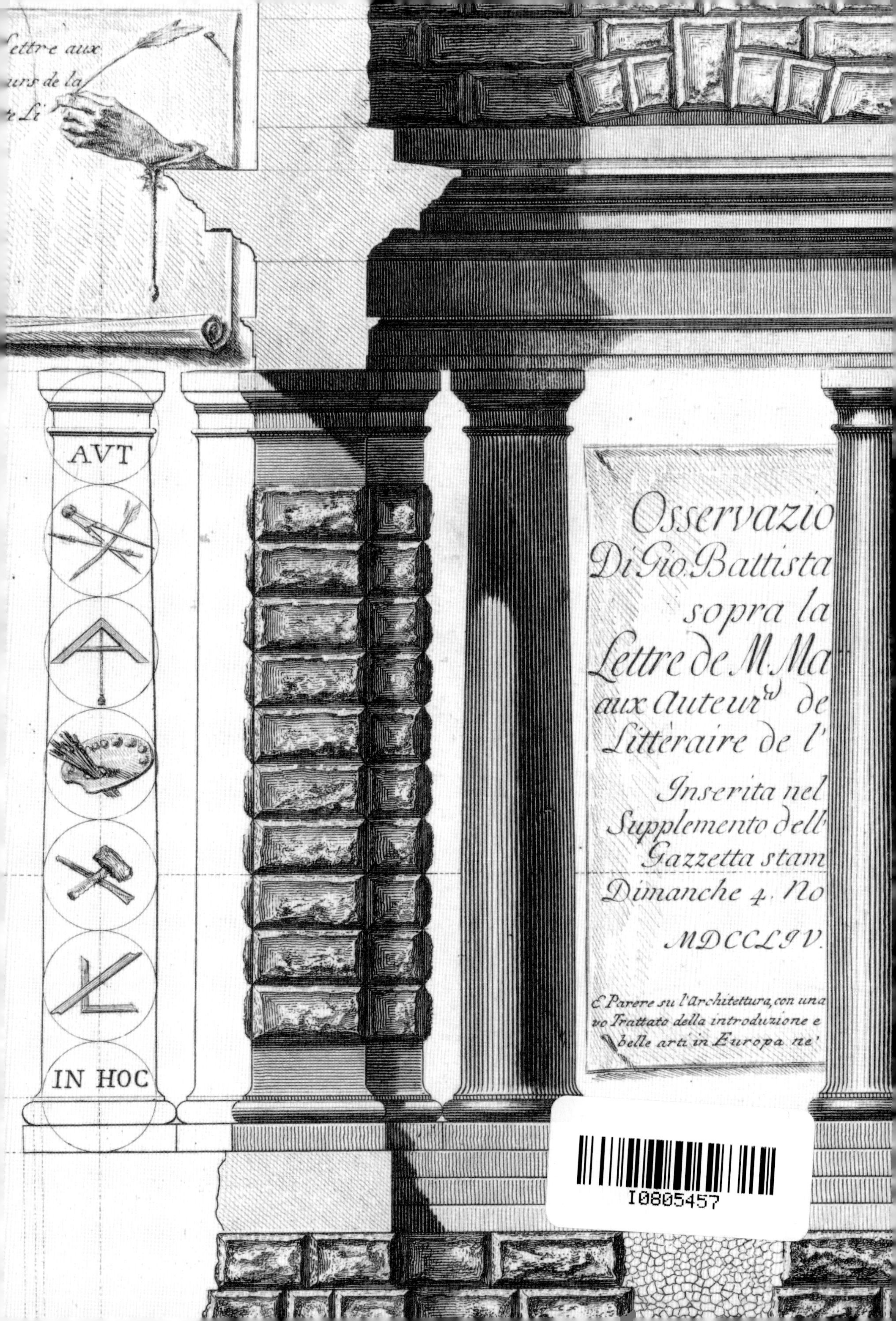
ettre aux
urs de la
AVT
IN HOC
Osservazio
Di Gio. Battista
sopra la
Lettre de M. Ma
aux Auteurs de
Littéraire de l'
Inserita nel
Supplemento dell'
Gazzetta stam
Dimanche 4. No
MDCCLIV.
e Parere su l'Architettura, con una
vo Trattato della introduzione e
belle arti in Europa ne'

Observations on the Letter of Monsieur Mariette

Published by the Getty Research Institute

Giovanni Battista Piranesi

Observations on the Letter of Monsieur Mariette

with
Opinions on Architecture, and a Preface to a New Treatise on the Introduction and Progress of the Fine Arts in Europe in Ancient Times

Introduction by John Wilton-Ely
Translation by Caroline Beamish and David Britt

Texts & Documents

The Getty Research Institute Publications Program
Thomas Crow, *Director, Getty Research Institute*
Gail Feigenbaum, *Associate Director, Programs*
Julia Bloomfield, *Head, Publications Program*

Texts & Documents
Julia Bloomfield, Kurt W. Forster, Harry F. Mallgrave, Thomas F. Reese, Michael S. Roth, and Salvatore Settis, *Publications Committee*

Observations on the Letter of Monsieur Mariette; with Opinions on Architecture, and a Preface to a New Treatise on the Introduction and Progress of the Fine Arts in Europe in Ancient Times
Francesco Dal Co, *Editorial Consultant*
Michelle Bonnice, *Manuscript Editor*

Translation of Giovanni Battista Piranesi, *Osservazioni sopra la lettre de M. Mariette aux auteurs de la* Gazette littéraire de l'Europe, *inserita nel supplemento dell'istessa gazzetta stampata dimanche 4. novembre MDCCLIV; e Parere su l'architettura, con una prefazione ad un nuovo trattato Della introduzione e del progresso delle belle arti in Europa ne' tempi antichi* (Rome: Generoso Salomoni, 1765)

Published by the Getty Research Institute, Los Angeles
Getty Publications
1200 Getty Center Drive, Suite 500
Los Angeles, CA 90049-1682
www.getty.edu

Printed in the United States of America

06 05 04 03 02 5 4 3 2 1

Cover: Giovanni Battista Piranesi, *Osservazioni . . .*, pl. III (detail). See page 134
Frontispiece: Giovanni Battista Piranesi, *Osservazioni . . .*, title page (detail). See page 125

Library of Congress Cataloging-in-Publication Data
Piranesi, Giovanni Battista, 1720–1778.
[Osservazioni di Giovanni Battista Piranesi sopra la lettre de M. Mariette aux auteurs de la Gazette littéraire de l'Europe. English]
Observations on the letter of Monsieur Mariette : with opinions on architecture, and a preface to a new treatise on the introduction and progress of the fine arts in Europe in ancient times / Giovanni Battista Piranesi ; introduction by John Wilton-Ely ; translation by Caroline Beamish and David Britt.
p. cm.—(Texts & documents)
Includes bibliographical references and index.
ISBN 0-89236-636-2
1. Architecture—Early works to 1800. 2. Architecture, Classical. 3. Architecture—Aesthetics. 4. Mariette, Pierre Jean, 1694–1774. 5. Architectural criticism—Europe—History—18th century. I. Wilton-Ely, John. II. Title. III. Series.
NA2515 .P57 2002
722'.7'0937–dc21

2002002595

Contents

ix Foreword

xi Acknowledgments

1 Introduction
John Wilton-Ely

Observations on the Letter of Monsieur Mariette; with Opinions on Architecture, and a Preface to a New Treatise on the Introduction and Progress of the Fine Arts in Europe in Ancient Times

87 Observations by Giovanni Battista Piranesi on the Letter of Monsieur Mariette to the Authors of the *Gazette littéraire de l'Europe,* Included in the Supplement of the *Gazette* Published Sunday, 4 November 1764

102 Opinions on Architecture: A Dialogue

115 On the Introduction and Progress of the Fine Arts in Europe in Ancient Times

125 Engravings for the *Observations*

142 Editorial Notes

154 Selected Bibliography

171 Illustration Credits

172 Index

Foreword

These three short texts by Giovanni Battista Piranesi (1720–78) represent one installment in a trilogy of works centering on the eighteenth-century Graeco-Roman debate to be published in the Texts & Documents series. It accompanies the two great archaeological and historical studies of Julien-David Le Roy (1724–1803) and Johann Joachim Winckelmann (1717–68).

The issues debated—always heatedly—were explosive in terms of their impact on the fine arts. Greece or Rome: Which rightly serves as the model for Western artistic practice? Which allows greater expressive power? Which possesses the aesthetic keynote for a new art challenging the limits of classicism?

Le Roy's *Ruins of the Most Beautiful Monuments of Greece* (1758; 2d ed. 1770) presented the first pictorial and literary survey of Greek architecture with its distinct and intriguing proportions. It is a young and intellectually detached survey of a culture still mysteriously remote in time and situated somewhere near the faint boundaries of Western art. Next Winckelmann's *History of the Art of Antiquity* (1764) offered an innovative approach to ancient works, laying out a history of styles in their gradual growth and somewhat precipitous decline. Greek art is understood to form the apex of the classical past, and all subsequent creations (including Roman copies) necessarily become inferior imitation. Piranesi responded in 1765 with his "Roman" defense. The culture of the classical Italians was never inferior to Greek culture, he contended; the Romans inherited their artistic talents not from the Hellenes but from the Etruscans. They were engineers of incomparable imagination and constructional daring; their works were inventive and sublime while those of the Greeks were merely pretty.

There emerged no clear victor in this dispute, except perhaps the dynamics of artistic development. Architects in the second half of the eighteenth century drew freely upon the competing sensitivities—ultimately reducing classical form to geometric severity (Claude-Nicolas Ledoux) while at the same time enlivening its frugal surfaces with emblematic nuance (Sir John Soane)—and the classical ideal transposed itself into a pluralistic historicism.

—Harry F. Mallgrave

Acknowledgments

The preparation of this volume owes considerable debts to a wide community of scholars with whom I have been in contact over the past thirty years of Piranesi studies, and it would be impossible to name here all who have enriched my understanding of the great Venetian. Many insights developed in exchanges with several generations of students as well as through fruitful discussions with colleagues during international conferences and work on three exhibitions devoted to Piranesi. Those scholars who have been of immediate assistance with regard to this publication include Robert and Susan Cockroft, Joseph Connors, Cara D. Denison, the late John Fleming, Christoph Luitpold Frommel, Silvia Gavuzzo-Stewart, Alvar Gonzáles-Palacios, Mario Gori Sassoli, Hugh Honour, Barbara Jatta, Elisabeth Kieven, Lesley Lewis, Heather Hyde Minor, Linda Murray, John A. Pinto, Andrew Robison, Frank Salmon, Damie Stillman, Marco Venturi, David Watkin, and Silla Zamboni.

I should like to pay tribute to the generous support given by staff and colleagues at two institutions where I held visiting research fellowships during the preparation of this work, namely, the Bibliotheca Hertziana, Rome, and the Center for Advanced Study in the Visual Arts, National Gallery of Art, Washington, D.C. The staff of various other institutions and libraries have also been of particular help, especially those at the British Library, the Courtauld Institute of Art, the Royal Institute of British Architects' British Architectural Library, the Society of Antiquaries, and the Warburg Institute, London; the Avery Architectural and Fine Arts Library of Columbia University and the Pierpont Morgan Library, New York; and the libraries of the American Academy in Rome and the British School at Rome.

In the development of my introduction, invaluable suggestions and additions have come from stimulating exchanges with the series editor Harry F. Mallgrave and editorial consultant Francesco Dal Co, while significant contributions have been made in the final stages by the manuscript editor Michelle Bonnice. This publication has also benefited from a remarkable empathy with the minds and personalities of Piranesi and Mariette in the translation contributed by Caroline Beamish and David Britt.

Last but not least, I owe a never-ending debt of gratitude to my wife, Valerie, whose own writing has been frequently and generously put aside in order to discuss and improve the text at critical moments.

—John Wilton-Ely

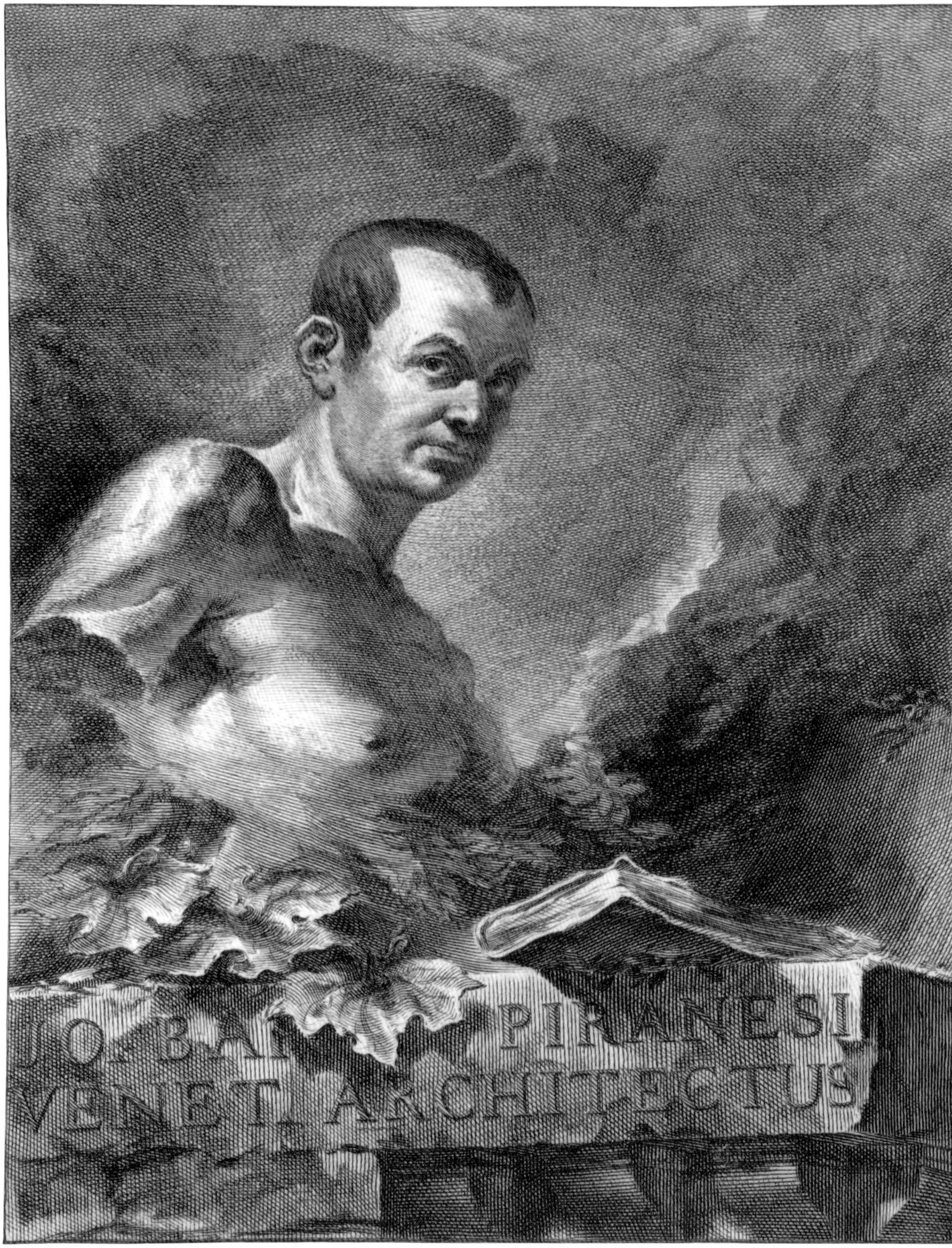

Fig. 1. Felice Polanzani (Italian, 1700–1783)
Jo. Bap. Piranesi Venet. Architectus, 1750, etching, 38 × 28.5 cm (15 × 11¼ in.)
From Giovanni Battista Piranesi, *Opere varie di architettura, prospettive, grotteschi, antichità* (Rome: n.p., 1750), frontispiece

Introduction

John Wilton-Ely

The movement of neoclassicism, which formed an integral part of the European Enlightenment in its radical questioning of received notions in all branches of human knowledge, was deeply involved with the emergence of new and far-reaching historical attitudes toward the past. The unprecedented archaeological discoveries made during the second half of the eighteenth century at sites ranging from southern Italy and the eastern Mediterranean to Egypt and the Near East challenged the conventions of classical design. The latter were represented by the enormously influential writings of the first-century B.C. Roman architect Vitruvius, whose *De architectura* was the only treatise on architecture to survive from antiquity. The freshly revealed archaeological material, as illustrated in an array of sophisticated and widely disseminated publications, not only fostered a revolutionary awareness of the plurality and relativity of historical styles but also led to the search for consciously original and contemporary forms of expression. The resulting concept of modernity set neoclassicism apart from past revivals of antiquity to which this radical movement was, nevertheless, closely related.

The quest for a consciously modern style was to involve strongly divergent approaches to architectural design, as strikingly focused in the Graeco-Roman debate. On one side was a relatively doctrinaire belief in formal severity and technical function—values that certain theorists traced back to the primitive origins of human history, grounded in Nature, and enshrined in the art and architecture of ancient Greece. On the other side, in strong reaction to this rationalist viewpoint, was a belief in creative diversity and an evolutionary system of design in which richness and complexity were essential values; each generation was seen to contribute innovations and fresh symbolic meanings in a progressive and open-ended process. This approach was exemplified, according to proponents of this position, by the architects and designers of the Roman Empire, who had assimilated and improved ideas derived from other cultures in their achievements. A contemporary nationalist dimension was to be added to this eighteenth-century debate, as there was a tendency for French and German theorists to advocate the superiority of the Greeks, while Italian scholars and architects attempted to demonstrate the essentially indigenous roots of Roman culture, which they argued was influenced primarily by the Etruscans rather than the early Greeks.

The prominent role of the architect and engraver Giovanni Battista Piranesi

(1720–78) in this debate was to lead him by the mid-1760s to abandon the narrow limits of this largely academic quarrel. Out of his complex polemical exchanges of the 1740s and 1750s was to emerge a challenging theoretical standpoint involving an eclectic system of design, potentially embracing all cultures, which he presented in "Parere su l'architettura" (1765; Opinions on architecture). By the time Piranesi published this dialogue, which is the central portion of the three-part work translated here, the controversy had reached new heights of learned dispute. However, his dominant idea of exploiting unfettered flights of the imagination had been a long-standing aesthetic conviction in Piranesi's professional career. It was manifested in his earliest publications involving engraved fantasies and speculative compositions, which complemented his achievements as a *vedutista* and an archaeologist. These conceptions were to prove an essential factor in Piranesi's impact on many foreign architects studying in Rome in the decades leading up to this critical publication, which, significantly, appeared as he began to receive commissions as a practicing architect and designer.[1]

The Formative Years: *Venice and Rome*

An inclination for controversy was endemic in Piranesi's character. His formative years were spent in Venice in the intellectual circle of his maternal uncle, the architect Matteo Lucchesi, where Piranesi was introduced to the debate regarding the Etruscan roots of Italic culture as well as to the achievements of ancient Roman technology.[2] Lucchesi, in addition to fulfilling architectural commissions, was a leading official (*vice-noto*) in the Magistrato delle Acque, the state organization responsible for the republic's harbor works and the vast walls of cyclopean masonry (*murazze*) protecting the Venetian lagoon from the predatory Adriatic. Besides concerning himself with the maritime structures of the ancient Romans, Lucchesi became involved in protracted antiquarian disputes, such as that provoked by the claim of the eminent Veronese scholar Scipione Maffei to have discovered an Etruscan entablature.[3] Close associates of Lucchesi included two of his colleagues in the Magistrato, Giovanni Scalfurotto and the latter's nephew Tommaso Temanza—a designer of a particularly radical nature who, in 1735, assisted his uncle in surveying and restoring the Roman Bridge and Arch of Augustus at Rimini.[4] Piranesi received a relatively conventional architectural training under Lucchesi, and later under Scalfurotto, in what amounted to a neo-Palladian revival. This training was offset, however, by the teachings of their friend, the Franciscan Carlo Lodoli, whose highly pragmatic ideas encouraged a radical questioning of conventional attitudes toward classical architecture as a whole.[5] Lodoli's iconoclastic teachings survive only in publications by his followers, yet it is clear that his advocacy of the stone constructions of the Etruscans, as inherited from the Egyptians and passed on to the Romans, and his willingness to challenge Vitruvius on the origins of architecture left a lasting impression on Piranesi. Moreover, the young architect's polemical cast of mind was soon to be combined with a formidable skill in conveying ideas and images by means of etched plates that was to establish him as one of the greatest topographical artists and engravers of all time. Indeed, images rather than words were to be Piranesi's natural medium of expression, and his visual originality swiftly outpaced, and at times even conflicted with, his powers of verbal justification. Arriving in Rome for the first time in 1740, he quickly acquired the rudiments of etching from Giuseppe Vasi, then the leading purveyor of souvenir views in Rome, as a means of livelihood and promptly began to convert the traditional *veduta* (topographical view) from an essentially factual record to a subtle vehicle for interpretation and powerful rhetorical expression.[6]

A reliance on the catalytic power of the image was already apparent in Piranesi's earliest independent publication, the suite of sixteen etched architectural fantasies featured in his *Prima parte di architetture, e prospettive* (Part one of architecture and perspectives).[7] Produced in 1743, within three years of his arrival in Rome, this prophetic work shows Piranesi already committed—as the dedicatory text makes clear—to the reform of contemporary architectural design. By this time Rome had become a major center for the intellectual ferment of the European Enlightenment. Apart from the radical *pensionnaires* at the Académie de France à Rome, there was an ever-increasing number of outstanding foreign architects, artists, designers, and scholars studying or seeking patronage, often under the aegis of the Grand Tour.[8] The church establishment itself contained a number of reformist clerics, sympathetic to Enlightenment thought and critical of the conventional traditions in the visual arts as well as literature and political thought. The city, moreover, was approaching the end of a considerable building boom that had produced Francesco De Sanctis's Spanish Steps, the initial stages of Nicola Salvi's Fontana di Trevi, Alessandro Galilei's Lateran facade, and Ferdinando Fuga's Palazzo della Consulta and facade for Santa Maria Maggiore.[9]

Piranesi, confronted by the grandeur of the ancient ruins but faced, as he perceived it, with a dearth of inspiring commissions, threw his architectural energies into the creative resources of his own imaginative world. As a number of surviving sketches and drawings reveal, he pioneered the architectural fantasy as an exploratory medium for experimental design as well as a means of communicating his original ideas to receptive colleagues.[10] In the *Prima parte*'s dedication, to his earliest patron, the Venetian builder Nicola Giobbe, Piranesi castigated the unimaginative designers of his time, as well as their clients, for neglecting the sheer inspirational potential of the antiquity that surrounded them. As he expressed it, "these speaking ruins have filled my spirit with images that accurate drawings, even such as those of the immortal Palladio, could never have succeeded in conveying.... Therefore, having the idea of presenting to the world some of these images, but not hoping for an architect of these times who could effectively execute some of them.... there seems to be no recourse than for me or some other modern architect to explain his ideas through his drawings."[11] Piranesi went on to thank Giobbe for not only giving him the run of his extensive collection of paintings, drawings, books, and engravings, as well as introducing him to leading architects,

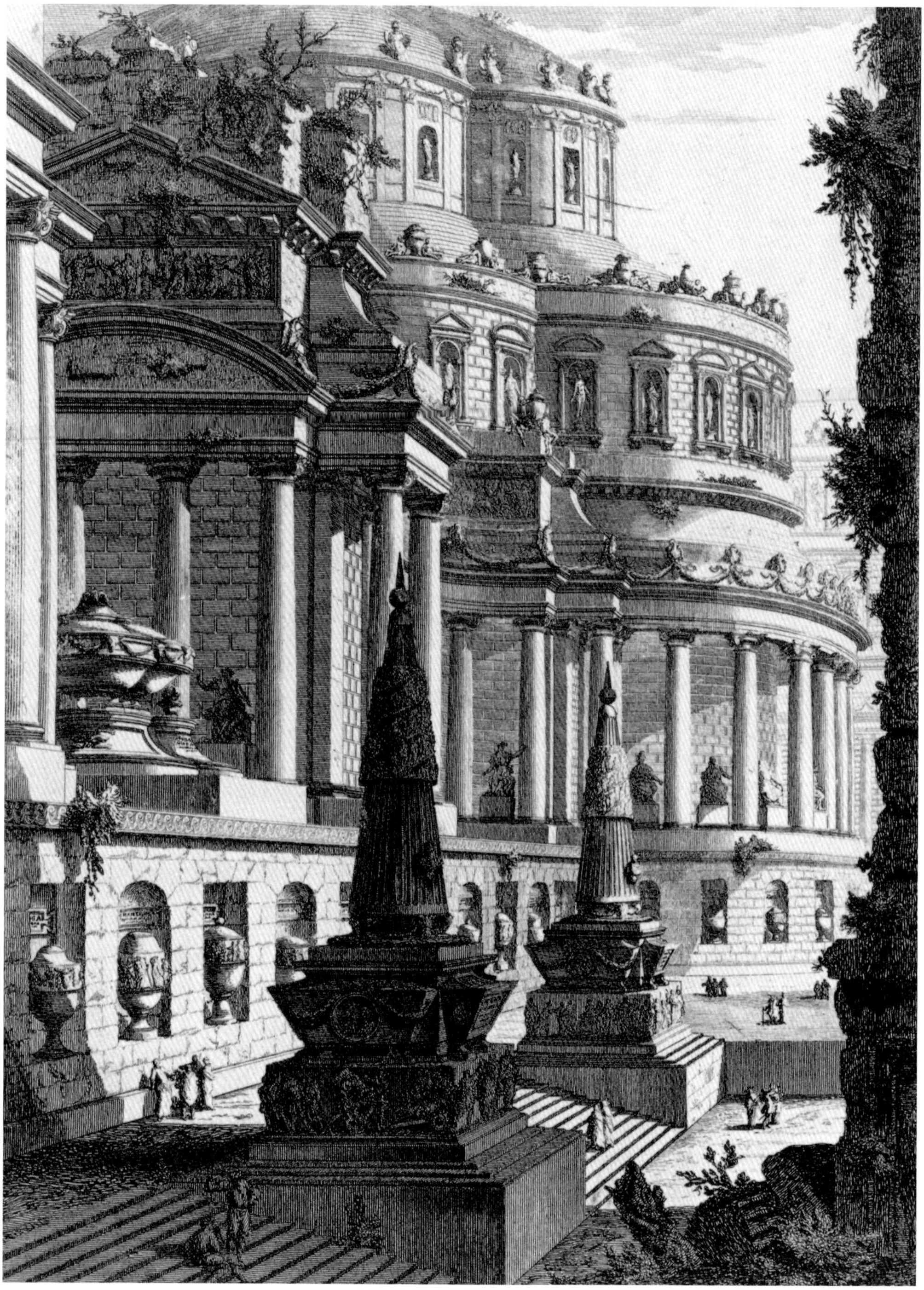

Fig. 2. Giovanni Battista Piranesi (Italian, 1720–78)
Mausoleo antico eretto per le ceneri d'un imperadore romano..., 1743, etching, 35 × 25 cm (13¾ × 9⅞ in.) From Giovanni Battista Piranesi, *Prima parte di architetture, e prospettive* (Rome: Stamperia de' Fratelli Pagliarini, 1743)

such as Salvi and Luigi Vanvitelli, but also showing him "how one can make praiseworthy use of the discoveries of our great predecessors in new forms."[12]

The critical stance of the *Prima parte* probably also reflects Piranesi's early involvement in the intellectual circle of the Tuscan cleric Giovanni Gaetano Bottari, whose villa, l'Archetto, was to be the focus of radical discussions strongly influenced by Jansenist beliefs and English empirical philosophy.[13] Bottari, who was librarian to the Corsini family (with access to an important collection of engravings) as well as the Vatican, was a leading member of a group of antiquarians and scholars who strongly disapproved of contemporary art and architecture on theoretical grounds. In their criticism of late baroque expression, they were to pioneer the way for neoclassical reform a generation before the arrival in Rome of Johann Joachim Winckelmann. Probably on the introduction of Bottari, Piranesi also became a member of the Accademia dell'Arcadia. Itself a focus of speculative debate, this literary society included the visual arts in its wide intellectual purview; indeed, Piranesi was to inscribe his Arcadian pseudonym, Salcindio Tiseio, on the fourth state of the frontispiece to the *Prima parte*.[14] Bottari was instrumental in extending the intellectual foundations, already laid by Lucchesi, Lodoli, and Temanza in Venice, of Piranesi's attitude to the classical past.

Piranesi's experimental activity, represented by the idiosyncratic compositions of the *Prima parte*, such as the *Mausoleo antico eretto per le ceneri d'un imperadore romano* (Ancient mausoleum erected for the ashes of a Roman emperor) (fig. 2), soon brought him into the circle of art and architectural students at the Académie de France. Then the liveliest center of research in Rome, the Académie was housed in the Palazzo Mancini, opposite Piranesi's print-selling business in the Corso. While there is no evidence that Piranesi ever had a formal connection with the Académie, his friendships with a number of the student *pensionnaires* and his involvement in their creation of temporary festival architecture in Rome as well as their exercises in ideal design are well documented.[15] Piranesi's conceptions were to influence a number of *pensionnaires*, as is evident in the radical and elemental forms of the festival designs by Louis-Joseph Le Lorrain and the imaginative breadth of Charles Michel-Ange Challe's fantasy compositions.[16] Meanwhile, Piranesi's fresh acts of speculative composition, based on his detailed studies of antique remains, appeared in a further group of etched fantasies collected together in the *Opere varie di architettura* (Selected architectural works) of 1750. Compositions such as the monumental *Parte di ampio magnifico porto* (Part of a spacious and magnificent harbor) (fig. 3) and the visionary *Pianta di ampio magnifico collegio* (Plan for a spacious and magnificent college) (fig. 4) were to make an exceptionally powerful impression on the generation of *pensionnaires* that included Charles de Wailly and Marie-Joseph Peyre. With the subsequent dispersal of these designers, Piranesi's seminal ideas gradually entered the mainstream of French neoclassical architecture, as demonstrated in the planning and the spatial and monumental treatment of exceptional buildings such as de Wailly's Château de Montmusard, near Dijon (1764–72),

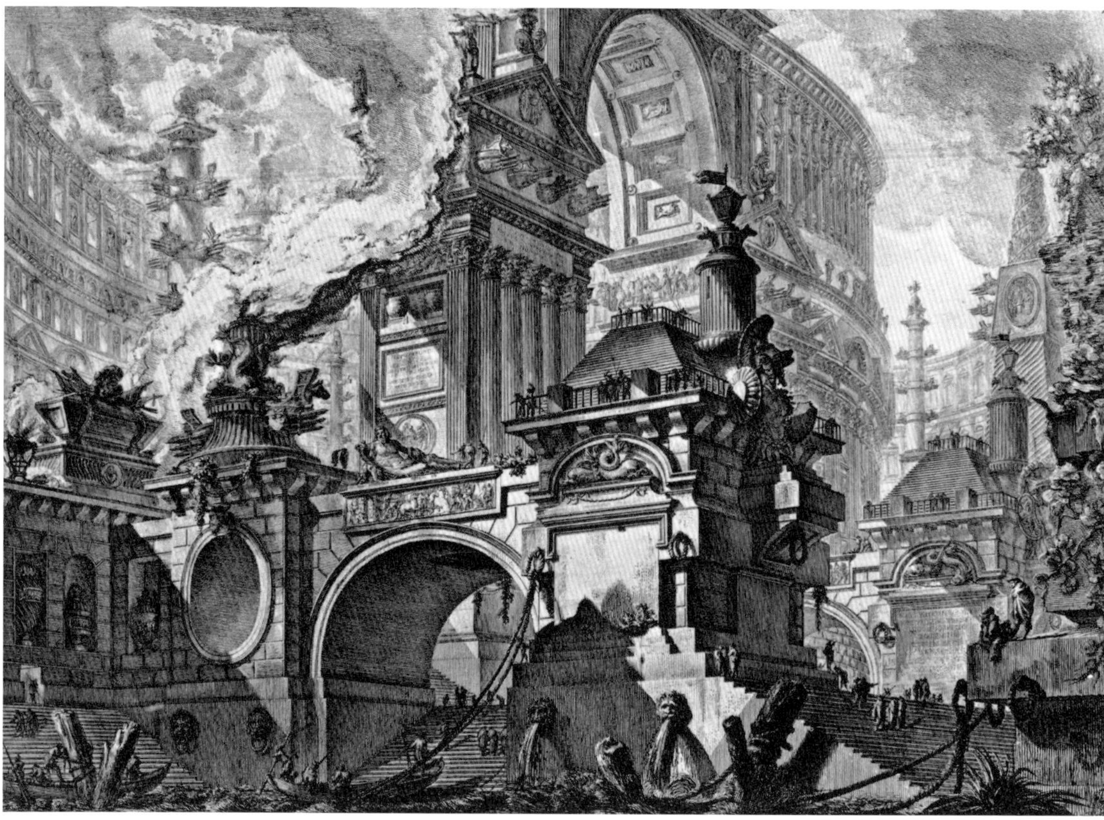

Fig. 3. Giovanni Battista Piranesi (Italian, 1720–78)
Parte di ampio magnifico porto all'uso degli antichi romani . . ., 1750, etching, 40 × 55 cm (15¾ × 21⅝ in.)
From Giovanni Battista Piranesi, *Opere varie di architettura, prospettive, grotteschi, antichità* (Rome: n.p., 1750)

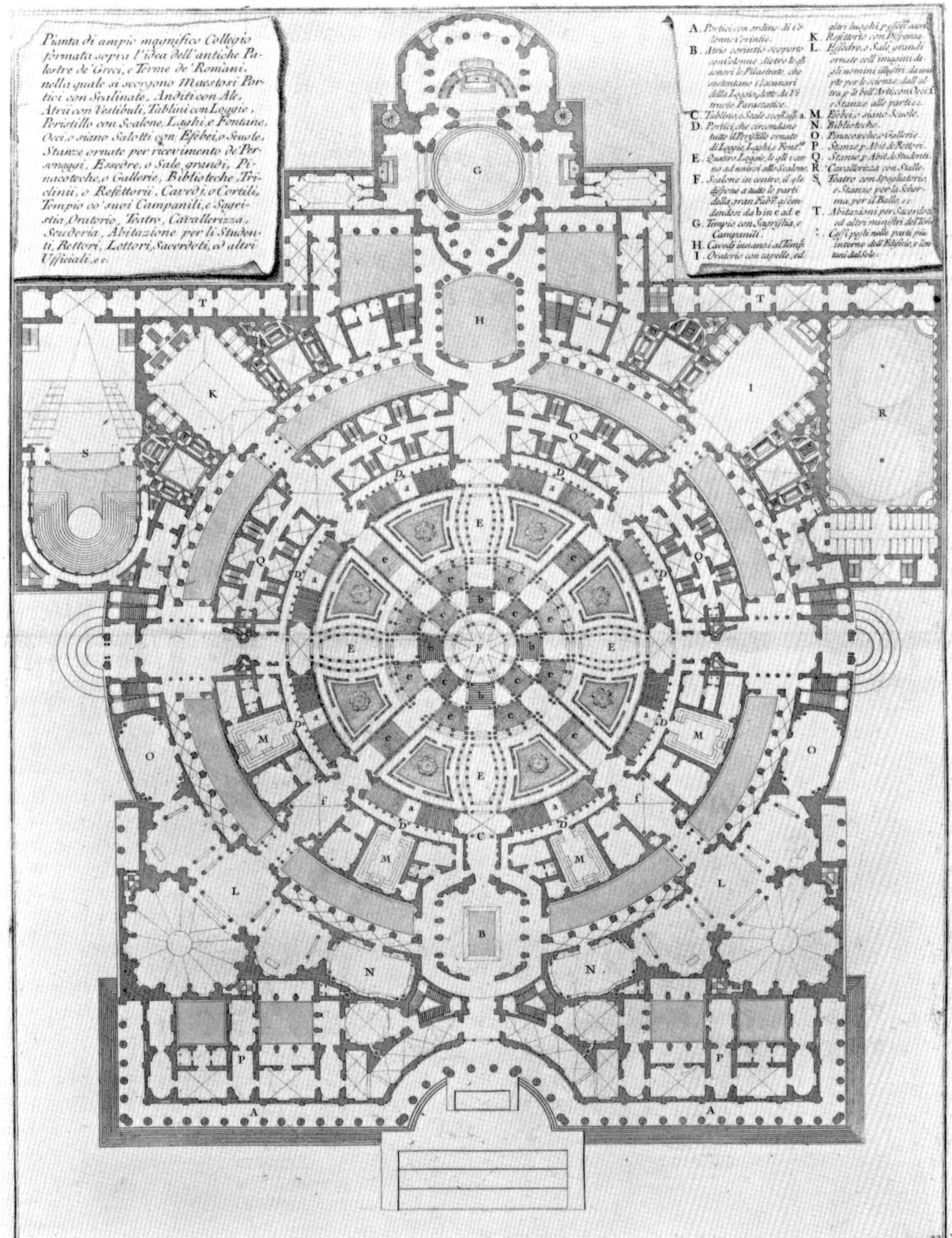

Fig. 4. Giovanni Battista Piranesi (Italian, 1720–78)
Pianta di ampio magnifico collegio . . ., 1750, etching,
61 × 45 cm (24 × 17¾ in.)
From Giovanni Battista Piranesi, *Opere varie di architettura, prospettive, grotteschi, antichità* (Rome: n.p., 1750)

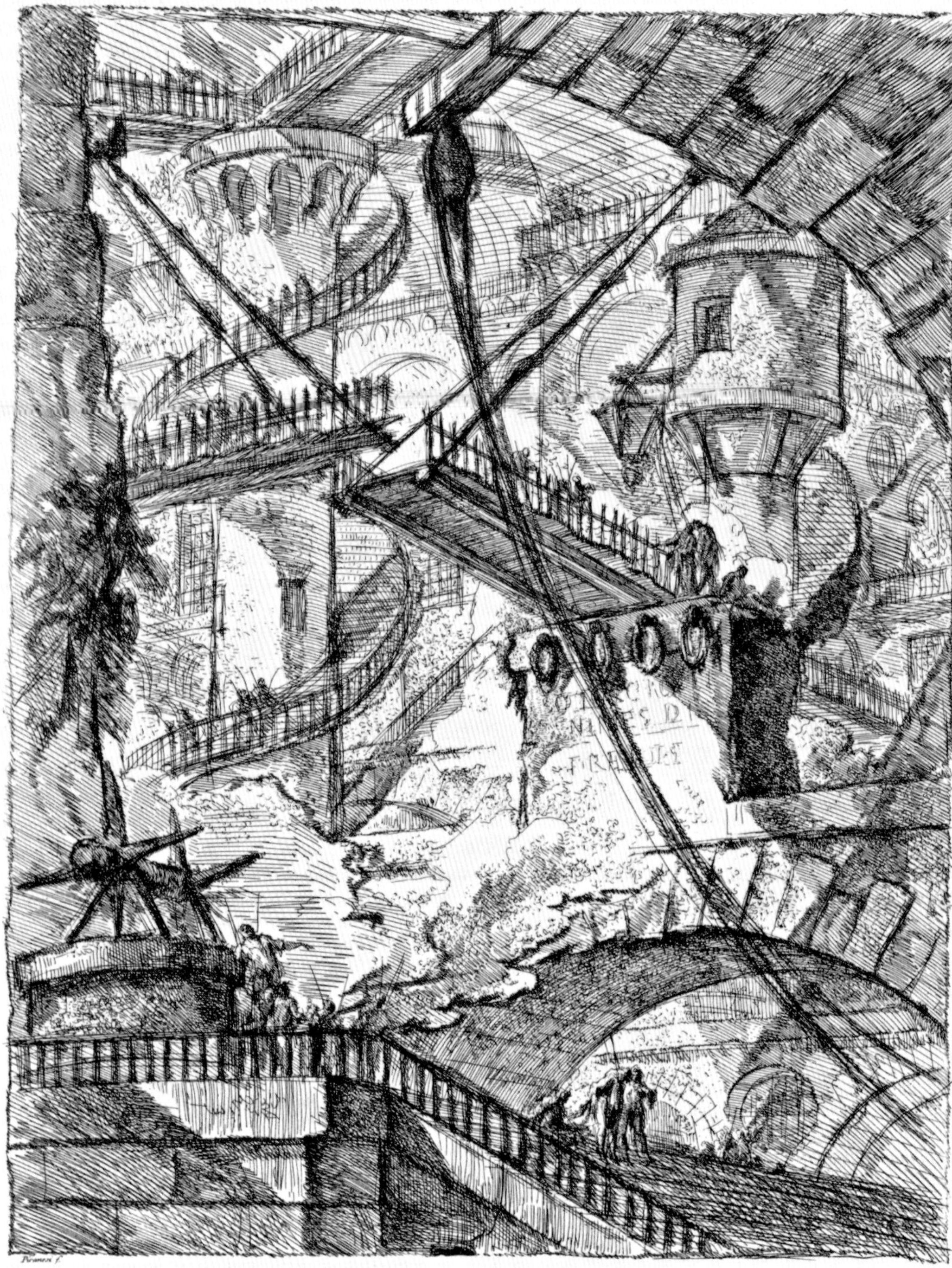

Fig. 5. Giovanni Battista Piranesi (Italian, 1720–78)
"The Drawbridge," ca. 1745–50, etching, 55 × 41 cm (21 ⅝ × 16 ⅛ in.)
From Giovanni Battista Piranesi, *Invenzioni capric di carceri* (Rome: Giovanni Bouchard, ca. 1745–50)

and his collaboration with Peyre on the theater of the Comédie-Française, Paris (1779–82; renamed the Théâtre de l'Odéon in 1797).[17]

The compositions of the *Prima parte* and other etched fantasies, as well as the surviving drawings of a similar nature, show Piranesi's intensely speculative use of the *capriccio* (fantasy) for architectural experiment. This activity was to be taken further with Piranesi's anonymous issue of a suite of fourteen etched fantasies, the *Invenzioni capric di carceri* (Fanciful images of prisons). As initially published around 1745, these appear to have been carried out largely as an exercise in conceptual analysis (fig. 5). However, Piranesi was to refashion these plates in the heat of the Graeco-Roman controversy and amplify the group by two additional compositions (see fig. 15) and by enhancing or adding certain arcane inscriptions. Reissued in 1761 as *Carceri d'invenzione* (Prisons of the imagination), and bearing Piranesi's name for the first time, this controversial suite of disturbing images was to have a longer and more extensive influence on the European imagination, literary as well as visual, than any other group of his graphic works.[18] The highly controlled use of perspective in the *Carceri* to evoke spatial ambiguity by means of an etching process of unparalleled freedom has been seen by Manfredo Tafuri to contain "the two poles of Piranesi's research—the evocation of a primordial *structurality* connected to the celebration of the *Lex romana,* of the idea of justice, and the disarticulation of the structure evoked."[19] Whatever interpretation of this initial state of these plates is adopted, it is essential to disregard the heavily loaded symbolism and penal imagery added in the later version and to regard these highly personal and intimate early works as primarily a means of visual exploration at a time when the young architect was attempting to push the boundaries of formal invention to entirely new levels of expression.

Antiquity for the Designer

Archaeological investigation was becoming increasingly important to Piranesi in the decade after his arrival in Rome, as reflected in the individually published plates of the *Vedute di Roma* (Views of Rome). The outstanding quality of these views led him to develop a prosperous business with Grand Tour visitors, but wishing to devote his graphic skills to more serious functions, Piranesi decided by the early 1750s to disseminate the artistic range and architectural achievements of ancient Rome through finely etched images for the benefit of a more specialist readership. Already in 1753 his admiration for the richness of Roman architectural decoration had led him to publish "for the use of painters, sculptors, and architects" the *Trofei di Ottaviano Augusto* (Trophies of Octavian Augustus), featuring two ornamental reliefs on the Capitoline Hill.[20] But as the scope of his inquiries expanded, it became clear that a far more ambitious work was required, and by 1755 Piranesi was developing a four-volume work that would provide a comprehensive survey of the surviving remains of Rome. Published in 1756, *Le antichità romane* (The antiquities of Rome) was to prove a landmark in the history of classical archaeology, not merely in terms of its thematic range and illustrative techniques but also in the application to a hitherto restricted field of study of a fresh and highly original mind capable of combining a technical understanding of engineering and architecture with imaginative faculties of the highest order.[21] Besides marking a major advance in the communication of archaeological discoveries, *Le antichità* directed attention in a visually striking way to largely neglected aspects of the classical past. Notable among these were the techniques of Roman building science and aspects of decoration and planning that lay outside the canons of Vitruvian orthodoxy. This approach reflected Piranesi's dual aim in creating *Le antichità*, which was both to record the vanishing past for scholars and to present antiquity as a fund of experimental ideas for the inspiration of his contemporaries. The work was therefore addressed to an extraordinarily wide audience, including not only antiquarians but also practicing architects, who predictably came in for some abrasive criticism from Piranesi.

The publication of *Le antichità* involved Piranesi with his first polemical activity. The dedicatee, the young Irish nobleman, James Caulfeild, Earl of Charlemont, seems to have promised to fund this highly ambitious and costly enterprise in exchange for fulsome recognition on its title pages, but after a small initial payment, the remainder apparently failed to materialize. There being no response to Piranesi's remonstrating letters to Charlemont, after the sale of forty copies the artist suppressed the title page of the first volume and reissued it with the earl's citation ceremonially deleted from the marble slab and his heraldic achievements defaced as if with a chisel; the subsidiary title pages in the other volumes were treated likewise. After further silence from Charlemont, in 1757 Piranesi issued the text of three letters in the *Lettere di giustificazione . . . a Milord Charlemont* (Letters of justification . . . to Lord Charlemont).[22] This pamphlet, which contained miniature versions of the initial and revised plates, was widely distributed among the author's colleagues and friends as well as influential figures ranging from the pope to key patrons and connoisseurs.[23] While the dispute was, in itself, of minor consequence, the intense language of Piranesi's introductory text indicates the extent to which Piranesi had begun to identify with the material of his archaeological studies by the early 1750s; the text also articulates the significant role that, in Piranesi's view, *Le antichità* should play for contemporary designers. An attack on Rome, as much as a slight from an unworthy patron, became in effect a personal affront to the artistic genius of the Romans as reborn in himself. As he claimed, "I believe . . . that I have completed a work that will pass on to posterity and endure so long as there are men curious to know the ruins which remain of the most famous city in the universe. . . . This work is not of the kind that remains buried in the crowded shelves of libraries. Its four folio volumes comprise a new system of the ancient monuments of ancient Rome. It will be deposited in many public libraries throughout Europe."[24]

During the 1750s Piranesi's extensive contacts with members of the Académie de France and its circle in Rome were largely supplanted by those with

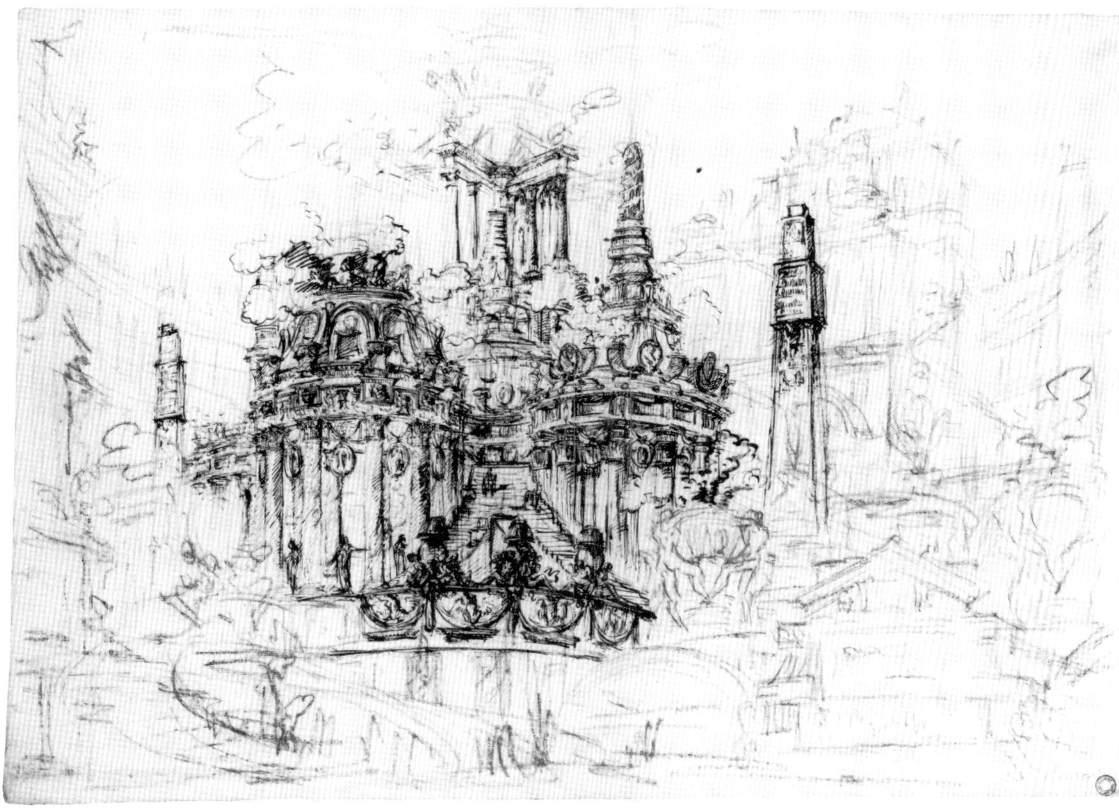

Fig. 6. Giovanni Battista Piranesi (Italian, 1720–78)
Imaginary architectural composition, late 1740s, pen and brown ink with wash over red chalk, 53.5 × 75 cm (21 1/8 × 29 1/2 in.)
London, Sir John Soane's Museum

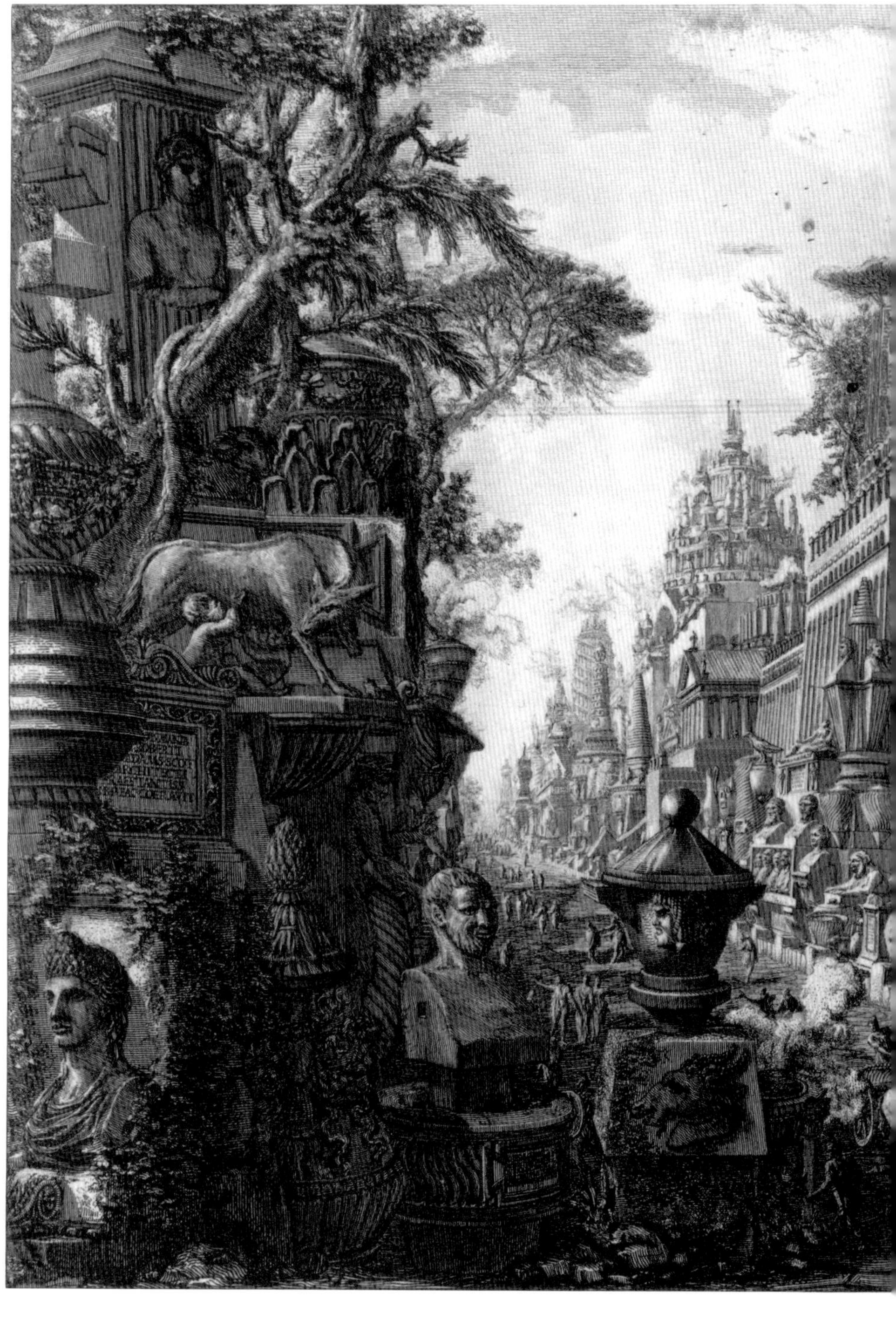

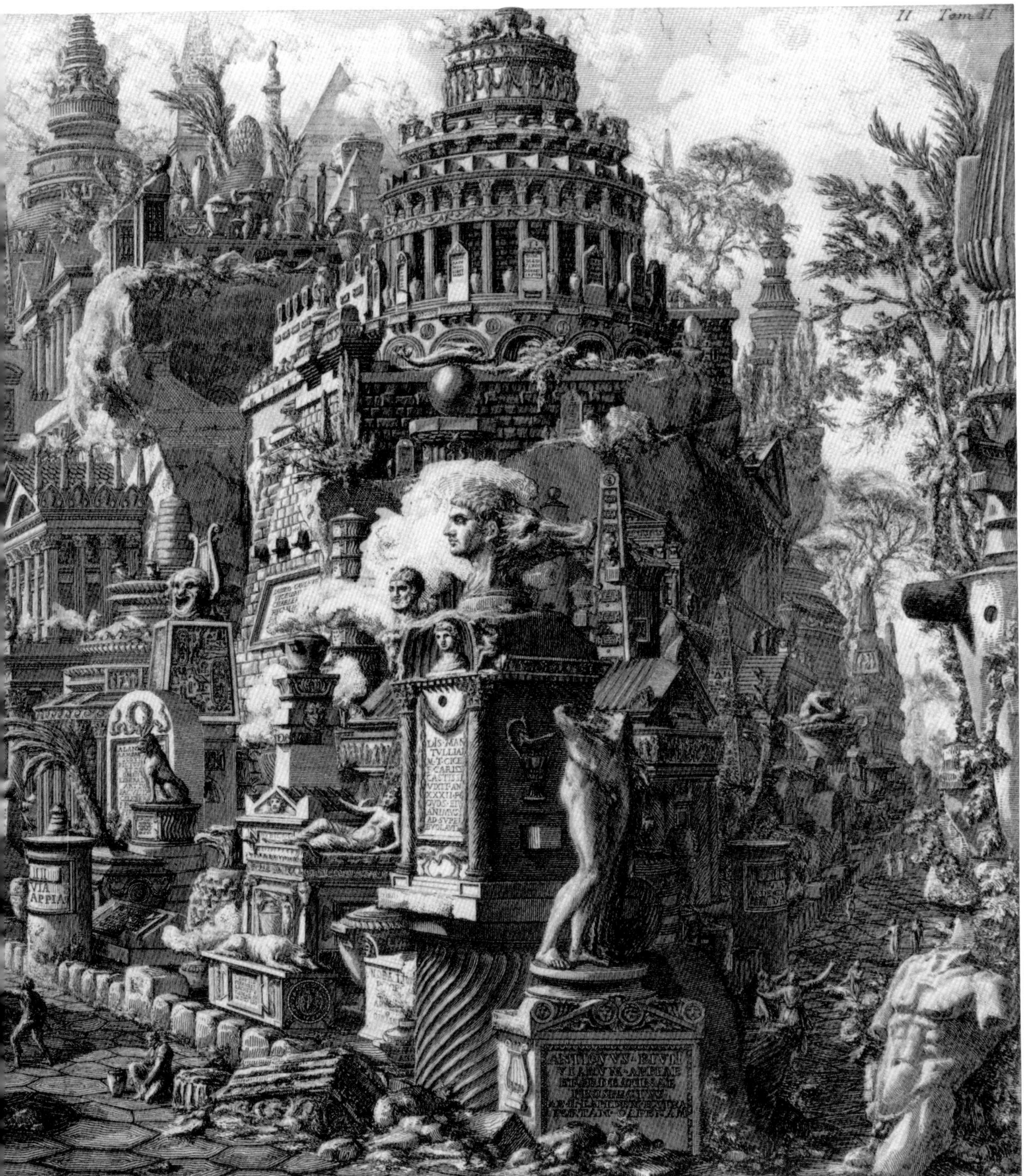

Fig. 7. Giovanni Battista Piranesi (Italian, 1720–78)
Antiquus Bivii Viarum Appiae et Ardeatinae Prospectus ad II Lapidem Extra Portam Capenam, 1756, etching, 39.5 × 64 cm (15½ × 25¼ in.)
From Giovanni Battista Piranesi, *Le antichità romane* (Rome: Stamperia di Angelo Rotilj [etc.], 1756), vol. 2, frontispiece

visiting British architects. William Chambers, Robert Adam, Robert Mylne, and George Dance the Younger all benefited from Piranesi's stimulating interpretations of the past. The diversity in response by these designers, who, unlike the French, came from a tradition of design that was inclined more to the pragmatic than the theoretical, is extremely informative. Chambers, whose work was already grounded in French avant-garde architectural training through his studies at Jacques-François Blondel's Parisian academy, regarded Piranesi's extravagant visions with considerable caution, although his designs for the major complex of public buildings at Somerset House, London (1776–86), were to reveal strong debts to the complex substructures of antiquity as interpreted in *Le antichità*.[25] Mylne's prize-winning design for Blackfriars Bridge, London (1760–69), owed much to Piranesi's analysis in *Le antichità* of ancient Roman technical construction.[26] Dance the Younger's monumental massing of his stern facades for Newgate Prison, London (1770–80), reflected ancient masonry patterns as interpreted by Piranesi, in both *Le antichità* and the refashioned plates of the *Carceri d'invenzione*.[27] Above all, it was Adam, with a shrewd eye for expanding his conventional architectural education and inheritance, who was to prove one of Piranesi's most susceptible pupils.[28] Shortly after meeting Piranesi in June 1755, Adam commented, "so amazing and ingenious fancies as he has produced in the different plans of the Temples, Baths and Palaces and other buildings I never saw and are the greatest fund for inspiring and instilling invention in any lover of architecture that can be imagined."[29] He went on to refer to two fantasy drawings that Piranesi was producing especially for him. These were similar if not identical to the two imaginary compositions, formerly belonging to Adam, that are now in the collection of Sir John Soane's Museum, London.[30] In one of these compositions (fig. 6), layer after layer of spatial boundaries, punctuated by strangely juxtaposed elements—colonnades, obelisks, vases, reliefs, and sinuous steps—lead the eye into infinity, challenging the logical, unitary system of Palladian design that Adam and his brothers had learned under their father. Returning to Britain in 1758, Adam soon proved to be one of the leading formal innovators of his age, with revolutionary designs ranging from large-scale ground plans and monumental structures, such as the country houses at Kedleston (circa 1760–70) and Syon (circa 1760–69), down to minute, fanciful, and delicate details of ornament in a wide range of domestic and public commissions in London.[31]

For all its didactic aims and parade of detached scholarship, certain aspects of *Le antichità* already reveal Piranesi's intense reactions to the early claims of the Greek Revival theorists. The febrile ornamental details of the archaeological fantasies of the Via Appia (fig. 7) and the Circus Maximus—the frontispieces to, respectively, the second and the third volumes of *Le antichità*, which were devoted to sepulchral monuments and tombs—clearly were intended as symbolic demonstrations of the superior fertility and range of Roman designers.[32] Apart from the sheer extent of its survival, this particular area of achievement provided plentiful evidence of invention and an

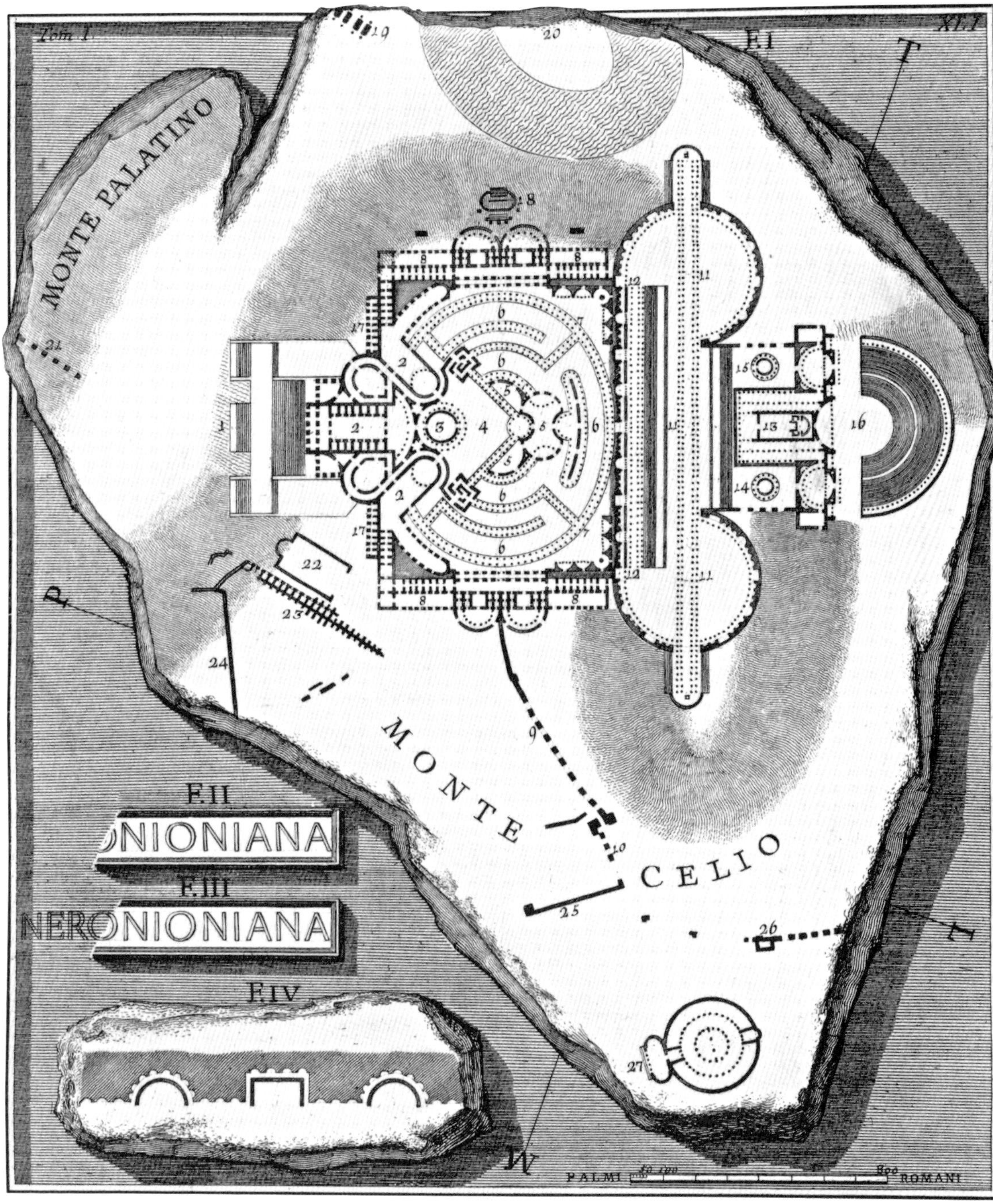

Fig. 8. Giovanni Battista Piranesi (Italian, 1720–78)
Rappresentasi nella figura I *il Ninfeo, di Nerone*..., 1756, etching, 35 × 23.5 cm (13¾ × 9¼ in.)
From Giovanni Battista Piranesi, *Le antichità romane* (Rome: Stamperia di Angelo Rotilj [etc.], 1756), vol. 1, pl. XLI

abundance of complex forms that Piranesi wished to impart to his fellow designers. (Significantly, Adam and his compatriot, the Scottish painter and scholar Allan Ramsay, were awarded inscribed tombs in the Via Appia fantasy.)[33] Moreover, among the 250 plates of this four-volume work, there is an appreciable number of highly speculative reconstructions and deliberate acts of structural and spatial exaggeration. These include images of the cyclopean scale of the assumed substructure of Hadrian's Mausoleum; the unparalleled complexity of a plan based on the few remains of the Temple of Divus Claudius, misidentified as the Nymphaeum of Nero (fig. 8); and the heroic technical apparatus allegedly used in the construction of the Tomb of Cecilia Metella. All devised as polemical statements with scant concern for veracity, they can be interpreted, at best, as images of "poetic truth."

Controversy: Della magnificenza ed architettura de' romani

By the mid-1750s, Piranesi could no longer ignore the published claims for Greek originality and assertions of the highly derivative and corrupt nature of Roman design. His first polemical salvo, the treatise *Della magnificenza ed architettura de' romani* (Concerning Roman architecture and magnificence), appeared in 1761,[34] with financial backing from the new Venetian pope, Clement XIII, the former Carlo Rezzonico. The British architects James Stuart and Nicholas Revett had issued their "Proposal" for publishing a survey of ancient Greek buildings, which would eventually appear as *The Antiquities of Athens* (1762–1816), several times from 1748 onward.[35] However, a more direct incentive for Piranesi to draw up a substantial publication on Roman design had been provided by the Jesuit priest Marc-Antoine Laugier's *Essai sur l'architecture* (Essay on architecture), which appeared in 1753.[36] Although derived from ideas advanced early in the century by Michel de Frémin and Jean-Louis, abbé de Cordemoy, this relatively modest book created a considerable impact by advancing a timely and rationalist philosophy of design in support of Greece.[37] Basing architecture on the fundamental principle of the imitation of nature, Laugier used Vitruvius's description of the rustic hut as a functional paradigm and demonstrated the evolution of wood to stone architecture as exemplified by the Greek Doric temple. Although Piranesi never refers specifically to Laugier in his publications, the impact of Laugier's ideas would have been inescapable in the circle of the Académie de France in which the Venetian still moved. Piranesi was later to claim that he had been provoked by the more superficial pamphlet praising Greek architecture, *The Investigator*, *Number 332,* issued anonymously in 1755 by his friend Allan Ramsay.[38]

Piranesi's new book was, therefore, well under way when, according to his letter to Mylne, the appearance of the French architect Julien-David Le Roy's *Les ruines des plus beaux monuments de la Grèce* (1758; The ruins of the most beautiful monuments of Greece) "contributed to its enlargement."[39] Swiftly following Stuart and Revett to Greece, Le Roy anticipated their publication by several years, producing the first sophisticated images of the Greek architecture of Athens to reach the West. According to Le Roy's supporting text, monumental architecture was a Greek creation, inherited from the Egyptians and taken over subsequently by the Romans, who had not only copied but also debased it. Referring to the classical orders, Le Roy asserted,

> it seems that the Romans lacked the kind of creative genius that allowed the Greeks to make so many discoveries. They did not create anything of note in the orders. The one that is attributed to their invention, the Composite, is only a fairly imperfect mixture of the Ionic and Corinthian, and by altering the proportions of the column from the Doric order and by multiplying the moldings of its entablature, they have perhaps made it lose a lot of its male character, which was its distinguishing feature in Greece.[40]

In Piranesi's *Della magnificenza*, the unwieldy and over-erudite text of more than two hundred pages in Italian and Latin bears the marks of scholarly help with its literary defense of Rome on the basis of Etruscan originality. However, Piranesi's attacks on Le Roy and Laugier—which rely primarily on the sequence of thirty-eight illustrations, several of them taking the form of elaborate foldout plates—are too intimately bound up with Piranesi's artistic concerns to be simply "ghosted," as was suggested at the time.[41]

Nevertheless, Piranesi's text needs to be considered in the context of contemporary Etruscan scholarship and archaeological inquiry, where cultural originality was already the subject of intense debate.[42] One of the earliest discussions of Etruscan art since antiquity occurred in the preface Giorgio Vasari wrote for the first edition of his *Le vite de' più eccellenti architetti, pittori et scultori italiani* (1550; Lives of the most eminent Italian painters, sculptors, and architects) to support his claims for the outstanding creative destiny of Tuscany. However, it was a Scottish historian, Thomas Dempster, who produced the pioneering study of this culture, *De Etruria regali* (On royal Etruria), written between 1616 and 1625 but first published between 1723 and 1726 by Thomas Coke, First Earl of Leicester. Apart from this work, it was the writings of the Neapolitan philosopher Giambattista Vico, already familiar to Piranesi from Lodoli's circle, that made the argument for the indigenous roots of Roman civilization, as derived from the Etruscans, and helped to promote a growing patriotic movement in Italy. In the Veneto, as already mentioned, Piranesi would have encountered as well the ideas of Scipione Maffei, author of the controversial *Trattato sopra la nazione etrusca e sopra gl'itali primitivi* (1739; Treatise concerning the Etruscan nation and the earliest Italians) and one of the earliest proponents of Etruscan studies in eighteenth-century Italy.[43] Promoted by this "Etruscheria," a series of early excavations had led to the foundation of the Accademia Etrusca at Cortona in 1727 and the Accademia Colombaria at Florence in 1735.[44] Meanwhile, new finds were evaluated in a substantial body of publications by scholars such as Filippo Buonarotti (who annotated Coke's publication of Dempster's study),

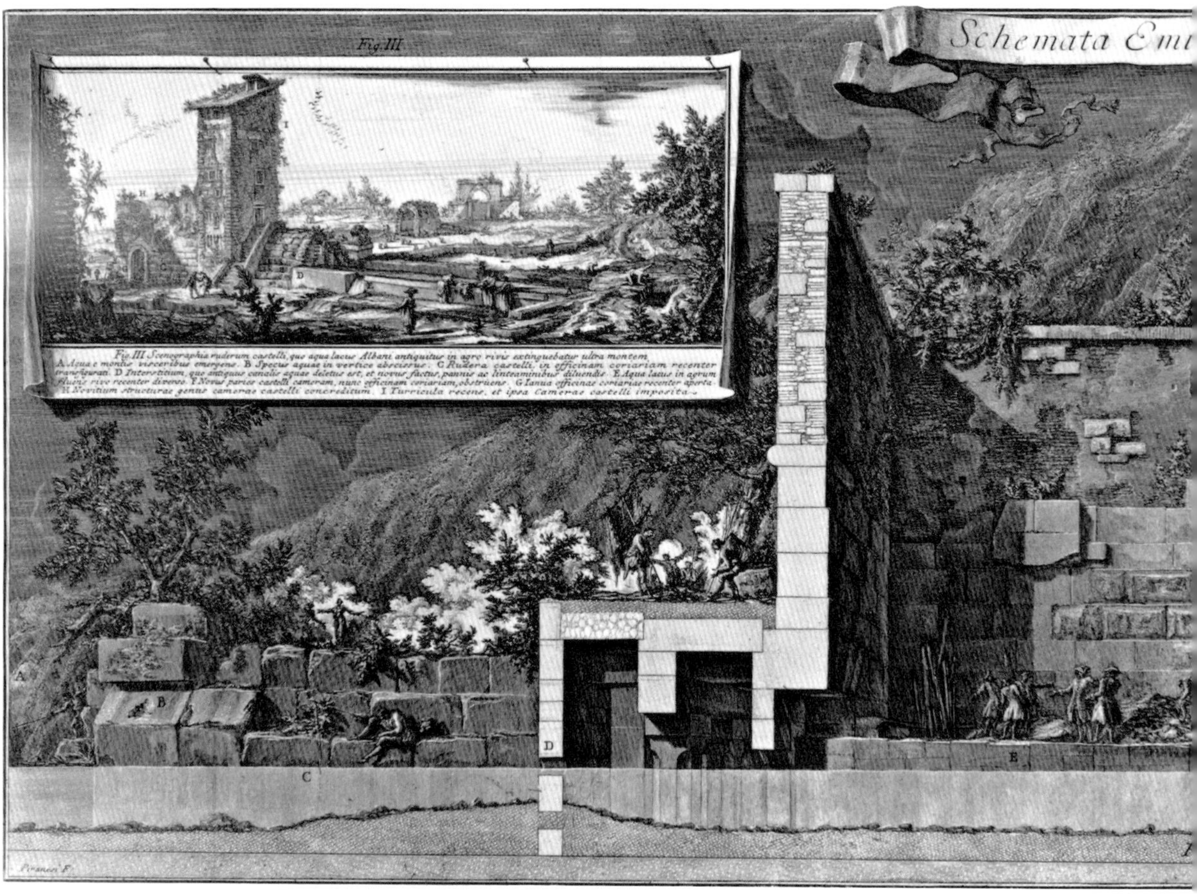

Fig. 9. Giovanni Battista Piranesi (Italian, 1720–78)
Schemata Emissarii Lacus Albani, 1761, etching, 39.7 × 110 cm (15⅝ × 43¼ in.)
From Giovanni Battista Piranesi, *Della magnificenza ed architettura de' romani . . .*
(Rome: n.p., 1761), pl. xxx

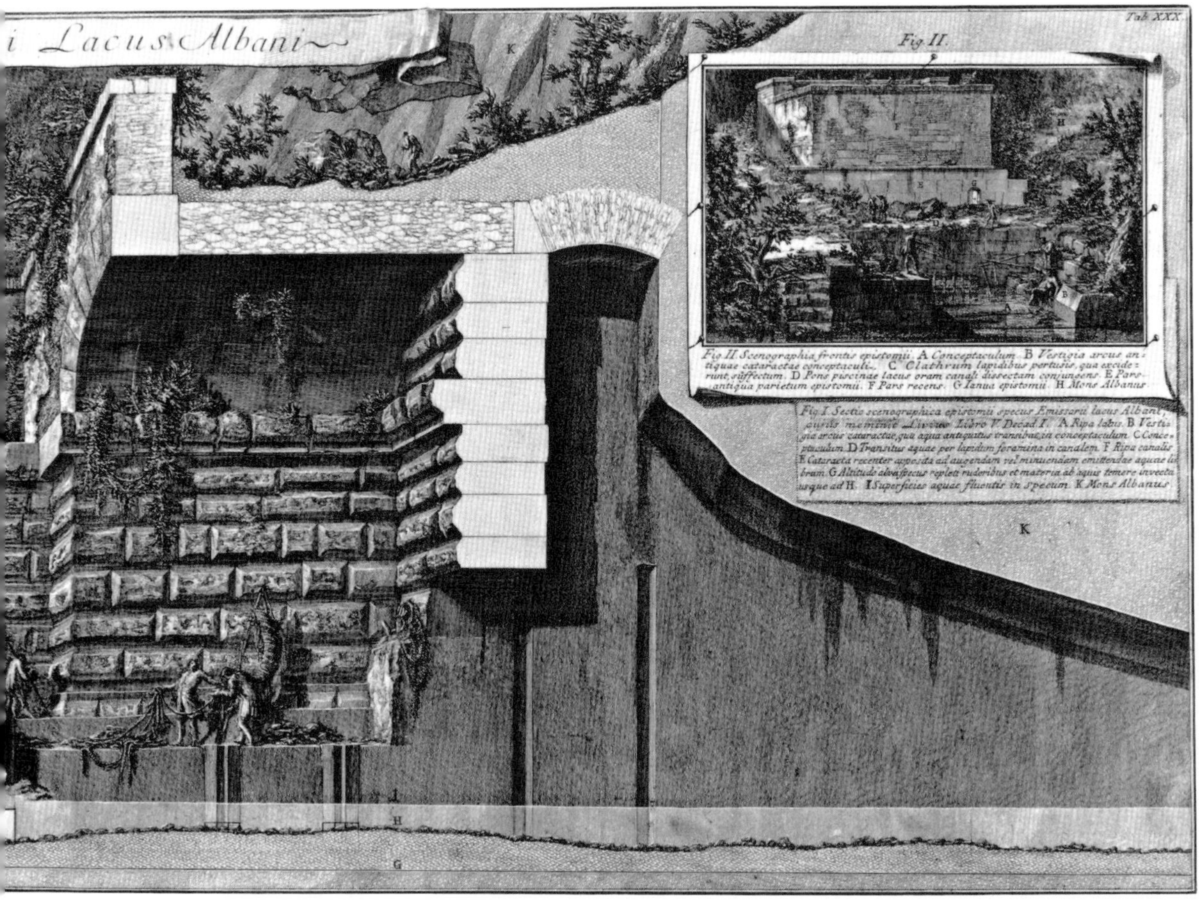
i Lacus Albani
Tab. XXX
Fig. II.
Fig. II. Scenographia frontis epistomii. A Conceptaculum. B Vestigia arcus an-
tiquae cataractae conceptaculi. C Clathrum lapidibus pertusis, qua excide-
runt, suffectum. D Pons piscinae lacus oram canali dissectam conjungens. E Pars
antiqua parietum epistomii. F Pars recens. G Ianua epistomii. H Mons Albanus.
Fig. I. Sectio scenographica epistomii specus Emissarii lacus Albani,
cujus meminit Livius Libro V. Decad. I. A Ripa lacus. B Vesti-
gia arcus cataractae, qua aqua antiquitus transibat in conceptaculum. C Conce-
ptaculum. D Transitus aquae per lapidum foramina in canalem. F Ripa canalis.
E Cataracta recenter apposita ad augendam vel minuendam emittendae aquae li-
bram. G Altitudo alvei specus repleti ruderibus et materia ab aquis temere invecta
usque ad H. I Superficies aquae fluentis in specum. K Mons Albanus.

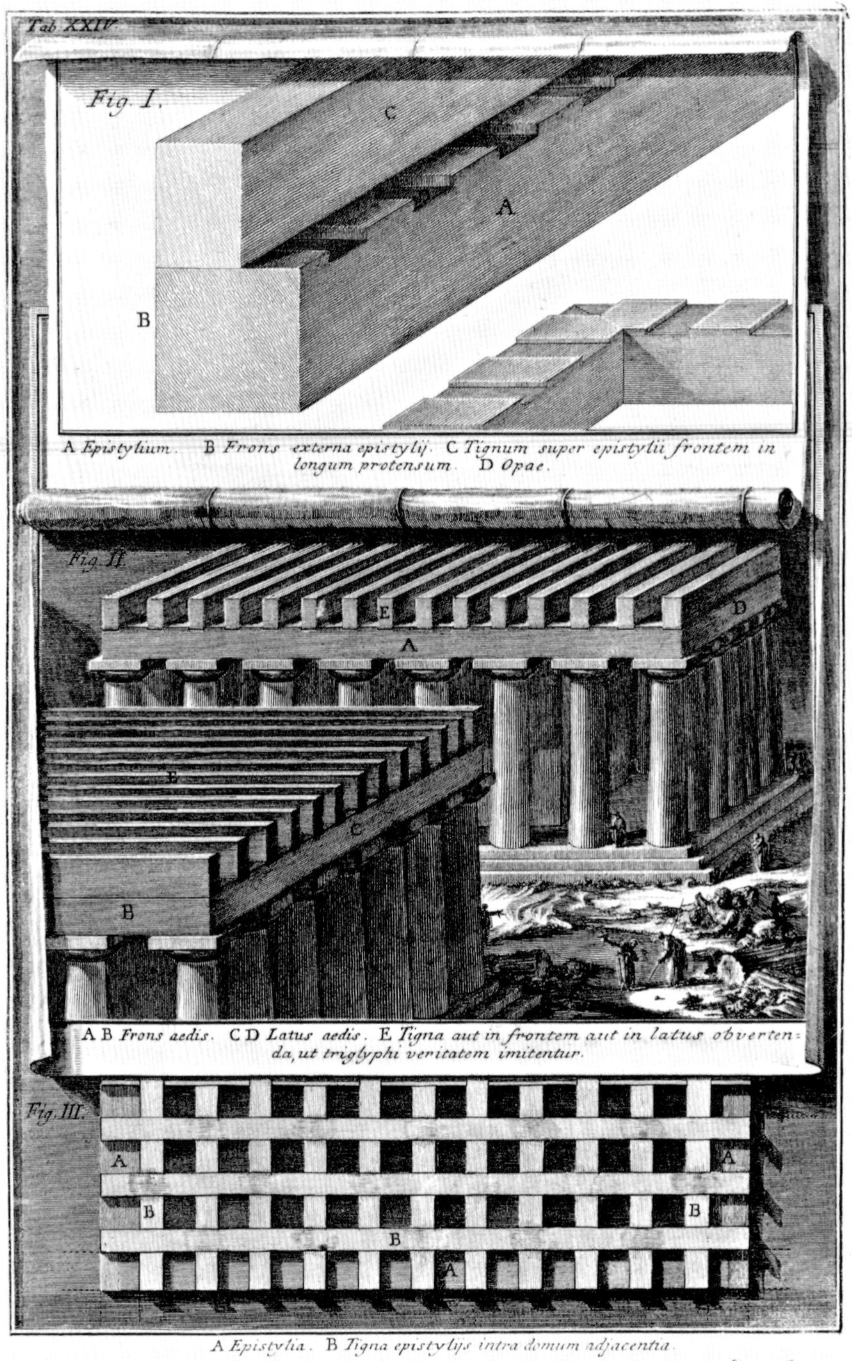

Fig. 10. Giovanni Battista Piranesi (Italian, 1720–78)
Three diagrams concerning Doric temple construction, 1761, etching, 37.5 × 23.5 cm (14¾ × 9¼ in.)
From Giovanni Battista Piranesi, *Della magnificenza ed architettura de' romani*... (Rome: n.p., 1761), pl. XXIV

Antonio Francesco Gori, Giovanni Battista Passeri, and Mario Guarnacci. In 1761 an Etruscan museum, bearing Guarnacci's name, was founded at Volterra with material from this scholar's extensive excavations. In the same year the leading British dealer in Rome, Thomas Jenkins, began exploring tombs at Chiusi and Corneto (Tarquinia), enabling Piranesi to accumulate fresh material for his polemical campaign.[45] In 1765 Piranesi visited Etruscan tombs at Corneto with another of his associates, the Scottish antiquarian James Byres, who would try unsuccessfully to publish his observations on the Etruscan remains found there. While the engraved plates for Byres's work, based on drawings of the tombs by Franciszek Smuglewicz, were soon in circulation, funds were not forthcoming, and the plates were eventually published posthumously without the text in 1842.[46] Piranesi was also in regular correspondence with Sir William Hamilton, from 1764 to 1800 envoy extraordinary to the Kingdom of the Two Sicilies in Naples, where this celebrated connoisseur was accumulating an outstanding collection of painted vases, then misidentified as Etruscan, which were to be published between 1767 and 1776.[47]

Piranesi's concern with the Etruscans was initially focused on their architectural achievements rather than their painted funerary interiors and vases. Responding to the stern rationalism of the French theorists' praise of Greece, in *Della magnificenza* Piranesi demonstrated the severity of Etruscan architecture and its survival in the utilitarian public works of Rome, as opposed to the "vana leggiadra" (vain prettiness), as he saw it, of Greek buildings, thus continuing the theme of heroic engineering he had celebrated in *Le antichità*. The relevant plates of *Della magnificenza*, therefore, included images of the cyclopean substructure of the Capitoline Hill, the monumental drainage works of the Cloaca Maxima in Rome, and the emissarium of Lago Albano (fig. 9). Such images were designed to demonstrate the functional grandeur, rooted in Etruscan engineering skills, of Roman structures. A series of images discrediting Laugier's thesis concerning the evolution from wooden to stone architecture by showing its patent illogicality (fig. 10) shows a clear debt to Lodoli's iconoclastic views as well as to his admiration of the Etruscan genius for stone construction.[48] Prominence is given also to the ancient origins of the Tuscan order as developing independently of the Greek Doric order and being of greater antiquity. (Lodoli believed that the Doric order had been invented by the Egyptians.)[49]

Predictably, the continuity between *Della magnificenza* and the first two decades of Piranesi's career is most significant in the visual aspects rather than the text of the treatise—namely, in the disproportionate emphasis given in over two-thirds of the plates in *Della magnificenza* to celebrating the imaginative richness and sheer variety of late imperial Roman ornament, even though certain examples did not met with Piranesi's unqualified approval. In many of these illustrations, Le Roy's austere line engravings of Attic detail are illusionistically attached to backgrounds crowded with Roman ornamental fragments rendered with the greatest luxuriance in texture and chiaroscuro.

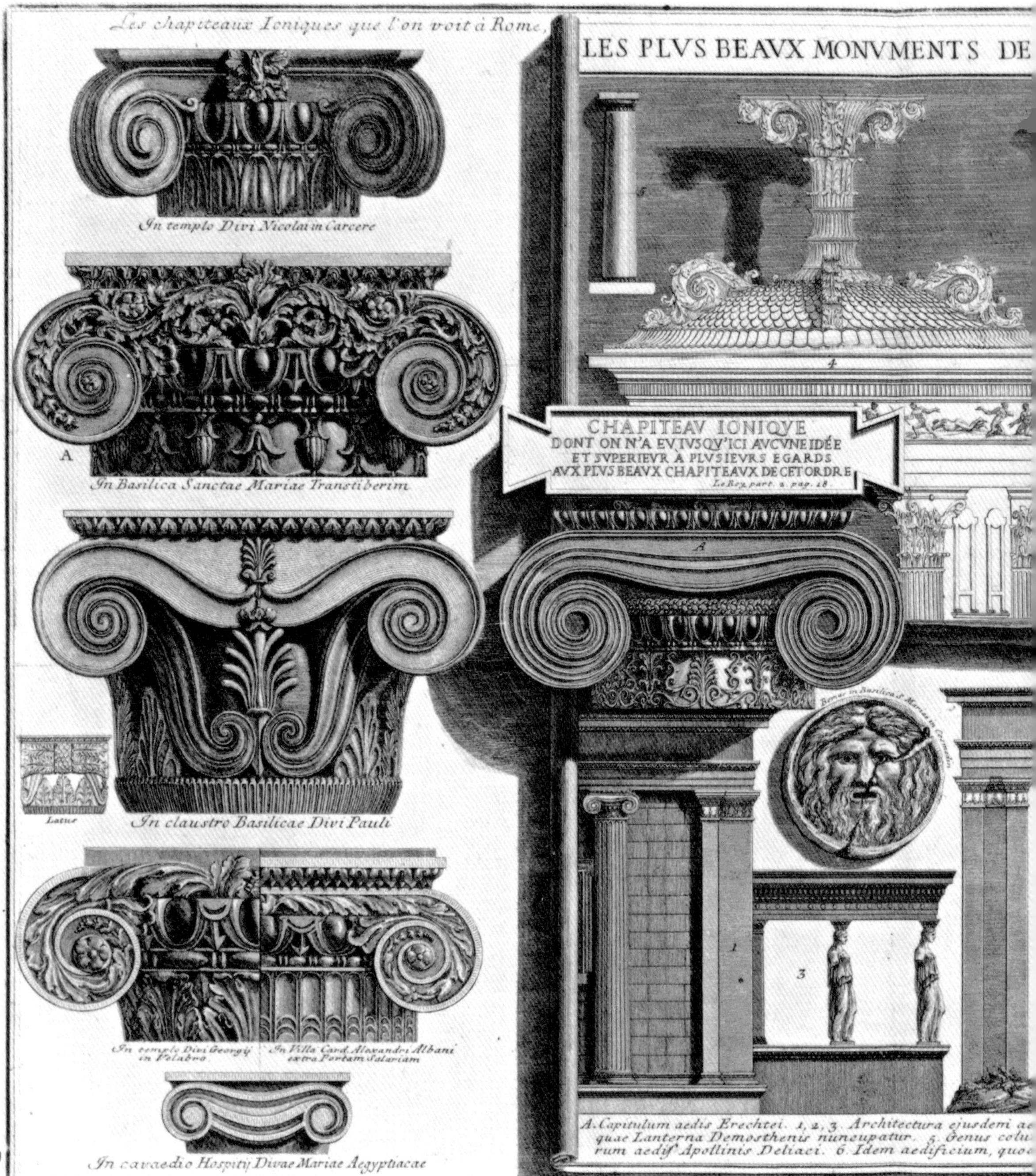

Fig. 11. Giovanni Battista Piranesi (Italian, 1720–78)
Various Roman Ionic capitals compared with Greek examples from Julien-David Le Roy's *Les ruines des plus beaux monuments de la Grèce* (1758), 1761, etching, 39 × 59 cm (15⅜ × 23¼ in.)
From Giovanni Battista Piranesi, *Della magnificenza ed architettura de' romani* . . . (Rome: n.p., 1761), pl. XX

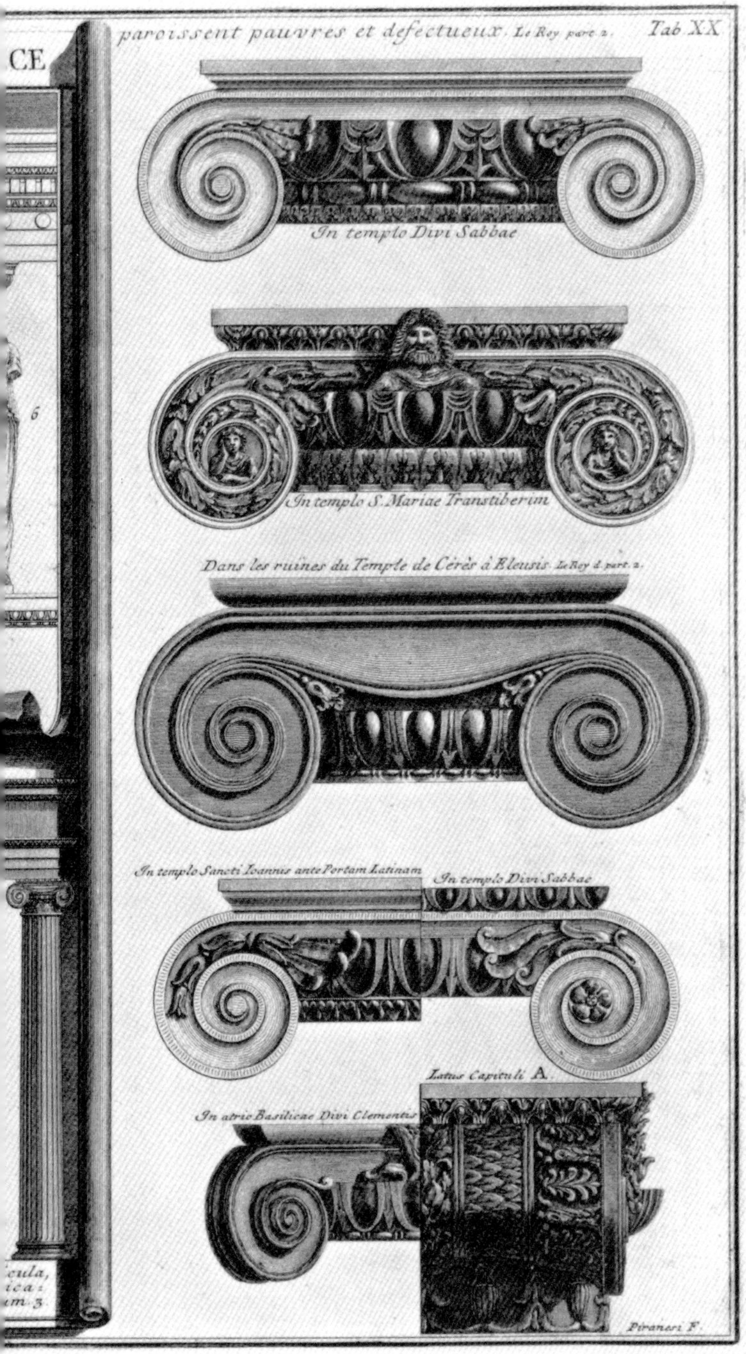
CE
paroissent pauvres et defectueux. Le Roy part 2.
Tab XX
In templo Divi Sabbae
In templo S. Mariae Transtiberim
Dans les ruines du Temple de Cérès à Eleusis. Le Roy 2. part. 2.
In templo Sancti Ioannis ante Portam Latinam
In templo Divi Sabbae
Latus Capituli A.
In atrio Basilicae Divi Clementis
Piranesi F.

Piranesi's quotations from Le Roy and satiric interpolations betray the Venetian's relish for Roman complexity, serving to demonstrate his assertion, in the text, that when the Romans eventually absorbed Greek taste they could not fail to correct and surpass it. In the case of the Ionic order, for instance, Piranesi selected relevant elements from Le Roy's plates, including the capital from the Erechtheion in Athens, pinned them illusionistically to a larger sheet, and surrounded them with a striking array of surviving Roman variants of the order (fig. 11). To emphasize the Frenchman's erroneous ways, Piranesi placed above the Erechtheion capital a plaque bearing Le Roy's assertion, "Chapiteau Ionique dont on n'a eu jusqu'ici aucune idée et superieur à plusieurs regards aux plus beaux chapiteaux de cet ordre" (A formerly unknown Ionic capital, which is superior in several respects to the most beautiful capitals of this order).[50] Just below the Erechtheion's capital, Piranesi placed an image of the Roman circular relief head from Santa Maria in Cosmedin; known colloquially as *La Bocca della Verità* (The Mouth of Truth), this relief, according to tradition, bit off the hands of those who told untruths.

In the ambitious text of *Della magnificenza* with its supporting images, it is clear that Piranesi had got out of his depth intellectually in pursuing certain arguments further than he probably intended at the outset. Contrary to his basic predilection for complexity as well as his own belief in artistic license, he had fought unwisely on the uncongenial and limited issue of function, determined by his French adversaries, rather than in accord with the material rapidly accumulating from his comprehensive studies. It comes as no surprise, therefore, that during the early 1760s he began to abandon an intellectual position made increasingly untenable and irrelevant by his own activities as a designer. Nevertheless, the polemical drive of *Della magnificenza* was sustained through a group of ambitious archaeological treatises, several of them growing out of studies connected with *Le antichità,* many evidently in preparation before the close of the 1750s.[51] As before, illustration played a dominant role, with highly technical plates being mixed with emotive and dramatic *vedute.* In *Rovine del Castello dell'Acqua Giulia* (1761; Ruins of the castellum of the Aqua Iulia), Piranesi continued his investigation of the Roman water system, while in *Descrizione e disegno dell'emissario del Lago Albano* (1762; Description and design of the emissarium of Lago Albano), he was to extract the maximum amount of information and drama through a brilliant sequence of technical plates combining plans, cross sections, elevations, reconstructions, and perspective views of the crater lake's drainage outlet. Other treatises on the antiquities of Albano, Castel Gandolfo, and the Etruscan site of Cori, all of them issued in 1764, expanded the heterogeneous ideas of *Della magnificenza,* as Piranesi pursued his defense of Rome and explored its Etruscan origins by the sheer weight and variety of evidence he presented rather than through any logical processes of argument.

The Infinite Fertility of the Imagination: Il Campo Marzio della Roma antica

One particular work of these years stands out, not only through its originality of approach but also by its key position in Piranesi's theoretical development: *Il Campo Marzio della Roma antica* (The Campus Martius of ancient Rome). Although published in 1762, the genesis of this ambitious work, like that of *Della magnificenza,* extended back into the previous decade, and it has an equally intricate connection to Piranesi's emerging artistic and polemical mission to fashion a new language of design. Significantly, as an exercise in speculative archaeology executed with contemporary architects in mind, the work originated in the highly productive relationship between Piranesi and Robert Adam.[52] Not only was the folio dedicated to the British architect (an exceptional gesture in itself) but much of its material was assembled during Adam's studies with Piranesi in Rome between 1755 and 1757. According to the considerable dedicatory preface, the author's objective was to examine the customs and environment of a vanished society through the study of its architectural remains. Here we may possibly see the influence of Vico, whose writings and ideas were the subject of much discussion by Lodoli and his circle during Piranesi's formative years in Venice.[53] In his most influential publication, *Principj di una scienza nuova* (Principles of a new science), first published in 1725, Vico rejected the Enlightenment belief in progress and advanced a theory of cyclical historical development, which accepted the inevitability of growth and decay. He also questioned the idea that human nature is unchangeable and universally the same. On the contrary, the philosopher argued, since human history is clearly subject to change, and all areas of society at a particular time, whether language, law, myth, or art, are interrelated, the surest way to understand the past is through imaginative study of its visible remains as well as its literature. Recognizing the need to relate written and archaeological evidence through creative acts of reconstruction, Piranesi set out to correlate literary references to the monumental area of central Rome and information from the surviving fragments of the Severan Marble Plan[54] with the results of a thorough physical examination of the site. The end product was a remarkable series of hypothetical reconstructions, presented in plan, elevation, and perspective, in which Piranesi's imaginative faculties were stretched to the full.

Il Campo Marzio opens with thirty-three pages of learned discussion of literary authorities, with parallel texts in Latin and Italian. There follows a group of maps showing, stage by stage, the evolution of this site from primitive beginnings in the marshy site bounded by the curve of the Tiber to a densely monumental townscape of the utmost complexity and grandeur. Although various surviving remains—such as the Pantheon, the theaters of Pompey and Marcellus, and the two imperial mausoleums—provide the reference points in this progression, the bounds of probability become increasingly remote as Piranesi proceeds, and the climax is provided by the virtual fantasy of the *Ichnographia* (Ground Plan) (fig. 12)—a vast six-plate plan purportedly

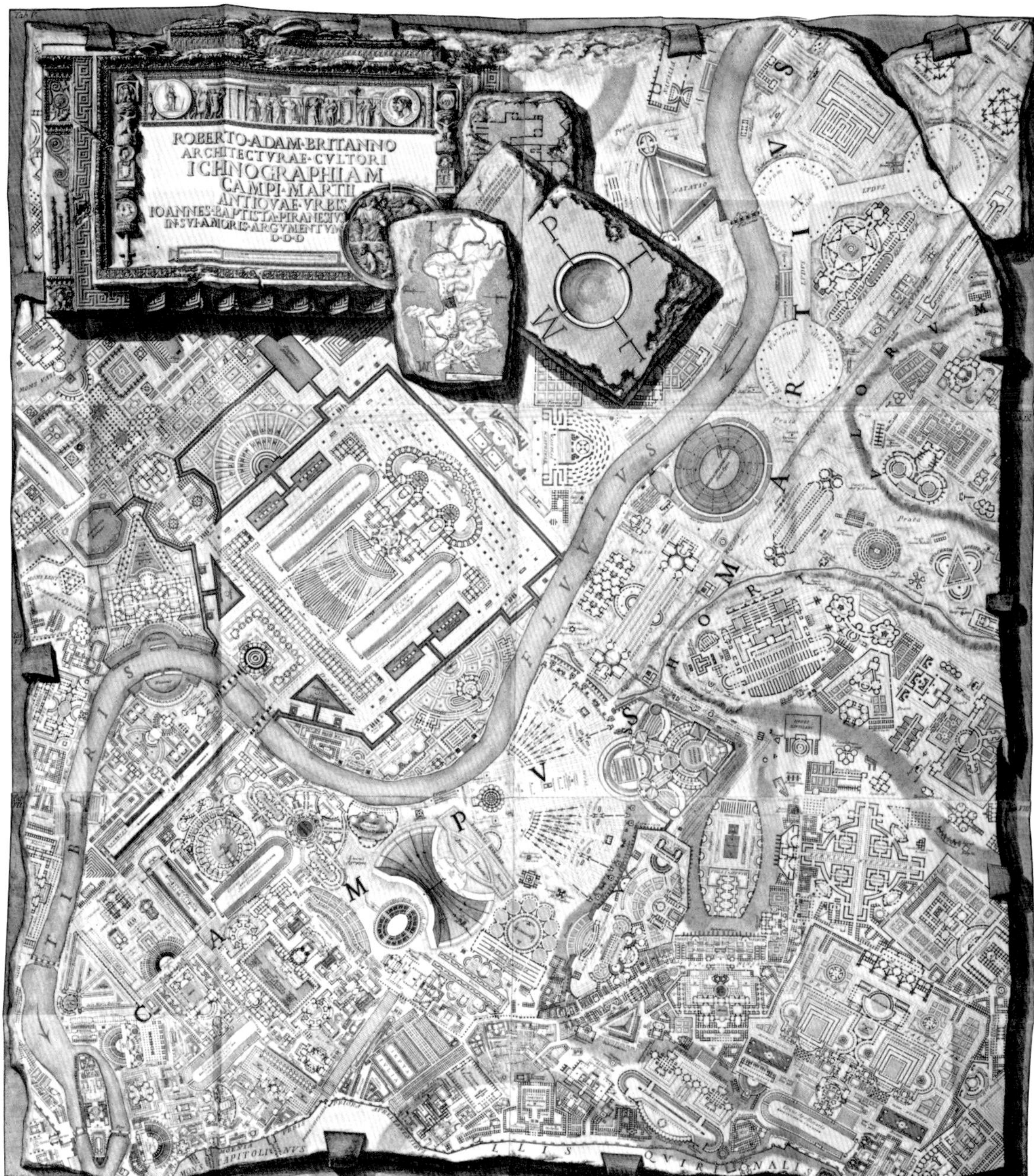

Fig. 12. Giovanni Battista Piranesi (Italian, 1720–78)
Ichnographiam Campi Martii Antiquae Urbis, 1762, etching, 135 × 117 cm (53⅛ × 46 in.)
From Giovanni Battista Piranesi, *Il Campo Marzio dell'antica Roma*... (Rome: n.p., 1762), pls. V–X

representing the Campus Martius under the late empire. The *Ichnographia* is supported by thirty-seven plates of *vedute* and detailed architectural surveys in which Piranesi presented the raw material on which this speculative act was based, often using the dramatic technique of isolating monumental fragments from the accretions of the medieval townscape. To conclude *Il Campo Marzio,* Piranesi added for the first time in his antiquarian reconstructions a series of aerial perspectives of selected parts of the *Ichnographia,* including one on the book's second title page.

While the fantasies and exaggerated images of *Le antichità* stand apart from the remainder of that work, as reflecting Piranesi's initial responses to the early claims of the Hellenists, these aerial perspectives and their source, the *Ichnographia,* follow naturally from the stated thesis of *Il Campo Marzio.* By this time, Piranesi had already begun to evolve a theoretical justification for his inclinations as an artist and no longer needed to resort to sophistry and ponderous academic justification, as in *Della magnificenza,* to justify his preoccupation with the ornate and the complex forms of antiquity. Like earlier planning fantasies such as the *Pianta di ampio magnifico collegio* of 1750 (see fig. 4) and the plan of the so-called Nymphaeum of Nero in *Le antichità* of 1756 (see fig. 8), the *Ichnographia* resulted from a brilliant conflation of ideas drawn from an exceptionally wide range of sources—imperial *thermae* (public baths), the Palatine complex, the Villa Adriana at Tivoli, and fanciful reconstructions by Pirro Ligorio, Giovanni Battista Montano, and Johann Bernhard Fischer von Erlach, to mention only a few. Whereas the *Collegio* plan had a Palladian basis and the reconstructed Nymphaeum of Nero a baroque character, the form of Piranesi's later exercise came remarkably close to contemporary developments in French neoclassical architecture, in which plans were generated by combining distinct geometric forms, derived from antiquity, into multiple patterns.[55] At the time, however, no other European designer had developed this speculative process to such extremes of ingenuity, and the *Ichnographia* was to provide an anthology of concepts that, as Piranesi clearly intended, stimulated the imagination of designers as varied as Adam, Jean-François de Neufforge, Etienne-Louis Boullée, Claude-Nicolas Ledoux, and Sir John Soane until the end of the century.[56]

No one could mistake the *Ichnographia* for a considered statement of archaeological fact. By way of countering such criticism, Piranesi states in the dedication to Adam:

> I am rather afraid that parts of the Campus that I describe should seem figments of my imagination and not based on any evidence; certainly if anyone compares them with the architectural theory of the ancients he will see that they differ greatly from it and are actually closer to the usage of our own times. But before anyone accuses me of falsehood, he should, I beg, examine the ancient [marble] plan of the city... he should examine the villas of Latium and that of Hadrian at Tivoli, the baths, the tombs, and other ruins outside the Porta Capena, and he will find that the ancients disobeyed the strict rules of architecture just as much as the moderns. Perhaps it is

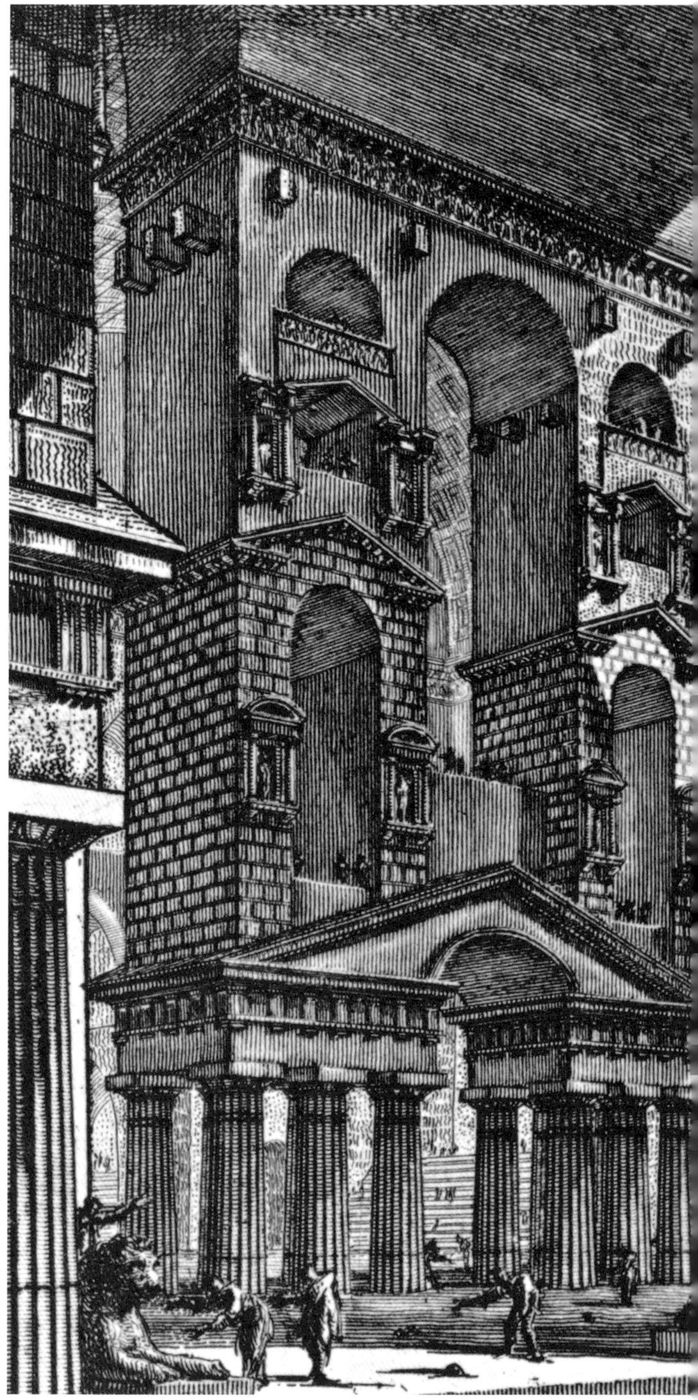

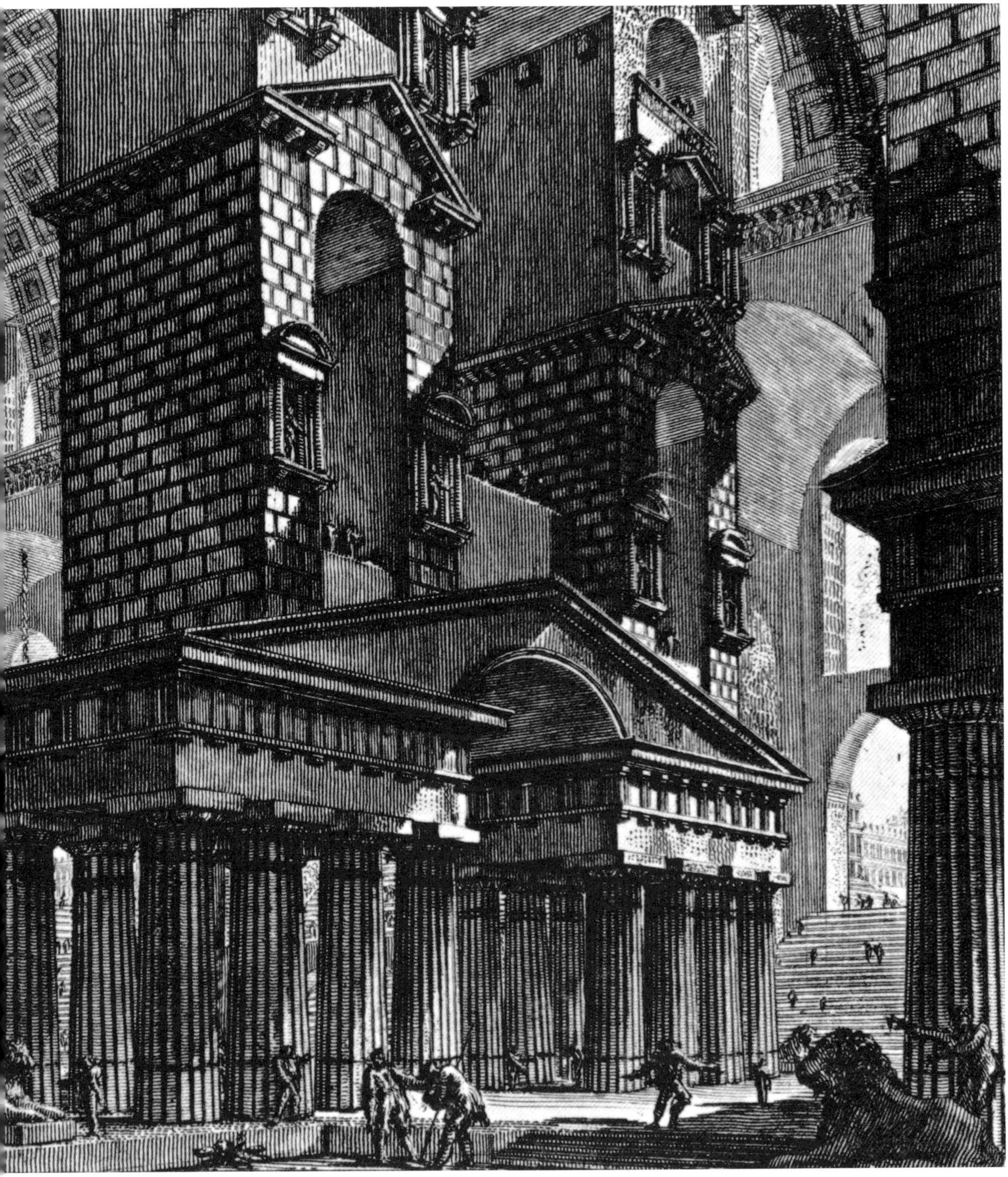

Fig. 13. Giovanni Battista Piranesi (Italian, 1720–78)
Appartenenze d'antiche terme con scale che conducono alla palestra, e al teatro, ca. 1761, etching, 14 × 20 cm (5 1/2 × 7 7/8 in.)
From Giovanni Battista Piranesi, *Opere varie di architettura, prospettive, grotteschi, antichità* (Rome: n.p., [1761])

> inevitable and a general rule that the arts on reaching a peak should gradually decline, or perhaps it is part of human nature to demand some license in creative expression as in other things; and it is not strange, if we find in that architects used things that we sometimes criticize in buildings of our times.[57]

Moreover, the folio represents, along with its theoretical justification, not only an artistic credo but also a fresh polemical response to the now-growing influence of Winckelmann, who, shortly after arriving in Rome from Dresden in 1755, became librarian to the outstanding patron and collector of antiquities, Cardinal Alessandro Albani.

Winckelmann's seminal essay *Gedanken über die Nachahmung der griechischen Werke in der Mahlerey und Bildhauer-Kunst* (1755; On the imitation of the painting and sculpture of the Greeks), which was published just before he left Germany, represented a major turning point in the development of the Greek Revival. His ideas were eventually to be elaborated in a more ambitious work, *Geschichte der Kunst des Alterthums* (1764; History of the art of antiquity), which, in many respects, laid the foundations of the modern conception of art history by offering a new system of stylistic analysis grounded in the cultural and social history of the ancient world.[58] Like Piranesi, Winckelmann, by combining an intense study of antiquity with imaginative acts of exceptional brilliance, had charged the classical past with a powerful new relevance for his contemporaries. While Laugier had denounced caprice and license as perversions of the primitive and austere ideals of Greek architecture, by the early 1760s the impact of Winckelmann's writings was establishing simplicity in the arts as a formal virtue in its own right. As a consequence, the field of debate in the Graeco-Roman controversy was beginning to shift from antiquarian issues to questions of aesthetics and style, where Piranesi was in a stronger position to respond. However, although Winckelmann accepted the theoretical justification for ornament in building in his *Anmerkungen über die Baukunst der alten Tempel zu Girgenti in Sicilien* (1762; Remarks on the architecture of the ancient temples at Agrigento in Sicily)—his only work specifically concerned with architecture—the German scholar traced a stylistic progression from the simplicity of Paestum to the grandeur of ancient Athens, followed by a sharp decline under the Romans, particularly at Palmyra and Baalbek, during the imperial age.[59] For him, an increased used of ornament, and, by inference, general complexity in design, coincided with a decline in taste. As he put it, "In architecture, beauty...consists principally in the *proportion:* for a building can become and be beautiful through that alone, without decoration."[60] He also wrote on another occasion, "Architecture suffered the same fate as the old languages, which became richer when they lost their beauty; this can be proved by the Greek as well as the Roman language, and as architects could neither equal nor surpass their predecessors in beauty, they tried to show that they were richer."[61] Piranesi, while accepting the evolutionary theory of architecture, argued in *Il Campo Marzio* quite to the contrary. By examining the role of a modern architect

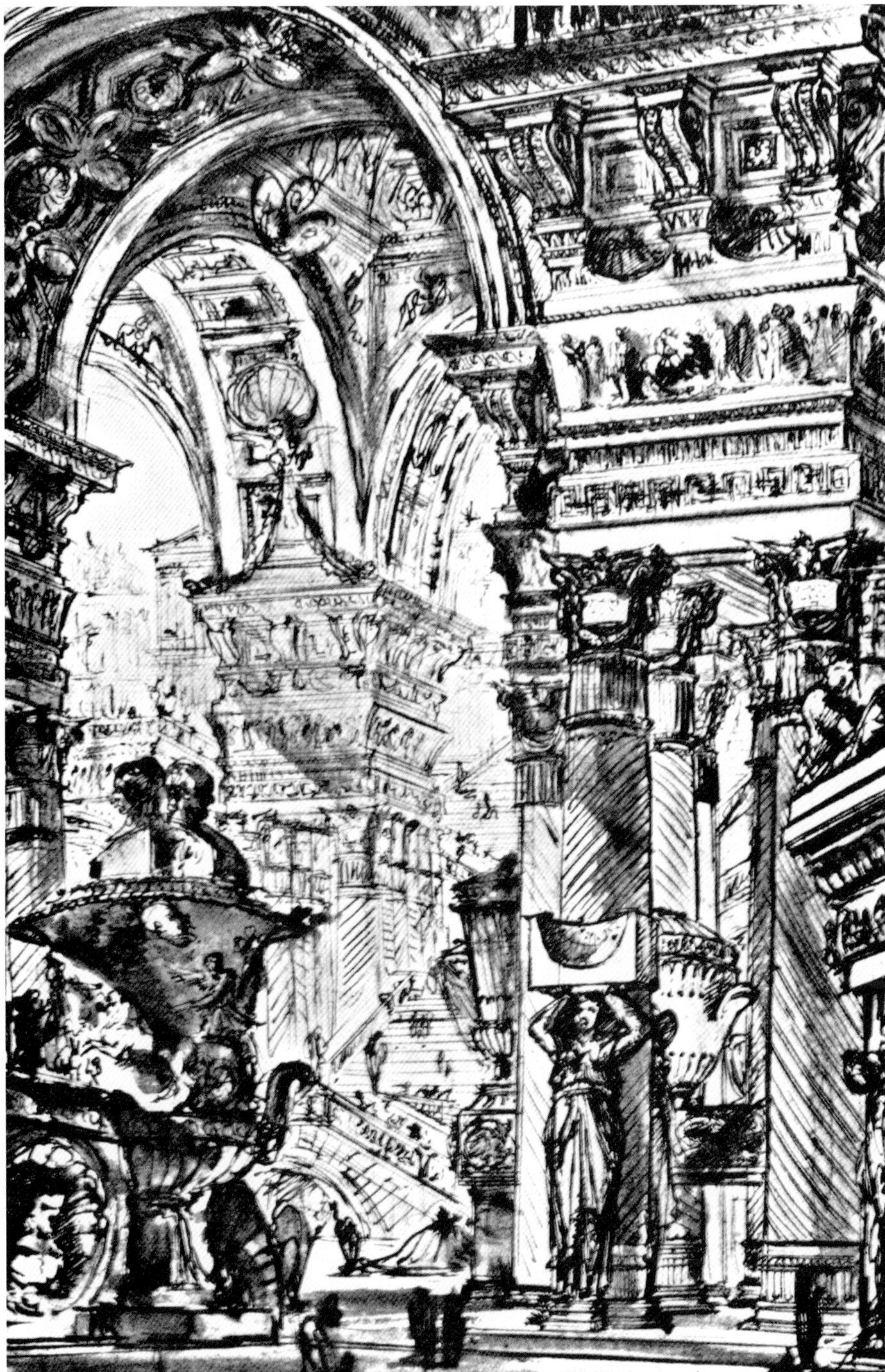

Fig. 14. Giovanni Battista Piranesi (Italian, 1720–78)
Architectural fantasy with monumental portico, ca. 1763, pen and brown ink and wash over red chalk, 58 × 36 cm (22⅞ × 14⅛ in.)
Bologna, Biblioteca Comunale dell'Archiginnasio

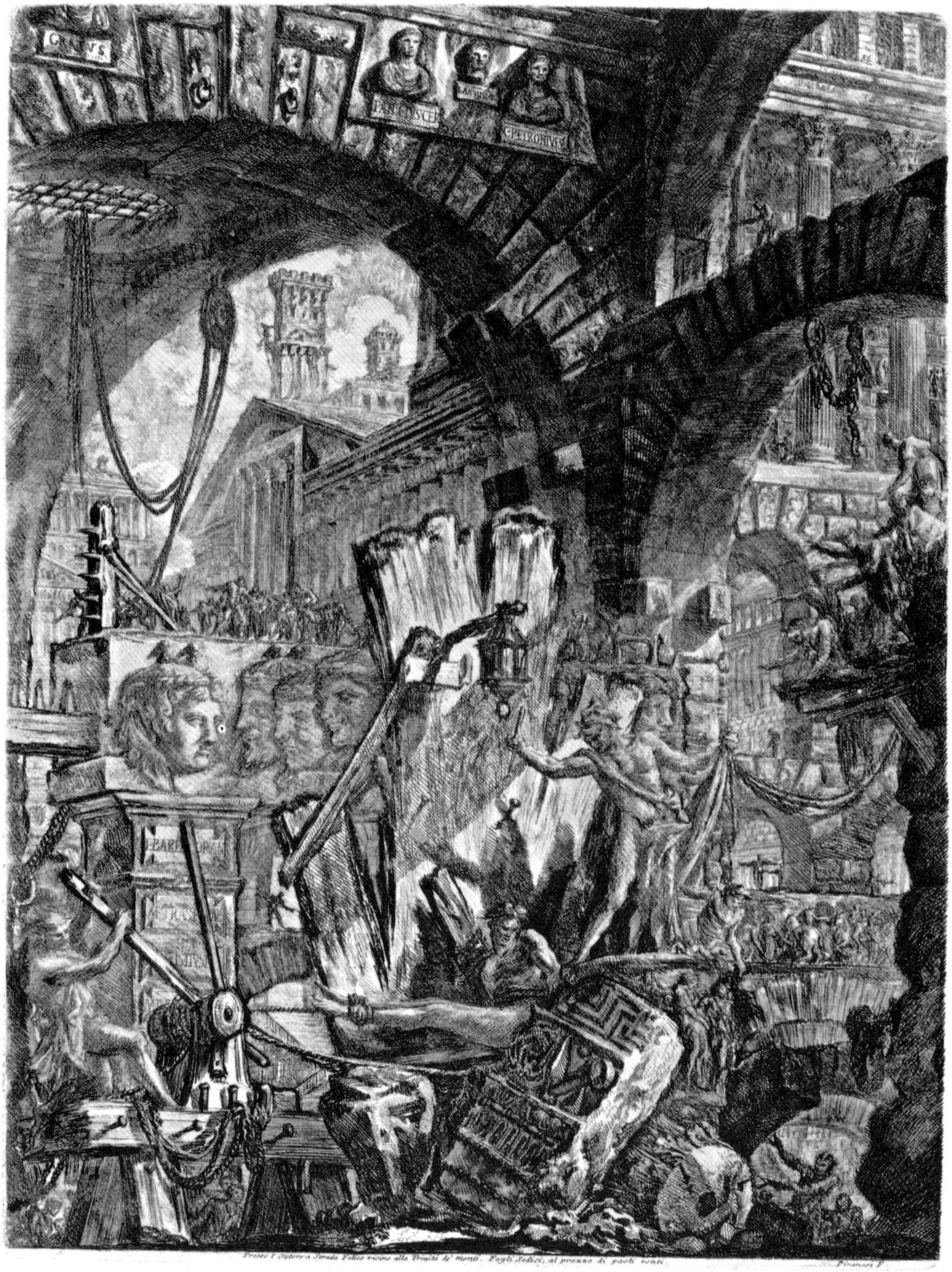

Fig. 15. Giovanni Battista Piranesi (Italian, 1720–78)
Prison interior: "The Man on the Rack," 1761, etching, 55.5 × 42 cm (21 7/8 × 16 1/2 in.)
From Giovanni Battista Piranesi, *Carceri d'invenzione* (Rome: n.p., 1761)

faced with a historic city such as Rome, which was constantly subject to flux and change, he drew lessons from the past that justified an eclectic rather than a restrictive and narrow philosophy of design. For him, the formal properties of movement and complexity in architectural and urban design, as well as in ornament, possessed the imaginative vitality that he considered to be the creative legacy of ancient Rome, a birthright not to be proscribed by the doctrinaire precepts of the Greek Revivalists.

Piranesi's search for new forms of expression, as adumbrated in the plates of *Il Campo Marzio,* led him to abandon his strictly exclusive attitude toward non-Italic styles. Some of his earliest attempts, through the experimental medium of the etched *capriccio,* to combine Greek and Egyptian with Roman motifs may be seen in a group of ten small plates that he added to the *Opere varie* during the early 1760s.[62] In one of these, *Appartenenze d'antiche terme con scale che conducono alla palestra, e al teatro* (Architectural elements of ancient baths with stairs that lead to the gymnasium and the theater) (fig. 13), the archaic Doric colonnades at Agrigento (which he probably derived from studies made by Mylne during his expedition to Sicily in the late 1750s) are daringly incorporated into a vaulted Roman interior. In another, *Portici tirati d'intorno ad un foro con palazzo regio* (Porticoes surrounding a forum with a royal palace), appear partly fluted Doric columns like those of the Temple of Apollo at Delos, as first illustrated by Le Roy in 1758. In one of the aerial reconstructions in *Il Campo Marzio* that features the Pantheon, Piranesi includes in the foreground a colonnade of caryatid figures derived from the Erechtheion. In contrast, many years later, at the end of his life when he came to record the three Greek Doric temples at Paestum in a folio of twenty particularly impressive *vedute,* posthumously completed and issued in 1778 by his son Francesco, Piranesi's aesthetic response to these gaunt forms was clearly prompted by their elegiac grandeur rather than by any formal inspiration.[63]

Meanwhile, Piranesi's fantasy drawings from the early 1760s continued to provide the means for exploring new compositional ideas, as the surviving examples suggest. One in the Biblioteca Comunale dell'Archiginnasio, Bologna (fig. 14), in contrast to the earlier etched *capricci* of the 1740s and 1750s, where anti-Vitruvian forms are tentatively introduced, shows a boldly imaginative range of formal ideas and aggressive violation of Vitruvian classical conventions. During this period, added to the dramatically refashioned plates of the *Carceri d'invenzione* of 1761 were two completely new compositions. One of these plates—"The Man on the Rack" (fig. 15), which features a distant building with a complex shouldered frieze and colonnade penetrating the tympanum area of the pediment—reveals this new formal language in the making.

Toward a New Architecture

By the time, therefore, that the collector and connoisseur Pierre-Jean Mariette (1694–1774) (fig. 16) unwittingly initiated a new phase in the Graeco-Roman controversy with a letter criticizing the arguments of *Della magnificenza* published in the *Gazette littéraire de l'Europe* in 1764, Piranesi had moved on to

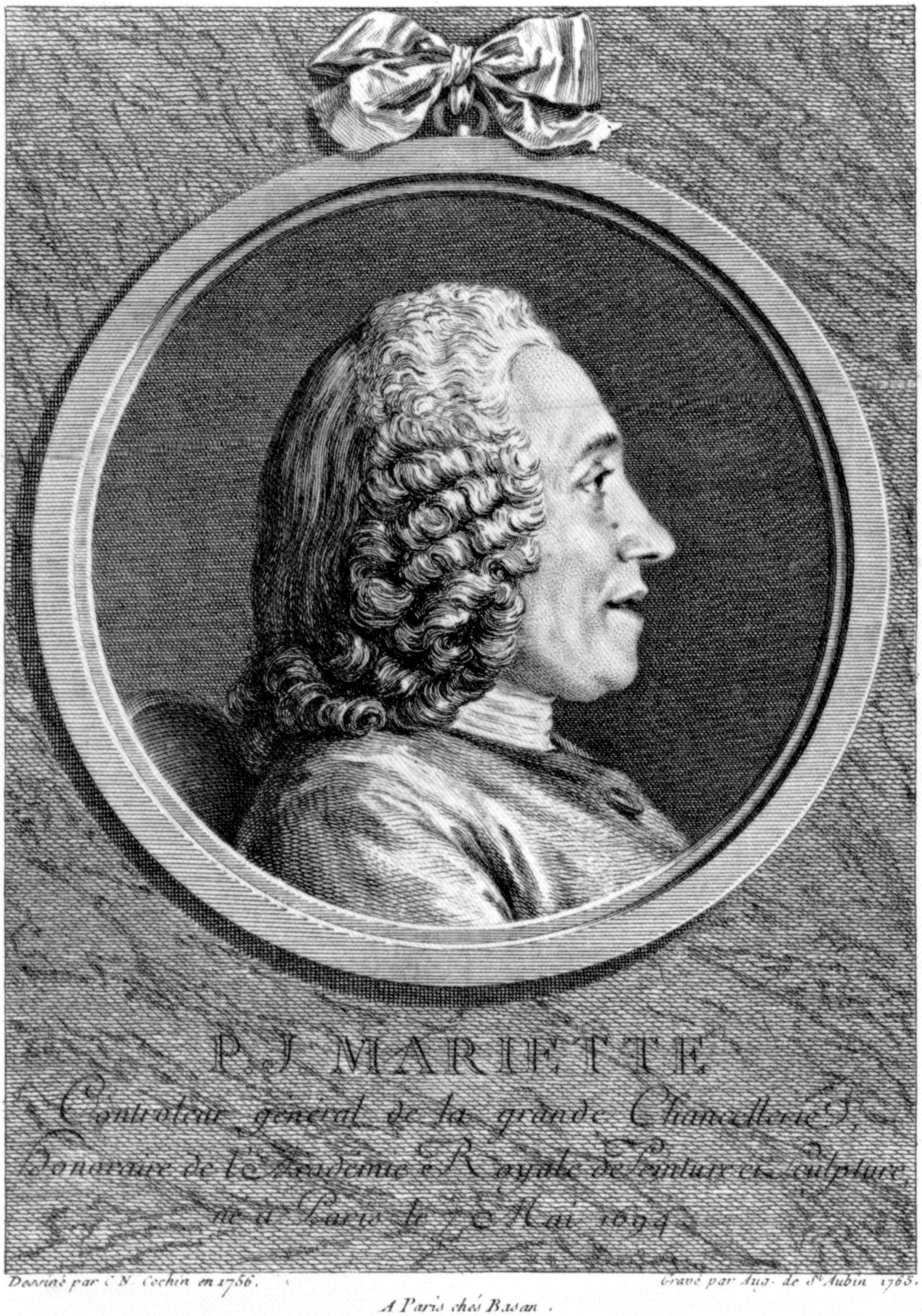

Fig. 16. Augustin de Saint-Aubin (French, 1736–1807), after Charles-Nicolas II Cochin (French, 1715–90)
P. J. Mariette, contrôleur général de la grande Chancellerie, honoraire de l'Académie royale de peinture et sculpture, né à Paris le 7 Mai 1694, 1765, engraving, subject: 17.1 × 12.2 cm (6¾ × 4¾ in.)
Paris, Institut Néerlandais, Collection F. Lugt

new concerns.[64] The Frenchman claimed that not only were the Etruscans in fact Greek colonists but also all Roman art had its roots in Greece and had been produced in Rome largely by Greek slaves. Moreover, he argued, Rome had ultimately debased Greek taste to a degree that rendered it ludicrous and barbarous: "nothing is produced that is not laden with superfluous and gratuitous ornament. All is sacrificed to luxury, and the result is a manner that rapidly becomes ridiculous and barbaric" (p. 98).[65] Previous French writing, as familiar to Piranesi in the works of Anne Claude Philippe de Tubières, comte de Caylus, had opposed the "grandeur" of the Etruscans to the "élégance" of the Greeks. Mariette, however, reflecting Winckelmann's criteria, considered that Roman art with its profusion of ornament had lost the Greeks' "belle et noble simplicité" (beautiful and noble simplicity).

Mariette's attack came just at the time when Piranesi's shift away from narrow issues of antiquarian scholarship toward the evolution of new modes of artistic expression, in emulation of Roman antiquity, coincided with a series of opportunities to practice as an architect and interior designer. In the mid-1760s, the enlightened patronage of Clement XIII and other members of the Rezzonico family gave him the kind of financial freedom and encouragement to experiment that had been absent in the 1740s when he was preparing the *Prima parte*.[66] A chance to apply his extremely original ideas on a monumental scale was provided in 1764 by the pope's commission to design an imposing tribune, complete with an elaborate papal altar (fig. 17), to terminate Borromini's nave at the Lateran Basilica (San Giovanni in Laterano).[67] It was an inspired choice: apart from providing this major opportunity for Piranesi to realize his belief in a novel language of a richly ornamental character, he was virtually alone among the designers of his time in being in complete sympathy with the baroque ideas and spirit of Borromini.[68] At an early stage in his career, Piranesi had already paid conscious tributes to the seventeenth-century designer in the imaginary compositions of the *Prima parte*.[69] Now, when it came to an opportunity to extend the Lateran nave, it was Borromini's example—his exceptional ability in modernizing a highly venerable building by means of a system of ingenious forms and highly developed ornamental *capricci* derived from an eclectic study of antiquity—that gave Piranesi the confidence to produce a dense concentration of equally idiosyncratic ornament in both the tribune and the papal altar.[70] Piranesi's various projects for this commission survive in a set of twenty-three highly finished presentation drawings, now in the Avery Architectural and Fine Arts Library of Columbia University. These drawings were reworked for presentation to the pope's nephew, Cardinal Giovanni Battista Rezzonico, in 1767 after the scheme had to be abandoned.[71]

While lack of money may have been partly responsible for the rejection of this ambitious undertaking, another key factor undoubtedly would have been contemporary criticism, conditioned by the growing restraint in taste associated with the Greek Revival, which found the language of Piranesi's design extravagant and highly idiosyncratic. The viewpoint of the more conventional

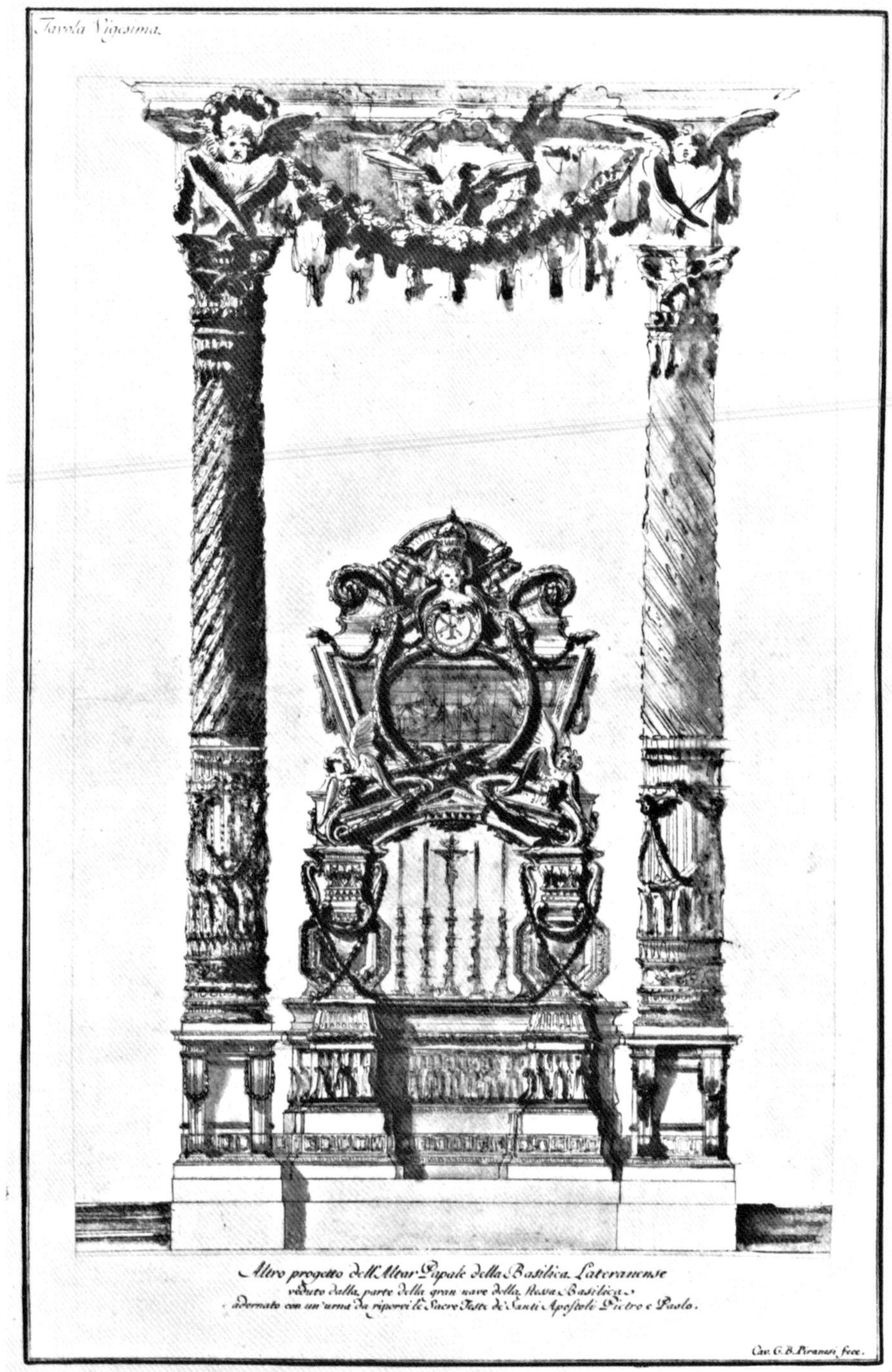

Fig. 17. Giovanni Battista Piranesi (Italian, 1720–78)
Alternative design for papal altar and baldachino, San Giovanni in Laterano, Rome, 1764, pen and brown ink over pencil guide lines, brown and gray washes, 85.9 × 53.9 cm (33⅞ × 21¼ in.)
New York, Columbia University, Avery Architectural and Fine Arts Library

members of the architectural profession was represented by Vanvitelli's dismissal of Piranesi (one of several in his surviving correspondence) in a letter of February 1764 referring to the Lateran tribune: "It is really amazing that the lunatic Piranesi dares to become an architect; I can only say that it is not an occupation for madmen."[72]

While Piranesi's decorative schemes for the papal summer residence at Castel Gandolfo, the Quirinal Palace, and the Palazzo Senatorio on the Capitoline Hill—commissioned, respectively, by Clement XIII, Cardinal Giovanni Battista Rezzonico, and Senator Abbondio Rezzonico—have all disappeared,[73] Piranesi's developing aesthetic can be seen in the highly unusual amalgams of symbolic forms in his one executed work of architecture: the reconstructed priory church of the Knights of Malta, Santa Maria del Priorato, and its adjacent piazza.[74] Developed during the same period as the various solutions for the Lateran tribune and deeply influenced by those concepts, this building complex prominently situated at the edge of the Aventine Hill was commissioned by Cardinal Giovanni Battista Rezzonico in his capacity as grand prior of the order. The work, carried out between 1764 and 1766, included a piazza lined with imposing stelae, or commemorative relief monuments, together with a church facade (fig. 18) where Piranesi's challenging new formal language was expressed with outstanding skill and ingenuity.[75] The nave culminates in an exceptionally unconventional high altar composed of two richly ornate sarcophagi, one behind the other, with the rear one supporting a third, which, in turn, supports a sphere (fig. 19); in the executed work, the latter is surmounted by a sculptural tableau of Saint Basil being borne heavenward by angels and putti. The concept of a sphere bearing a group of figures possessed a particular fascination for Piranesi; it appears in many of his drawn and etched architectural *capricci* where, characteristically, so many of his most original ideas were first introduced and developed.[76] The inspiration of Borromini recurs not only in the complex rib system of the nave's vault, which in its diagonal rhythms and use of oblique light recalls the former's ceiling for the Cappella dei Re Magi at the Collegio de Propaganda Fide in Rome, but also in the way historic tombs of the Knights of Malta are skillfully incorporated within a series of strangely formed ornamental cartouches that emulate the seventeenth-century master's similar treatment of the ancient monuments in the nave aisles of the Lateran Basilica.[77]

During this intensely productive period, Piranesi was also designing suites of furniture, schemes of interior decoration, and elaborate chimneypieces; and he was exploring a novel use of Egyptian forms in his painted mural decorations for the Caffè degli Inglesi in Piazza di Spagna, Rome—a pioneering work that, like other such extreme experiments, attracted much abuse from contemporary critics.[78] In the production of these works, Piranesi, while fully aware of his innovatory role, looked back on historic precursors in the idiosyncratic uses of antiquity. The imaginative synthesis of disparate forms in mannerist architecture clearly inspired the strange appliqués on the facades and monuments of the Aventine buildings. In particular, Piranesi was to pay

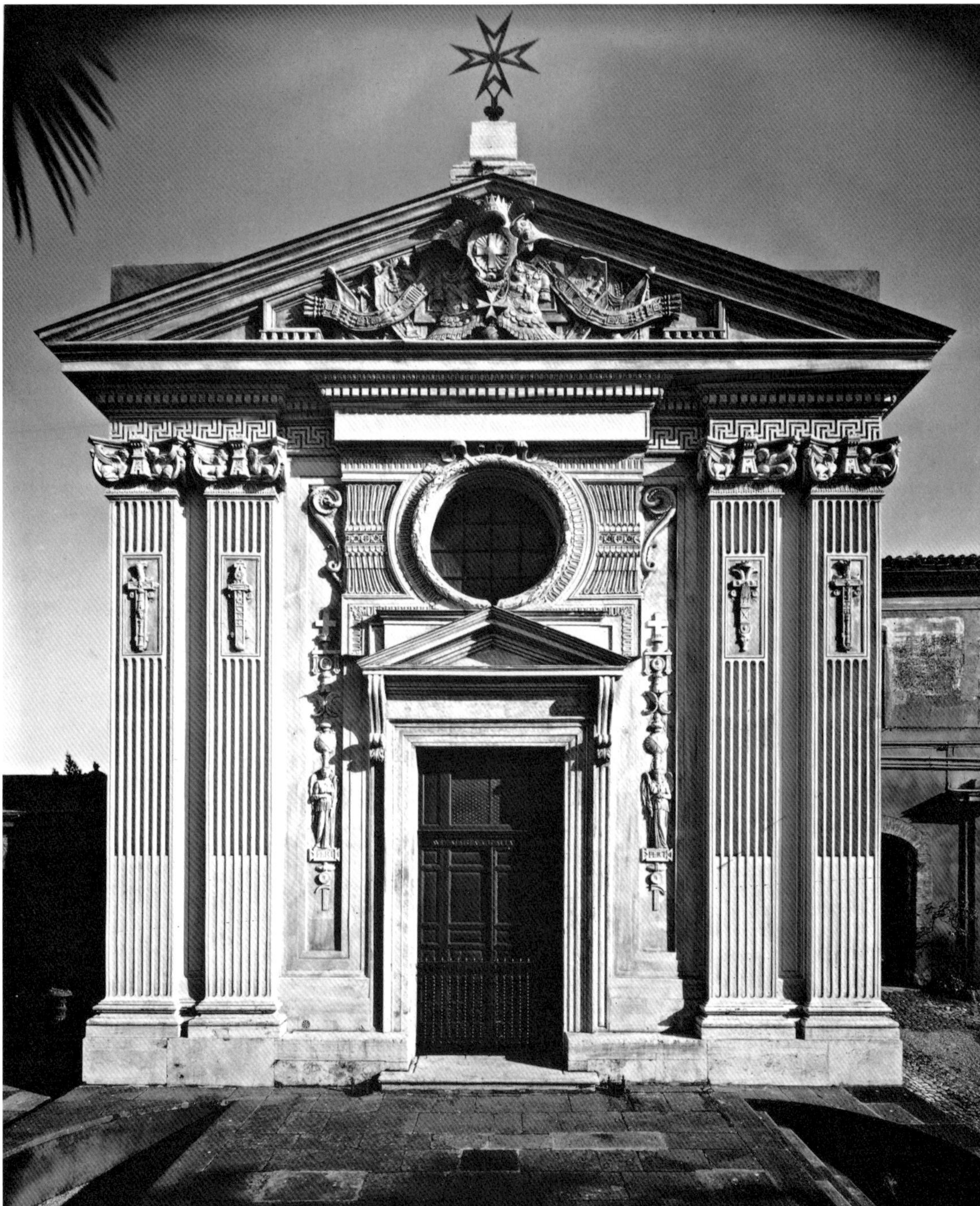

Fig. 18. Giovanni Battista Piranesi (Italian, 1720–78), architect
Facade, Santa Maria del Priorato, Rome

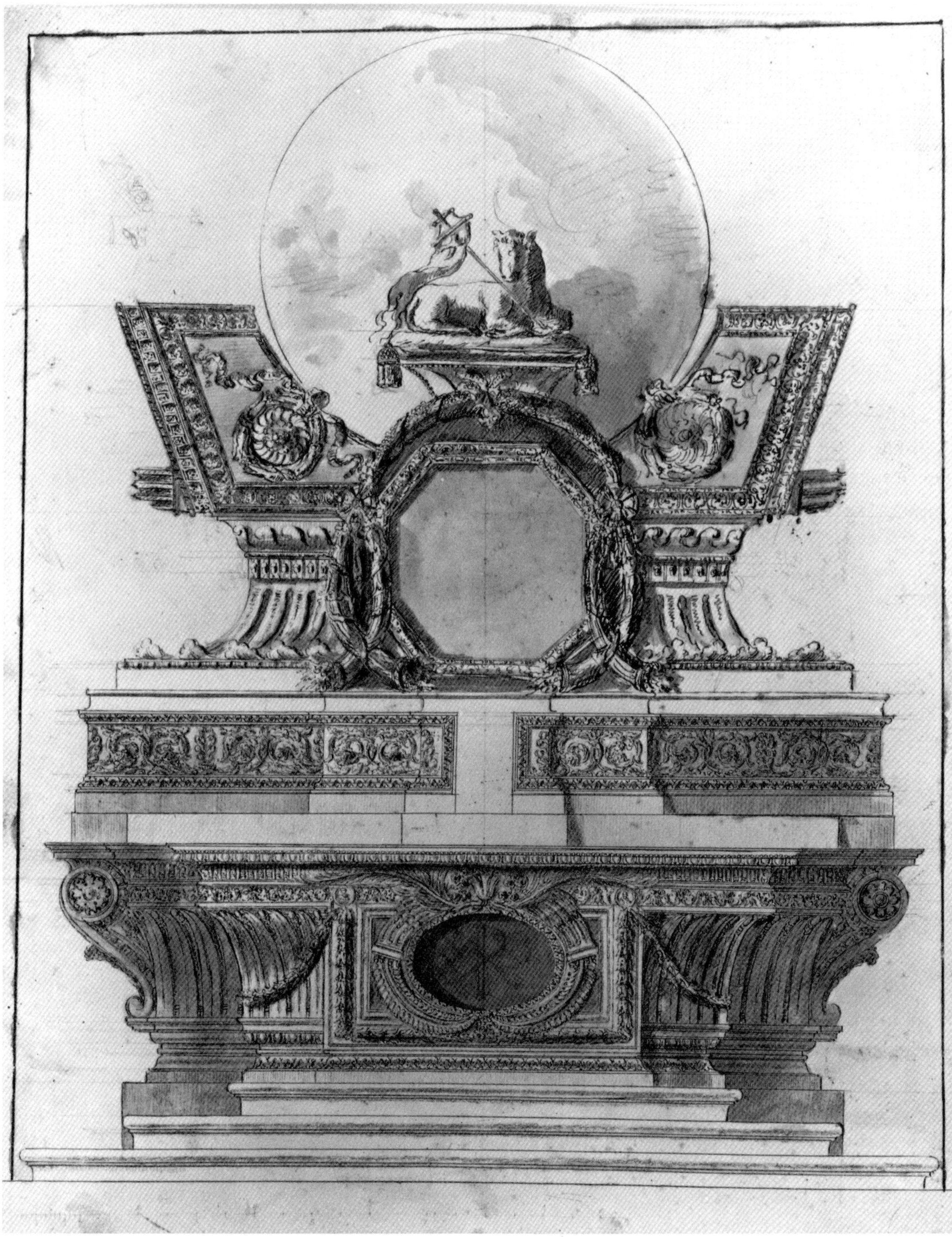

Fig. 19. Giovanni Battista Piranesi (Italian, 1720–78)
Design for the lower part of the high altar, Santa Maria del Priorato, Rome, 1764–65, pen and brown ink with india ink wash over black chalk, additions in black chalk and pencil, 47.1 × 36.6 cm (18½ × 14⅜ in.)
New York, Pierpont Morgan Library

tribute to the inventive handling of antique decoration in Ligorio's Casino di Pio IV at the Vatican and in Baldassare Peruzzi's Palazzo Massimo alle Colonne in his later writings.[79]

The Osservazioni

When Piranesi responded to Mariette's attack with three interconnected works published as one volume in 1765, his intellectual position was therefore fully adjusted to his artistic development. The ostensible subject of the title page (see p. 125) heralding the *Osservazioni sopra la lettre de Monsieur Mariette*... (Observations on the Letter of Monsieur Mariette...) is the Tuscan order as an original invention of the Etruscans, fully independent of the Doric and displaying all the primal authority attributed to Laugier's rustic hut. This presentation had a particular resonance in the current debate: both Le Roy and Blondel considered the Tuscan order simply a degenerate version of the Greek Doric, while Adam himself was later to state that the Tuscan was "no more than a bad and imperfect Doric."[80] The issue of artistic originality was more profound, however, as the two contrasting insets on the left side of the plate indicate. Mariette's left hand beginning his letter, under the statement "aut cum hoc" (either with this), is placed above a column of the tools of the artist and architect, accompanied by the words "aut in hoc" (or on this). By inference, the discussion of such matters is now beyond the reach of armchair critics like Mariette and can be resolved only by active designers like Piranesi who are in far closer contact with the creative spirit of antiquity through modern practice.

Although Piranesi could not resist publishing a detailed, line-by-line refutation of Mariette in the first essay, entitled "Osservazioni sopra la lettre de Monsieur Mariette...," and continued the theme of Etruscan origins of Roman civilization in the final essay, entitled "Della introduzione e del progresso delle belle arti in Europa ne' tempi antichi" (On the introduction and progress of the fine arts in Europe in ancient times), the main weight of his defense rests on the "Parere su l'architettura."[81] Like Ramsay's dialogue in *The Investigator,* this essay takes the form of a debate between two architects concerning the role of ornament in architecture. The rigorist, Protopiro, essentially represents the ideals of Laugier and is clearly committed to Winckelmann's view of Hellenic austerity as reflected in Mariette's letter. His opponent, Didascolo, advocates Piranesi's belief in the creative license of the designer, in "the crazy liberty of following his own caprice" (p. 104)—Didascolo's ironic description of Piranesi—as triumphantly demonstrated in the works of Borromini and Gian Lorenzo Bernini.[82]

The central theme of the "Parere" is the tyranny of theory over the speculative processes of the unfettered imagination. As Tafuri has pointed out, Piranesi here "attacks the principles of absolute linguistic coherence that are founded on naturalism. Blondel, Cordemoy, Laugier and Algarotti are all caustically challenged."[83] Contrary to Tafuri's interpretation, however, the debate does not end in disillusionment on both sides. Under attack is a naturalism that is founded on a deliberate and restrictive reading of the primitive origins of architecture and that makes no allowance for the irrational, for the infinite and arbitrary fertility of natural processes of creation, as Piranesi valued them. Through Didascolo he satirizes the logical consequences of reducing architecture to a minimalist and sterile system:

> Let us observe the walls of a building from inside and outside. These walls terminate in architraves and all that goes with them above; below these architraves, most often we find engaged columns or pilasters. I ask you, what holds up the roof of the building? If the wall, then it needs no architraves; if the columns or pilasters, what is the wall there for? Choose, Signor Protopiro, Which will you demolish? The walls or the pilasters? No answer? Then I will demolish the whole lot. Take note: *buildings with no walls, no columns, no pilasters, no friezes, no cornices, no vaults, no roofs.* A clean sweep (p. 106).[84]

Another area of attack in the "Parere" is the danger of a doctrinaire philosophy of design that enables buildings to be created by a mechanical process of composition where a system of finite rules dispenses with intellectual endeavor and allows no scope or freedom for the individual imagination. If one were to follow that path to its logical conclusion, Piranesi believed, there would simply be no need for architects at all. As Didascolo puts it,

> Let us imagine the impossible: let us imagine that the world—sickened though it is by everything that does not change from day to day—were gracefully to accept your monotony; what would architecture then become? *A low trade, in which one would do nothing but copy,* as a certain gentleman has said. So that not only would you and your colleagues become extremely ordinary architects, as I said before, but further you would be something less than masons. By constant repetition, they learn to work by rote; and they have the advantage over you, because they have the mechanical skill. You would ultimately cease to be architects at all, because clients would be fools to use an architect to carry out work that could be done far more cheaply by a mason (pp. 110–11).[85]

The workings of the imagination as inspired by antique prototypes are exemplified by Didascolo's reference to James Adam's design of a British order for a projected Houses of Parliament in London, which was also mentioned in Mariette's letter. Following his elder brother Robert on the Grand Tour, James had met Piranesi in Rome during April 1762, when he had proudly showed the artist various designs for the Parliament scheme. The capital of the order concerned (fig. 20), which was published some years later in *The Works in Architecture of Robert and James Adam* (1773–79), was devised according to Piranesi's precepts. It combined features of the British royal coat of arms (principally a lion and a unicorn flanking the crown) with ideas from the capital of the Templum Mars Ultor in Rome.[86] At this time Piranesi himself had incorporated the castle of the Rezzonico arms, between

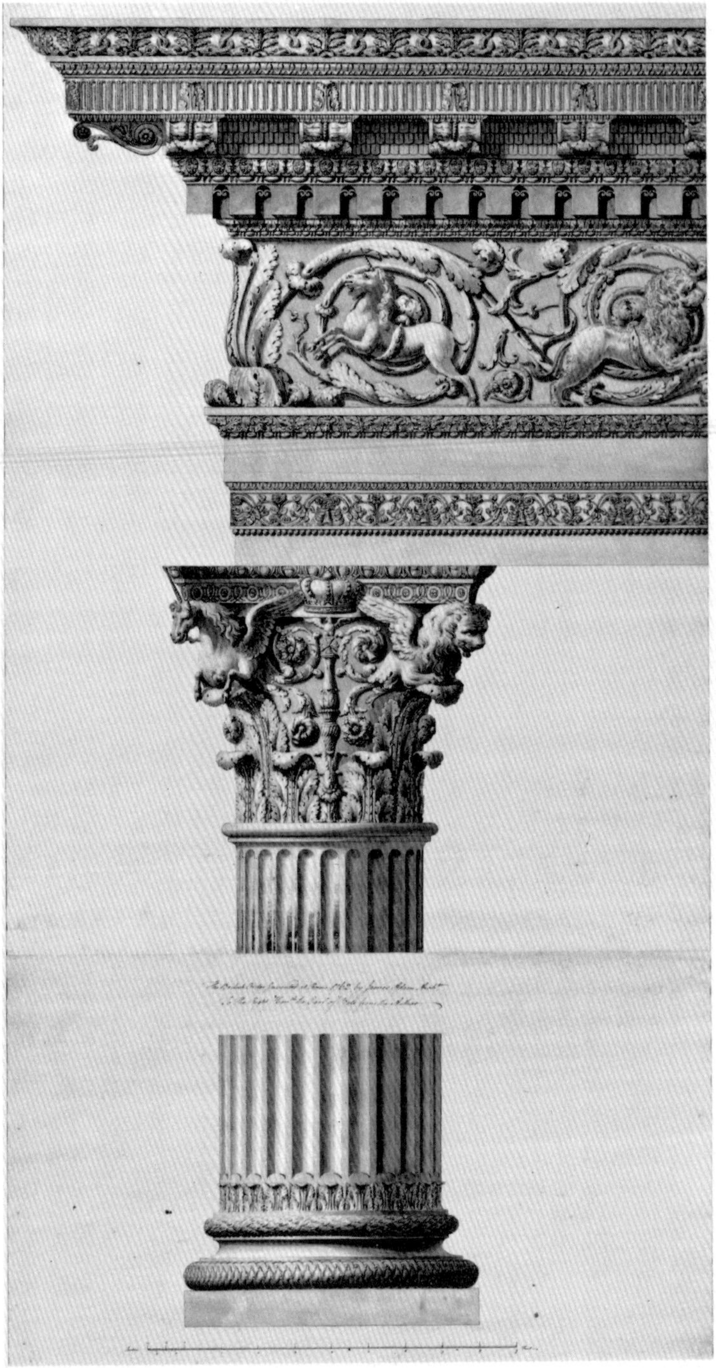

Fig. 20. James Adam (British, 1732–94)
The British Order Invented at Rome, 1762, pen and ink with watercolor, 106 × 60 cm (41⅜ × 23⅝ in.)
New York, Columbia University, Avery Architectural and Fine Arts Library

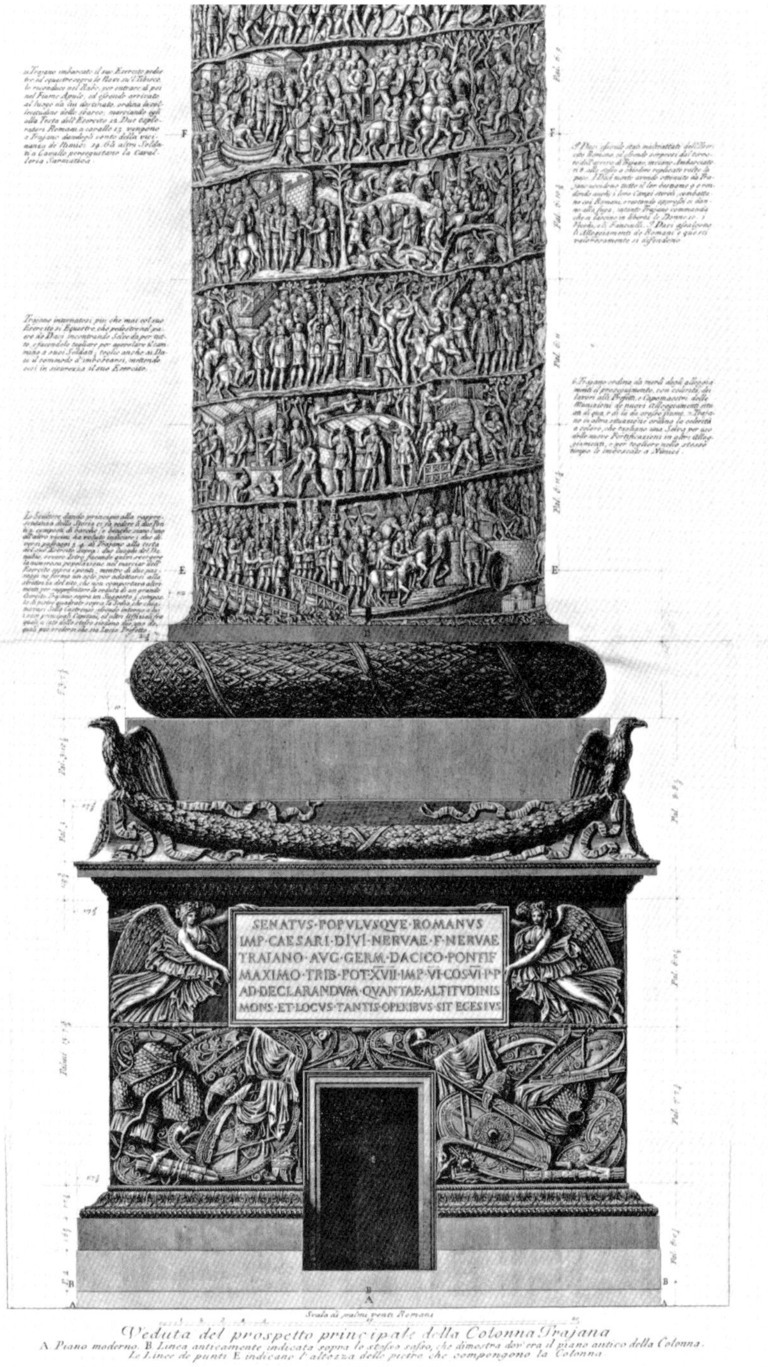

Fig. 21. Giovanni Battista Piranesi (Italian, 1720–78)
Veduta del prospetto principale della Colonna Trajana (detail), 1774, etching, 285 × 46.5 cm (112¼ × 18¼ in.)
From Giovanni Battista Piranesi, *Trofeo o sia magnifica colonna coclide di marmo*. . . (Rome: n.p., 1774–79), pl. III

confronted Sphinxes, in the capitals of his Aventine church, following the stylistic precedent of the Pamphili dove inserted by Borromini in the order he used for the facade of the family's palace in Piazza Navona, Rome.

By way of a final indictment of the endless potential for mediocrity in the rigorists' system of strictly functional design (a theoretical anticipation of the familiar Miesian adage "Less is more"), Piranesi ridiculed, through Didascolo, the intellectual poverty implicit in system-led design:

> Show me designs by any of the rigorists, anyone who thinks he has conceived a wonderful design for a building; and I warrant he will look more foolish than the man who works to please himself—yes, more foolish—because the only way he could imagine a building without irregularities is when four upright poles with a roof—the very prototype of architecture—can remain entire and unified at the very moment of being halved, varied, and rearranged in a thousand ways; in short, when the simple becomes composite, and one becomes as many as you like (p. 106).[87]

Toward the end of the debate, Didascolo returned to the rigorists' censure of ornamented construction, which not only struck at the heart of Piranesi's theoretical artistic beliefs but also ignored some of the greatest surviving achievements of imperial Rome. In particular, Didascolo cited the richly detailed bas-reliefs covering the columns of Trajan (fig. 21) and of Marcus Aurelius, which were to feature in the fully illustrated folio on the three monumental relief columns in Rome that Piranesi was to issue between 1774 and 1779.[88]

Polemics and Fantasy

Predictably, it was through the images of the "Parere" that Piranesi's most forceful arguments were expressed. When the *Osservazioni* appeared in 1765, its three essays were embellished by relatively modest vignettes that simply reinforced the meaning of the texts. Three of these, as in Piranesi's earlier publications, feature compositions of antique fragments: heading the "Osservazioni" (see p. 126) is a particularly inventive Roman capital, incorporating sirens and dolphins, which Piranesi found lying in the courtyard of the Palazzo Gabrielli; at the head of the "Introduzione" (see p. 129) is an Etruscan antefix consisting of rams locked in conflict, inscribed as belonging to the English (actually Irish) artist Matthew Nulty;[89] and the book's colophon (see p. 130) features objects grouped around two coins, the smaller stamped with one of the warrior Dioscuri, the larger with the helmet of Minerva, goddess of wisdom. More central to the arguments of the "Parere," and unprecedented among the artist's vignettes, however, are the three representing examples of highly monumental buildings—the scale being indicated by the minute human figures grouped on stairways or in entrances. These edifices are assertively anti-Vitruvian compositions, each being assembled from exceptionally disparate elements in which profusion of ornament is the primary focus.

The first one, heading the "Parere" (see p. 127), is composed in what can only be described as a collage of disturbingly discordant forms contrived for polemical effect. It takes the form of a temple facade, covered with a wealth of sculptural elements in relief, and an attached Tuscan colonnade surmounted by a disproportionate upper story bearing an inscription to the Society of Antiquaries of London ("REI ANTIQUARIAE LONDINENSI SAC"), to which Piranesi had been elected in 1757.[90] Flanking screen walls, bearing tapering columns decorated with reliefs, partly obscure flanking freestanding Tuscan porticoes. A number of the decorative forms used here appear as well in Piranesi's contemporary proposals for the Aventine complex, including inscribed stelae as well as the panpipe and the serpent motifs, which, in a later publication, Piranesi was to claim were Etruscan in origin.[91]

A second temple composition, which appears as the tailpiece for the "Parere" (see p. 128), also consists of a prominent portico and two flanking screen walls. Here the building's proportions are more conventional, but the variety of ornament—involving rich passages of relief in friezes and panels, freestanding sculptural forms, and a range of diverse columns, spiral and scale-patterned—can be traced back to mannerist sources such as Peruzzi or Ligorio. Far closer still to Cinquecento mannerism is the third composition (see p. 131), printed on the page after the book's colophon. This depicts a particularly complex palace facade where Vitruvian conventions and Palladian proportions are abandoned in a design that has considerable resemblances to the formal innovations of Raphael's vanished Palazzo Branconio dell'Aquila in Rome, as preserved in an engraving by Pietro Ferrerio.[92] Here one of the most striking conceits is the screenlike sequence of aediculae whose triangular and segmental pediments are supported by square posts bearing what appear to be hieroglyphics and flanked by paired Egyptian telamones, which face one another across each doorway. As in the previous two compositions, ornament is applied to structure rather than integral to it, and these vignettes are clearly devised to support Piranesi's belief in the autonomy of an ornamental system in its own right.

Far more dramatic and polemically significant is the suite of six large plates of imaginary compositions (see pls. IV–IX) that appears to have been added to the "Parere" after 1767, that is, after Clement XIII conferred on Piranesi the order of the Sperone d'Oro (Golden Spur) for his work on the Aventine church, allowing the architect to style himself "Cavaliere," as he inscribed these plates, which were numbered at some later date.[93] By this point in his artistic development, Piranesi's tentative essays in his new system of eclectic design had been fully explored in working out the ornamental programs for the Aventine and Lateran commissions and in his various designs for interiors and the applied arts in the mid-1760s. Thus, for all their polemical distortion, these compositions are more monumentally assured and possess a greater vigor and grandeur than the earlier vignettes and are characteristic of his graphic style of the later 1760s. They also possess a considerable amount of esoteric symbolism that continues to tax the iconographic ingenuity of scholars who consider that there are distinct messages still to be unraveled. Moreover, it is possible to discern in these important additions to the "Parere" a far more personal language of composition that, although it often involves specific borrowings, is totally Piranesi's own. This is the language reflected not only in his designs for the Aventine piazza's reliefs and monuments as well as the church's facade and high altar but also in the intricate decorative system of his designs for the Lateran tribune. While two of the additional plates show complete buildings, the remainder are devoted to sections of facades and a funerary monument where the ornamental language is rendered with unparalleled complexity and detail. Large preparatory studies in pen and ink survive for at least four of the etched designs as well as for two equally ambitious compositions that were not engraved.[94]

Following the order of the numbered suite, reproduced here, this series of plates begins with an elevation and plan of a relatively conventional facade with an attached Tuscan order bearing a pediment with a rusticated tympanum (see pl. IV), as if representing a point of formal departure for the sequence of compositional scherzos that follow. In marked contrast, the following image (see pl. V), which depicts a portion of a larger composition, suggests the upper part of a religious structure. A frieze depicting warriors and priestesses making sacrifice is supported by a complex design of tapering pilasters decorated with acanthus reliefs, ambivalently superimposed on relief panels and an inner colonnade. The plethora of ornament mixes conventional classical elements with reliefs of a veiled Minerva, a sword in scabbard, a snake-legged giant, a crouching tiger, naturalistic dolphins, feet in sandals (with a coiled snake), and Egyptian winged scarabs. Here the extremes in scale of juxtaposed elements could hardly be greater, perhaps because Piranesi copied a number of the figures enclosed in borders from engraved hard stones in the collection of the Venetian connoisseur Anton Maria Zanetti, published by Gori in 1750.[95] The inscription is an epigraph from the prologue to Terence's *Eunuchus:* "AEQUUM EST VAS COGNOSCERE ATQUE IGNOSCERE QUAE VETERES FACTITARUNT SI FACIUNT NOVI" (You should know this and make allowances if the moderns do what the ancients used to do).[96]

After the brittle play of sharply defined textures and surfaces of plate V, a distinct change of mood is signified by the next composition (see pl. VI), where another portion of a monumental structure is registered with far stronger effects of chiaroscuro and plasticity. This solemn edifice, without windows but conveying the impression of having a domed roof with oculus, is articulated on its lower level by a powerfully rusticated and uncharacteristically tapered Ionic order possessing an almost Egyptian effect of grandeur. A vigorous band of reliefs runs across this attached order, which is fluted solely at the base. The upper part of the composition consists of a complex superstructure of figurative reliefs and projecting panels on consoles, with disjunctions and contrasts in ornamental forms similar to the previous plate.

In the succeeding composition, the focus changes to what appears to be a elaborate funerary monument (see pl. VII), shown on a far larger scale than in the preceding images and even more vigorously defined. The main part, which appears to derive from a tomb in Santa Maria Gloriosa dei Frari, Venice, features a sarcophagus with a strigilate surface on which is superimposed a relief of an eagle bearing a snake in its beak.[97] Above this particular feature are two sets of panpipes, flanked by groups of profile heads in relief; the outermost are women facing inward, the inmost are two pairs of helmeted warriors facing outward, with one on each side having as well a (skewed) Janus form. At the top, separated from the lower half by a neutral area, is a more conventional relief of four robed female figures posed in the fashion of the Borghese *Dancers* and wreathing two terminal figures. Above this relief is an inscription from Ovid's *Metamorphoses:* "RERUMQUE NOVATRIX EX ALIIS ALIAS REDDIT NATURA FIGURAS" (And Nature, the great renewer, ever makes up forms from other forms).[98]

The following design (see pl. VIII) shows the left-hand portion of the *piano nobile* (upper floor) of a palatial building, articulated by an attached Greek Ionic order framing alternate bays with aediculae and supporting a massive superstructure that features a vast segmental pediment and plethora of reliefs and ornamental forms derived from Roman and Etruscan sources. The inscription from Le Roy—"POUR NE PAS FAIRE DE CET ART SUBLIME UN VIL METIER OU L'ON NE FEROIT QUE COPIER SANS CHOIX" (So as not to make this sublime art into a vile profession where one would only copy without choice)—displayed at the heart of this composition (and also quoted in the "Parere" text) is supported by the sheer fecundity of invention surrounding it. The motifs used in this structure range from conventional sources, such as the confronted griffins from the Templum Antoninus and Faustina, Rome, and *aplustria* (ornamental warship terminals) from a naval relief in the Museo Capitolino's collection (a much-used source for the Aventine reliefs), to strange zoomorphic motifs combining shells with rams' heads. As with the *Carceri* plates, ambiguity is skillfully used to enhance the visual power of the design. For example, the gesticulating robed figure on the far left of the cornice may represent either a human being or a statue, thus affecting our sense of the building's scale. Similarly, the freely rendered group of entwined dolphins in the inverted segmental frieze at the top have an uncanny realism in contrast to the adjacent stylized figures. There are also frequent jumps in scale from one element to another, and a disconcerting play of surface planes, as demonstrated by the uncertain location of the blank panels that incorporate the pediments of the aediculae between the columns yet also appear to extend across the columns themselves.

The sixth and final composition (see pl. IX), which presents the complete facade of a temple, develops all the formal complexity and ambiguity of the preceding plates and is polemically crowded with the widest range of stylistic sources at Piranesi's command. Anticipating his critics, the artist places at the top of the plate a defensive inscription from Sallust's *Bellum Igurthinum:* "NOVITATEM MEAM CONTEMNUNT, EGO ILLORUM IGNAVIAM" (They despise my novelty, I their timidity). As Joseph Rykwert has pointed out, the context of this quotation reveals the extent to which Piranesi was prepared to use recondite literary texts to defend the challenging nature of his inventive style. The quotation comes from a speech by the outsider Gaius Marius to the Roman Senate after he had risen to the consulship during the Jugurthine War. In the preceding paragraph of Sallust's account, Marius had attacked the nobles, the *homines preposteri* (those who put things last), who on assuming office relate the deeds of their ancestors or quote Greek manuals on warfare. Marius confronts such armchair theorists, dependent on inherited privilege, with his own sense of worth, derived from decision and active experience: "If the patricians justly despise me, let them also despise their own ancestors, whose nobility, like mine, had its origin in meritous deeds."[99]

In this culminating plate of the "Parere," Piranesi demonstrates the sovereignty of an ornamental language that throws into question all previous conventions and rational theories, especially those attributed by his rigorist opponents to classical Greek architecture and to primal nature. While the columnar forms espoused by the functionalists are displayed in a range of ornamental versions, their structural integrity is deliberately neutralized by an extensive frieze in the form of a frame superimposed on the facade. In front of this frame and the columns are placed, almost in suspension, two rectangular plaques depicting winged victories bearing and flanked by reliefs. The hermetic symbolism in these reliefs is found throughout the composition, especially in the central panel imposed over the pediment, where seven figures preside over a sacrificial altar. Beneath this group are knotted serpents above a Sphinx between lion's paws above the horned head of Jupiter Ammon. To either side of this panel is a winged caduceus overlaid by clasped hands, which some scholars have interpreted as having Masonic significance.[100] As elsewhere in this suite of plates, the composition contains references to the Aventine facade—here, the knotted snakes and the ornamental swords in scabbards attached to the spirally fluted columns that flank the entrance, framing four diminutive figures in a disconcerting leap in scale.

The fact that Piranesi was working on other versions of these plates but rejected them is borne out by the two unexecuted compositions surviving in preparatory pen and ink studies for imaginary temple facades, already mentioned. The study held by the Kunstbibliothek, Berlin (fig. 22), possesses the same compositional boldness as the executed versions and uses the same framing frieze motif as plate IX, but it incorporates the baseless Greek Doric colonnade, and there are also signs of Egyptian forms in the doorway framed by the colonnade.[101] In the drawing at the British Museum, London (fig. 23), however, the temple composition is perhaps even more extreme than in the etched works.[102] Here the artist devised an exceptionally strange interpretation of a Doric colonnade, with superimposed linked dolphins, setting it in front of a segmental arch and below a superstructure where the disproportionate scales of the various reliefs make no concessions to rational design. The reliefs include a theatrical mask on a circular panel placed between facing men's heads on a rectangular panel surmounted by confronted Sphinxes, the

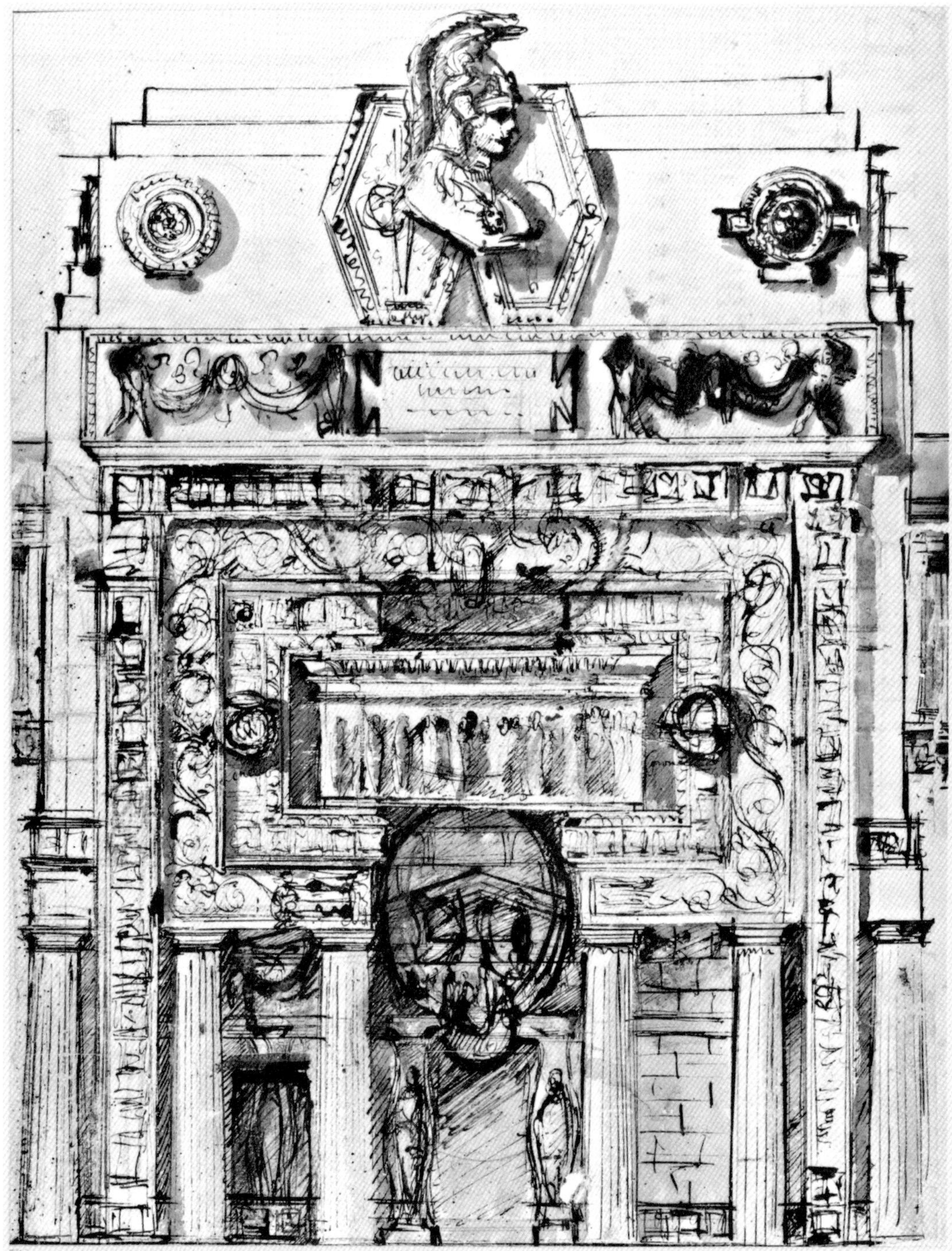

Fig. 22. Giovanni Battista Piranesi (Italian, 1720–78)
Unexecuted design for "Parere su l'architettura," after 1767, pen and brown and black inks, and brown wash, 62.5 × 43.8 cm (24⅝ × 17¼ in.)
Berlin, Kunstbibliothek

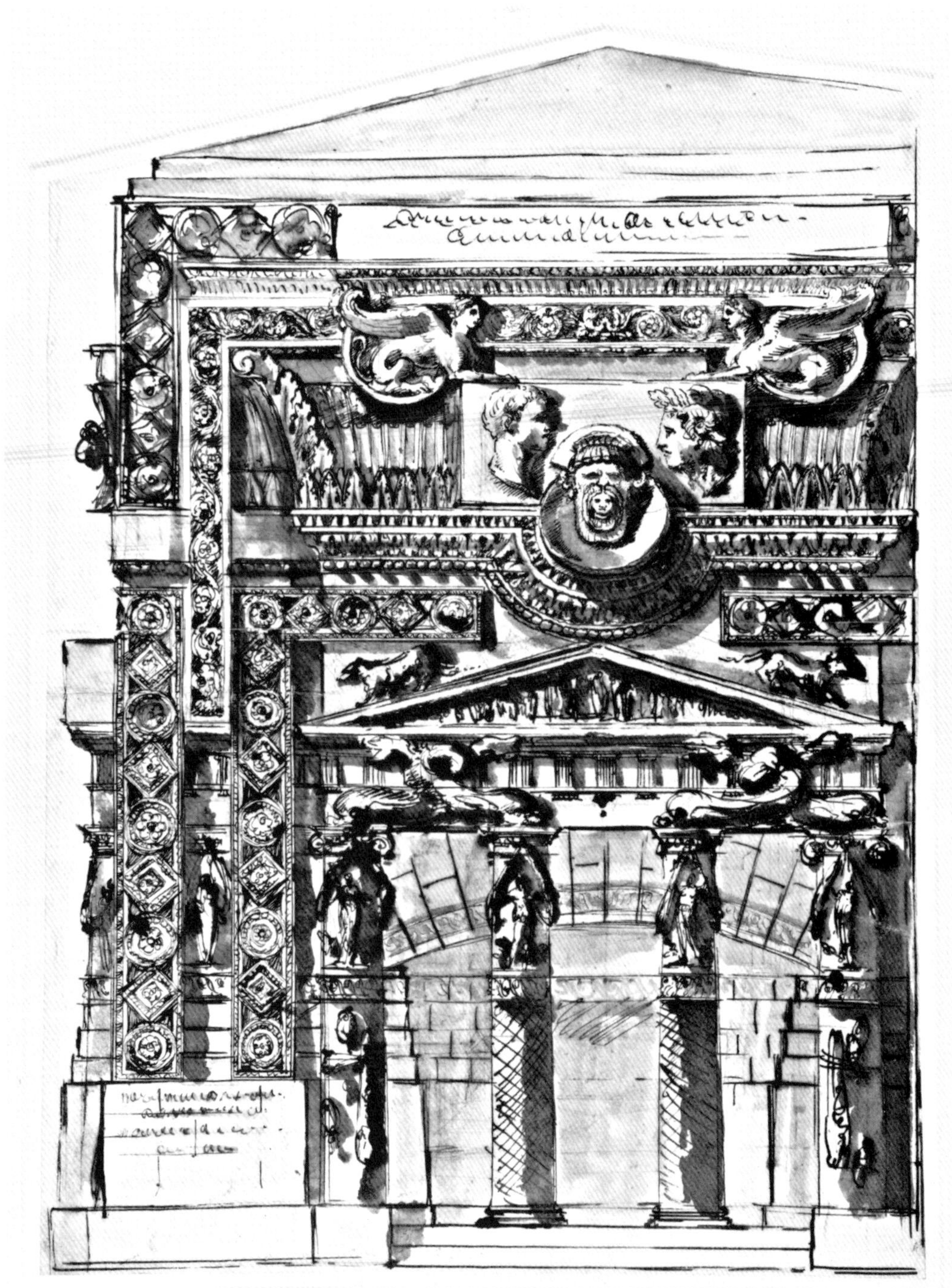

Fig. 23. Giovanni Battista Piranesi (Italian, 1720–78)
Unexecuted design for "Parere su l'architettura," after 1767,
pen and brown ink with wash over red and black chalk outline,
66.2 × 46.7 cm (26 × 18⅜ in.)
London, British Museum

latter derived from an antique source that Piranesi quoted in *Della magnificenza* and also used on the Aventine facade. This bizarre composition, which is set below a panel evidently intended for an inscription, is superimposed on a willfully enlarged pilaster capital of flutes and acanthus, whose antique source was also illustrated in *Della magnificenza* on the same plate as the Sphinxes.[103]

Despite its ambitious title, the final essay of Piranesi's *Osservazioni* merely repeats Piranesi's theories regarding the originality of Italy. Supporting his contentions are three plates illustrating the extensive range of relief patterns invented by the Etruscans for their tombs at Corneto (Tarquinia) and Chiusi (see pls. I–III). These had been partly derived from the research, mentioned earlier, of James Byres, who was preparing a history of the Etruscans, as well as from visits to Corneto by Thomas Jenkins in 1761 and by Piranesi himself in 1765.[104] A satiric caption placed next to the lowest two Etruscan friezes in the first of these plates poses the question, "A historical problem of interest to tailors/stonecutters. Were the Etruscans or the Greeks the inventors of these sorts of trimmings, which Piranesi found in Tuscany in the caves of Corneto and Chiusi."[105] Whatever the answer, Piranesi immediately applied what he had seen in the Etruscan tombs of Tuscany in his contemporary work. The fretted band of the large fragment inscribed with Etruscan letters in the middle of the third plate (see pl. III) is used on the frieze of the Aventine church facade (see fig. 18).

Final Testament: Diverse maniere

By the end of the 1760s Piranesi was in a position to review his practical achievements as a designer, and his final publication in the Graeco-Roman controversy was to take the form of an illustrated demonstration of his new aesthetic in action, the folio *Diverse maniere d'adornare i cammini ed ogni altra parte degli edifizj . . .* (*Divers Manners of Ornamenting Chimneys and All Other Parts of Houses . . .*) of 1769. Its introductory text, presented in three languages, is followed by a considerable number of etched designs for chimneypieces as well for furniture and portions of complete decorative schemes. These plates illustrate several executed commissions, including two chimneypieces for British clients, various works for members of the Rezzonico family, and two wall compositions from the painted Egyptian scheme of the Caffè degli Inglesi.[106] The preparation of certain of these designs can be traced back to the years 1764 and 1765, and a number of the etched prints were already in circulation among colleagues and patrons by 1767. Like the compositions in the additional plates for the "Parere," these compositions, and the chimneypiece designs in particular (fig. 24), clearly were exaggerated in their complexity for polemical effect. However, unlike the former imaginative designs, those in the *Diverse maniere* were also intended as ornamental "collages" from which ideas and motifs could be selected for reuse, which was in fact done by architects as diverse as Adam, Dance the Younger, François-Joseph Bélanger (fig. 25), and Charles Percier and Pierre-François-Léonard Fontaine.[107]

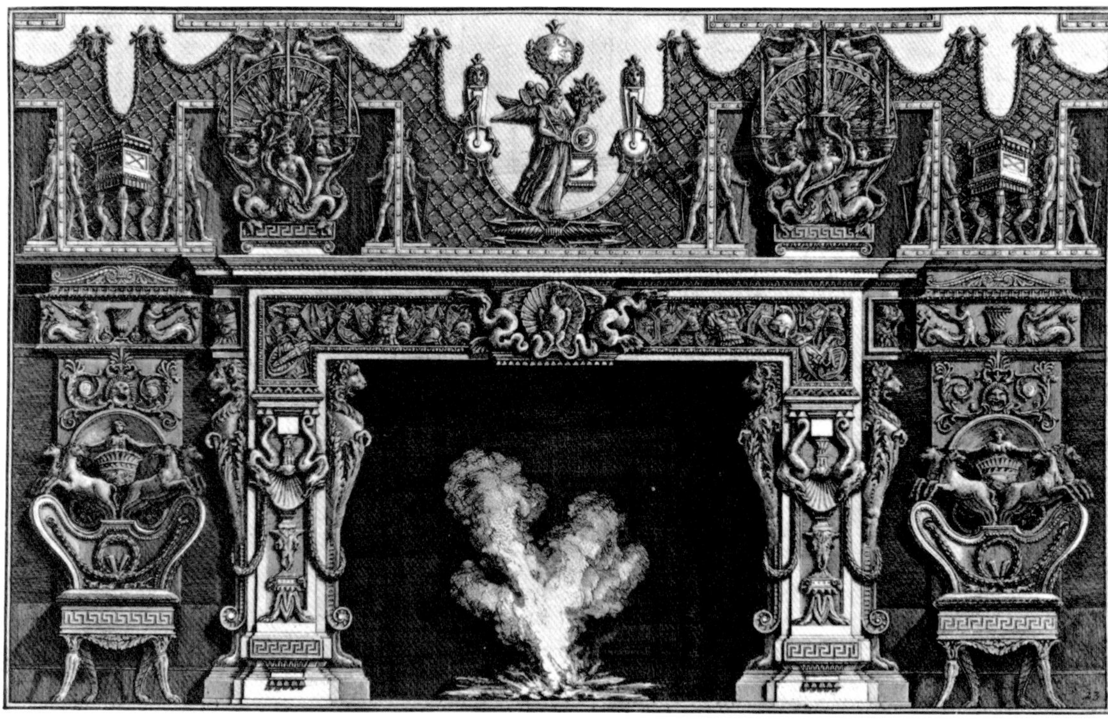

Fig. 24. Giovanni Battista Piranesi (Italian, 1720–78)
Design for a chimneypiece, with flanking chairs, 1769, etching, 24 × 38 cm (9½ × 15 in.)
From Giovanni Battista Piranesi, *Diverse maniere d'adornare i cammini ed ogni altra parte degli edifizj . . .* (Rome: Stamperia Generoso Salomoni, 1769)

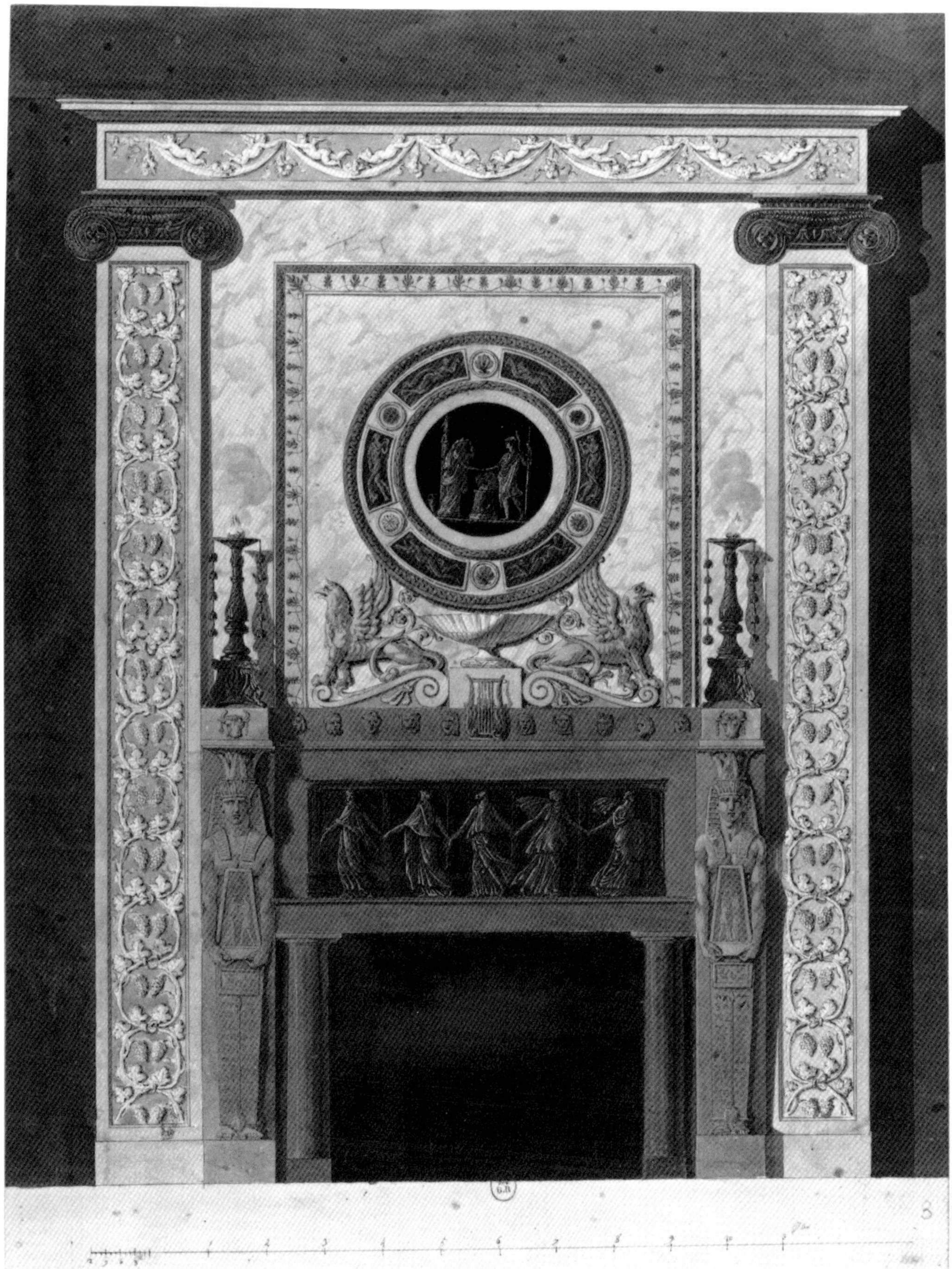

Fig. 25. François-Joseph Bélanger (French, 1744–1818)
Design for a chimneypiece in the Egyptian taste, ca. 1770–80, pen and black ink, watercolor, and wash, 45.6 × 33 cm (18 × 13 in.)
Paris, Bibliothèque Nationale de France

The volume was, appropriately, dedicated to Cardinal Giovanni Battista Rezzonico as the model of a sympathetic and enlightened patron of modern design. Unlike *Della magnificenza* or the *Osservazioni*, it was directed not toward the critics and antiquaries of an earlier phase of debate but, by parallel texts in Italian, French, and English, to an international audience of clients and practicing designers. The prefatory text to the sixty-seven plates is entitled, in Piranesi's English, "An Apologetical Essay in Defense of the Egyptian and Tuscan Architecture" and represents a considered summing up of his theories of creative license with respect to both antiquity and nature. In this essay, Piranesi drew attention to the creative eclecticism of the Romans, who had first utilized Etruscan ideas and then had proceeded to absorb Greek and Egyptian material into their own living, ever-changing system of design. In particular he justified the complexity and multiplicity of forms in his designs on the basis of aesthetic control rather than academic orthodoxy. He also sought to explain the boldness and a certain stiffness in Egyptian art (reflected in many of the etched designs) with a remarkably advanced defense of stylization in architectural forms.[108] His confidence in opening up a new approach to the understanding and application of Egyptian sources for contemporary design is expressed in a letter of 1768 to Thomas Hollis of the Society of Antiquaries in London, which accompanied a group of proof plates intended for the *Diverse maniere*. "You will see in this work," he wrote, "something that has been hitherto unknown. For the first time Egyptian architecture makes its appearance, for the first time I stress, because until now the world has thought that it consisted of nothing but pyramids, obelisks, and vast statues, and concluded that these were insufficient to form a basis for architectural ornament and design."[109]

In the course of the "Apologetical Essay," Piranesi returned to a defense of the Etruscans, arguing not simply on historical and literary grounds but on grounds of the creative abstraction of their designs, which be believed were based on natural patterns, such as found in sea shells (which he illustrated from examples in the Florentine collection of Niccolo Gualtieri).[110] His own designs for furniture among the etchings of the *Diverse maniere* were clearly grounded in the belief that fertility in composition, such as expressed by both the Etruscans and the Egyptians in fanciful as well as sacred ornamental works, was based on a close study of natural forms. In at least two instances, rare preparatory studies by Piranesi for pieces of furniture show, in the one case, how an etched sconce had evolved from studies of tree branches and, in the other, how the legs of a side table—produced for Cardinal Giovanni Battista Rezzonico and surviving in two executed examples—were evolved from the freely sketched natural form of an animal's leg structure.[111]

Toward the close of the "Apologetical Essay," Piranesi makes a final plea for a new system of design, one unconstrained by doctrinaire theory but sanctioned by usage from the past and inspired by nature. As he expressed it in the English version of his text:

> Must the Genius of our artists be so basely enslaved to the Grecian manners, as not to dare to take what is beautiful elsewhere, if it be not of Grecian origin? But let us at last shake of[f] this shameful yoak, and if the Egyptians, and Tuscans present to us, in their monuments, beauty, grace, and elegance, let us borrow from their stock, not servilely copying from others, for this would reduce architecture and the noble arts [to] a pitiful mechanism, and would deserve blame instead of praise from the public, who seek for novelty, and who would not form the most advantageous idea of an artist, as was perhaps the opinion some years ago, for a good design, if it was only a copy of some ancient work. No, an artist, who would do himself honour, and acquire a name, must not content himself with copying faithfully the ancients, but studying their works he ought to show himself of an inventive, and, I had almost said, of a creating Genius; And by prudently combining the Grecian, the Tuscan, and the Egyptian together, he ought to open himself a road to the finding out of new ornaments and new manners. The human understanding is not so short and limited, as to be unable to add new graces, and embellishments to the works of architecture, if to an attentive and profound study of nature one would likewise join that of the ancient monuments.[112]

Legacy and Reception

In the many examples of Piranesi's later influence, through his theoretical writings and images, on the leading designers of neoclassicism, no more striking demonstration can be found than the later style of Robert Adam, where there is a similar degree of extreme experiment, venturing beyond the boundaries of conventional taste.[113] This is embodied in the exceptional series of "Etruscan" rooms Adam produced in the 1770s, and epitomized by the most complete surviving example, at Osterley Park House, Middlesex (fig. 26).[114] Adam, after his highly successful debut in the 1760s at Kedleston Hall and Syon House, mentioned earlier, was faced with increasing competition for fashionable patronage from younger designers such as James Wyatt. In attempting to retain his market leadership by devising a novel and attractive style, from the 1770s onward the architect followed the principles advocated in the "Parere" and *Diverse maniere* by consciously developing a mode of expression derived from the archaeological evidence found in the Vesuvian cities as well as from the ornamental forms and colors of the so-called Etruscan vases of Hamilton's collection.[115] Adam was to create at least eight such interiors, including the dressing room he completed at Osterley in 1775, where a striking unity of design, encompassing walls, ceiling, doors, furniture, carpet, chimneyboard, and curtains, achieved the complete coherence of the modern style advocated by Piranesi.

Adam, however, remained an exception even among those neoclassical designers who derived inspiration from the innovatory concepts and compositions of the *Diverse maniere*, and Piranesi's idiosyncratic ideas were regularly ridiculed and maligned by the more conservative architects, artists, and critics of the time. According to the British artist James Barry, writing in 1769 to the

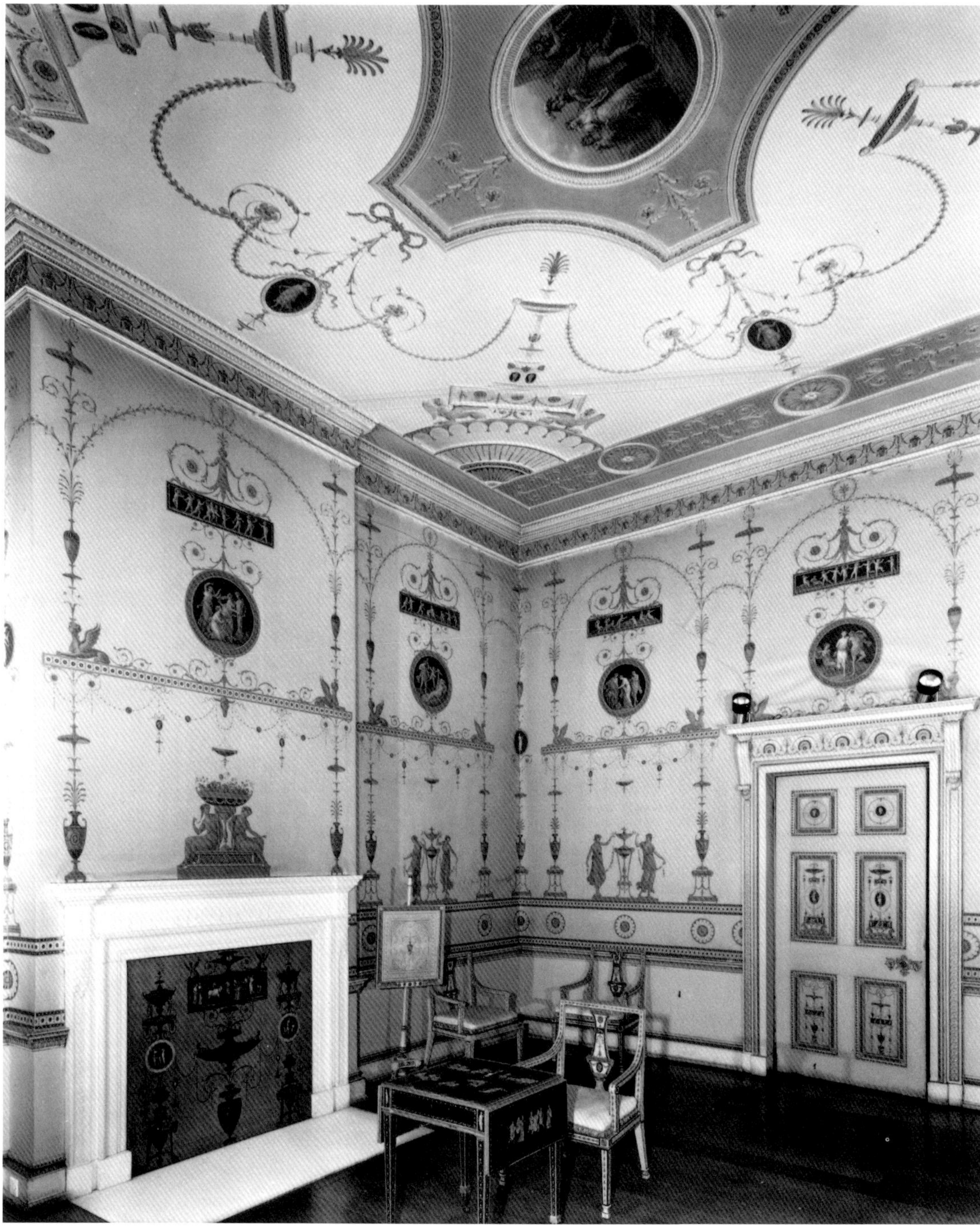

Fig. 26. Robert Adam (British, 1728–92), architect
Etruscan dressing room, Osterley Park House, Middlesex, London

politician and theorist Edmund Burke, Piranesi "will go down to posterity with deserved reputation, in spite of his Egyptian or other whimsies, and his gusto of architecture flowing out of the same cloacus as Borromini's, and other hair-brained moderns."[116] However, the critic Horace Walpole, disenchanted with the more experimental character of the Adam style, saw Piranesi's images as a valuable corrective. In the fourth edition of his *Anecdotes of Painting*, published in 1780, he observed, almost certainly with the magisterial fantasy of the *Parte di ampio magnifico porto* in mind (see fig. 3),

> This delicate redundance of ornament growing into our architecture might perhaps be checked, if our artists would study the sublime dreams of Piranesi, who seems to have conceived visions of Rome beyond what it boasted even in the meridian of its splendor. Savage as Salvator Rosa, fierce as Michael Angelo, and exuberant as Rubens, he has imagined scenes that would startle geometry, and exhaust the Indies to realize. He piles palaces on bridges, and temples on palaces, and scales Heaven with mountains of edifices. Yet what taste in his boldness! what grandeur in his wildness! what labour and thought both in his rashness and details![117]

By the last decades of the eighteenth century, as the discipline of a new academic orthodoxy replaced flights of the imagination as the basis for architectural design, a fresh generation of theorists was swift to condemn Piranesi's visionary language, whether in his writings or his executed works. Francesco Milizia could not bring himself to mention the architect of Santa Maria del Priorato by name in his *Roma, delle belle arti del disegno* (1787; Rome, the fine arts of design); while Giovanni Lodovico Bianconi, a devoted follower of Winckelmann, when producing Piranesi's obituary in 1779, had characterized the Aventine complex in the following terms: "Oh how different is *The design from the actual execution of the building!* The work turned out to be overloaded with ornaments which, even though taken from antiquity, were not in harmony with one another. The church of the Priorato will certainly please many, as it must above all have pleased Piranesi who always regarded it as a masterpiece, but it wouldn't have pleased Vitruvius or Palladio if they returned to Rome."[118] Only a few years earlier an equally negative reaction to Piranesi's Aventine church had been expressed by the marquis de Sade on a visit to Rome in 1775: "this church has been recently embellished by the architect Piranesi, who has weighed down the temple with ornaments taken from antiquity, systematically confused and handled with a hardness that wearies the eyes and which will always appear unpleasant."[119]

It is predictable that Piranesi's maverick and idiosyncratic theories of design were equally unacceptable to one of the high priests of French classicism, Antoine-Chrysostome Quatremère de Quincy. During his first visit to Rome, which began in 1776, he made the acquaintance of Piranesi, who clearly had a significant impact on his early studies of the city's classical remains, even if the aesthetic theories of Winckelmann were to prove far more decisive in his later intellectual development. While his voluminous writings make no reference at all to Piranesi as designer, the Frenchman testified in his architectural dictionary, which appeared from 1788 onward, to the value of Piranesi's archaeological publications in providing evidence of license in antiquity. Regularly citing him as "cet illustre dessinateur" (this distinguished draftsman), Quatremère de Quincy commented in the entry on the Composite order, "Piranesi's collection of antique fragments could furnish us with still more examples of the fertile imagination of the ancients, in the composition of their capitals and in the decoration of the Corinthian."[120] Similarly, he cited in the entry on carpentry Piranesi's observations and plates in *Della magnificenza* relating to Laugier's theories on the transference of wooden systems of construction to stone in the Doric temple, and originally he had intended to use the etchings concerned to illustrate this entry.[121]

This selective appreciation was also evident when the major Regency designer Sir John Soane lectured, from 1809 onward, as Professor of Architecture at the Royal Academy of Arts in London and had to confront the achievements of Piranesi, who had been such a catalytic force in his early development and whose engraved surveys of antique detail provided him with such rich visual resources.[122] While Soane's bold and highly radical forms of classicism were abundantly displayed throughout his works, particularly in the ornamental details, expressive sequences of spaces, and interior vaulting of his major commission, the Bank of England, London (1788–1833), he felt bound to warn his students that

> novelty, although a bewitching siren, has bounds; variety, with all her charms, has limits. In both, the artist must show moderation and sound judgement, not overstepping the modesty of nature lest he should fall into the excesses of Borromini and those of his school who, like Piranesi, passing by the fine examples of antiquity, carried what they called the powers of invention so far as to lose sight entirely of the simple and unaffected grandeur of those ancient compositions which have stood the test of ages, and will continue to be admired as the standard of pure taste so long as any true feeling for art remains.[123]

Throughout the nineteenth century and for most of the twentieth, Piranesi's theoretical ideas and highly imaginative forms were largely neglected in favor of the romantic vision of a ruined past in the *Vedute di Roma* and the emotional intensity of a confined and menacing world in the *Carceri d'invenzione*, which a long line of writers, from Samuel Taylor Coleridge to Marguerite Yourcenar, has mined for literary inspiration or psychological metaphor.[124] Significantly, it was during the 1970s, when new inquiries into the nature of architectural language began to be developed by scholars and theorists such as Maurizio Calvesi, Manfredo Tafuri, and Joseph Rykwert, that Piranesi's importance in the exploration of profound issues of meaning in architecture was recognized. In this intellectual climate, a close examination of the full range of his remarkable technical and formal expression resulted in a fresh awareness of its integral relationship to his polemical writings.[125] It is a sure indication of Piranesi's protean genius that the profound issues raised by the *Osservazioni* will continue to be relevant as long as the complexity and contradictions inherent in architecture continue to provoke a wider debate on the creative processes of the imagination.

Notes

1. Attention was first significantly directed to Piranesi as a practicing architect in the pioneering article by Werner Körte, "Giovanni Battista Piranesi als praktischer Architekt," *Zeitschrift für Kunstgeschichte* 2 (1933): 16–33. This was followed up many years later by Rudolf Wittkower, "Piranesi as Architect," in [Robert O. Parks et al.], *Piranesi*, exh. cat. (Northampton, Mass.: Smith College Museum of Art, 1961), 99–109. For a more recent assessment, see John Wilton-Ely, *Piranesi as Architect and Designer* (New York: Pierpont Morgan Library; New Haven: Yale Univ. Press, 1993).

2. For the Venetian architectural world of Piranesi's early years, see Elena Bassi, *Architettura del Sei e Settecento a Venezia* (Naples: Edizioni Scientifiche Italiane, 1962); Rudolf Wittkower, *Art and Architecture in Italy, 1600 to 1750*, 3d rev. ed. (Harmondsworth, England: Penguin, 1973), 386–89; Manlio Brusatin, *Venezia nel Settecento: Stato, architettura, territorio* (Turin: Giulio Einaudi, 1980); and Lionello Puppi, "Appunti sulla educazione veneziana di Giambattista Piranesi," in Alessandro Bettagno, ed., *Piranesi tra Venezia e l'Europa* (Florence: Leo S. Olschki, 1983), 217–64. For Lucchesi, see also Manlio Brusatin, ed., *Illuminismo e architettura del '700 Veneto*, exh. cat. (Resina, Treviso, Italy: Grafiche Giorgio Paroni, 1969), 65–66.

3. For Lucchesi's Etruscan polemic against Maffei, see Matteo Lucchesi, *Riflessioni sulla pretesa scoperta del sopraornato Toscano: Espostaci dall'autore dell'opera* Degli anfiteatri, e singolarmente del veronese (Venice: Presso Stefano Monti, 1730). For Maffei, see Giuseppe Silvestri, *Un europeo del Settecento: Scipione Maffei* (Treviso: Canova, 1954).

4. For Scalfurotto and Temanza, see Brusatin, *Venezia nel Settecento* (note 2).

5. Fresh light on Piranesi's Venetian training, and on the likely influence of the ideas of Lodoli as well as the intellectual ambience in which Piranesi grew up, can be found in Joseph Rykwert, *The First Moderns: The Architects of the Eighteenth Century* (Cambridge: MIT Press, 1980), 315–26; and Brusatin, *Venezia nel Settecento* (note 2). For Lodoli in general, see Francis Haskell, *Patrons and Painters: A Study in the Relations between Italian Art and Society in the Age of the Baroque*, rev. ed. (New Haven: Yale Univ. Press, 1980); Joseph Rykwert, "Lodoli on Function and Representation," *Architectural Review*, July 1976, 21–26; and Edgar Kaufmann Jr., "Memmo's Lodoli," *Art Bulletin* 46 (1964): 159–75. For a stimulating interpretation of Piranesi's response to Lodoli's ideas, see Emil Kaufmann, "Piranesi, Algarotti and Lodoli (A Controversy in Eighteenth Century Venice)," *Gazette des beaux-arts*, 6th ser., 46 (1955): 21–28.

6. Piranesi's radical development of the *veduta* and his use of etching as a means of communicating technical information about antiquity are discussed in John Wilton-Ely, *The Mind and Art of Giovanni Battista Piranesi* (London: Thames & Hudson, 1978). See also John Wilton-Ely, *Giovanni Battista Piranesi: The Complete Etchings* (San Francisco: Alan Wofsy Fine Arts, 1994), esp. vol. 1.

7. A detailed discussion of the plates of the *Prima parte* (and the *Opere varie*) is provided in Andrew Robison, *Piranesi—Early Architectural Fantasies: A Catalogue Raisonné of the Etchings* (Chicago: Univ. of Chicago Press, 1986). See also Jörg Garms, "Considérations sur la *Prima parte,*" in Georges Brunel, ed., *Piranèse et les Français: Colloque tenu à la Villa Médicis, 12–14 mai 1976* (Rome: Edizioni dell'Elefante, 1978), 265–80, where the role of the dedicatee, Nicola Giobbe, is also discussed. Evidence of the extent of Piranesi's preparatory work on the architectural design of certain compositions in the *Prima parte,* as found in one of two notebooks at Modena, is discussed in Silla Zamboni, "Due quaderni di Piranesi scoperti nella Biblioteca Estense di Modena," *Studi romani: Rivista trimestrale dell'Istituto di studi romani* 27 (1979): 332–34.

8. A comprehensive survey of the artistic world of eighteenth-century Rome and its intellectual milieu, as well as the phenomenon of the Grand Tour, is to be found in Edgar Peters Bowron and Joseph J. Rishel, eds., *Art in Rome in the Eighteenth Century,* exh. cat. (London: Merrell, 2000). See also Andrew Wilton and Ilaria Bignamini, eds., *Grand Tour: The Lure of Italy in the Eighteenth Century,* exh. cat. (London: Tate Gallery Publishing, 1996).

9. The architectural scene in Rome during Piranesi's lifetime is examined in Elisabeth Kieven, "Roman Architecture in the Time of Piranesi, 1740–1776," in Cara D. Denison, Myra Nan Rosenfeld, and Stephanie Wiles, *Exploring Rome: Piranesi and His Contemporaries,* exh. cat. (New York: Pierpont Morgan Library; Montreal: Centre Canadien d'Architecture/Canadian Centre for Architecture, 1993), xv–xxiv; and John A. Pinto, "Architecture and Urbanism," in Edgar Peters Bowron and Joseph J. Rishel, eds., *Art in Rome in the Eighteenth Century,* exh. cat. (London: Merrell, 2000), 113–21. See also Wittkower, *Art and Architecture* (note 2), 376–83; and Marica Mercalli, "L'architetto si presenta: Note iconografiche su alcuni ritratti del secolo XVIII," in Bruno Contardi and Giovanna Curcio, eds., *In Urbe Architectus: Modelli, disegni, misure: La professione dell'architetto Roma 1680–1750,* exh. cat. (Rome: Àrgos, 1991), 229–38.

10. Piranesi's use of the architectural fantasy as a medium for personal experiment is examined in John Wilton-Ely, *Piranesi,* exh. cat. (London: Arts Council of Great Britain, 1978), 24–26; and John Wilton-Ely, "El diseño a través de la fantasía: Los dibujos 'Capricci' de Piranesi," in Mariano J. Ruiz de Ael, ed., *Arquitecturas dibujadas: I jornadas internacionales sobre el estudio y conservación de las fuentes de arquitectura, Vitoria-Gasteiz, mayo 1994* (Vitoria-Gasteiz, Spain: Centro Vasco de Arquitectura, 1996), 81–92.

11. See "Original Text of *Prima parte* and English Translation," in [Dorothea Nyberg, ed.], *Giovanni Battista Piranesi: Drawings and Etchings at Columbia University,* exh. cat. (New York: Avery Architectural Library/Department of Art History & Archaeology, Columbia University, 1972), 115–18: "tali immagini mi hanno riempiuto lo spirito queste parlanti ruine, che di simili non arrivai a potermene mai formare sopra i disegni, benchè accuratissimi, che di queste stesse ha fatto l'immortale Palladio. . . . Quindi è ch'essendomi venuto in pensiero di farne palesi al Mondo alcune di queste: ned essendo sperabile a un Architetto di questi tempi, di poterne effettivamente esequire alcuna. . . . altro partito non veggo restare a me, e a qualsivoglia altro Architetto moderno, che spiegare con disegni le proprie idee."

12. "Original Text" (note 11), 116, 118: "come si possa in nuove forme fare lodevole uso de' ritrovati de' nostri maggiori."

13. For Bottari and his intellectual milieu, see *Dizionario biografico degli Italiani*, s.v. "Bottari, Giovanni"; Haskell, *Patrons and Painters* (note 5), 347–60; and Augusta Monferini, "Piranesi e Bottari," in Anna Lo Bianco, ed., *Piranesi e la cultura antiquaria, gli antecedenti e il contesto: Atti del convegno, 14–17 novembre 1979* (Rome: Multigrafica, 1983), 221–29. On the character of Bottari and on Roman Jansenism, see Enrico Dammig, *Il movimento giansenista a Roma nella seconda metà dell secolo XVIII* (Vatican City: Biblioteca Apostolica Vaticana, 1945); and Ernesto Codignola, *Illuministi, giansenisti e giacobini nell'Italia del Settecento* (Florence: "La Nuova Italia" Editrice, 1947). See also Heather Hyde Minor, "Rejecting Piranesi," *Burlington Magazine* 143 (2001): 412–19.

14. The significance of the Arcadians in eighteenth-century Rome, particularly as related to architectural thinking, is explored in Sandro Benedetti, "L'architettura dell'Arcadia, Roma 1730," in *Bernardo Vittone e la disputa fra classicismo e barocco nel Settecento: Atti del convegno internazional promosso dall'Accademia delle scienze di Torino . . . , 21–24 settembre 1970* (Turin: Accademia delle Scienze, 1972), 337–91; see also Sandro Benedetti, "Per un'architettura dell'Arcadia: Roma 1730," *Controspazio* 3, nos. 7–8 (1971): 2–17. See also Maurizio Calvesi, "Saggio introduttivo," in Henri Focillon, *Giovanni Battista Piranesi*, ed. Maurizio Calvesi and Augusta Monferini, trans. Giuseppe Guglielmi (Bologna: Alfa, 1967), iii–xlii; and Jonathan Scott, *Piranesi* (London: Academy Editions, 1975), 51–52, 307 n. 10. In the fourth state of the *Prima parte* title plate, the full reference to Piranesi's association with this literary society, which met in the Bosco Parrhasio on the Janiculum, is "fra gli Arcadi / Salcindio Tiseio" (among the Arcadians / Salcindio Tiseio); see Robison, *Piranesi* (note 7), 68, where the fourth state of the title plate is dated to 1748/49.

15. For Piranesi's participation in the fireworks display celebrating the recovery of the *pensionnaire* sculptor Jacques Saly in 1746, see Richard P. Wunder, "A Forgotten French Festival in Rome," *Apollo* 85 (1967): 354–59, which also describes the background to temporary designs by the *pensionnaires* for the biennial festival of the *Chinea*.

16. Piranesi's critical impact on the *pensionnaires* of the Académie de France à Rome is examined in John Harris, "Le Geay, Piranesi and International Neo-Classicism in Rome, 1740–1750," in Douglas Fraser, Howard Hibbard, and Milton J. Lewine, eds., *Essays in the History of Architecture Presented to Rudolf Wittkower* (London: Phaidon, 1967), 189–96.

17. For the spread of Piranesi's ideas among eighteenth-century French architects, see Allan Braham, "Piranesi as Archaeologist and French Architecture in the Late Eighteenth Century," in Georges Brunel, ed., *Piranèse et les Français: Colloque tenu à la Villa Médicis, 12–14 mai 1976* (Rome: Edizioni dell'Elefante, 1978), 67–71; Allan Braham, *The Architecture of the French Enlightenment* (London: Thames & Hudson, 1980) (for a discussion on the Château de Montmusard and the Comédie-Française, see pp. 94–102); and Robin Middleton and David Watkin, *Neoclassical and Nineteenth Century Architecture* (New York: Abrams, 1980).

18. The literature on the analysis and interpretation of the two *Carceri* suites is

considerable. A bibliography (publications up to 1992) appears in Wilton-Ely, *Complete Etchings* (note 6), 1:48. The most important pioneering study remains Ulya Vogt-Göknil, *Giovanni Battista Piranesi:* Carceri (Zurich: Origo, 1958). Important new insights are to be found in Robison, *Piranesi* (note 7); and Silvia Gavuzzo-Stewart, *Nelle carceri di G. B. Piranesi* (Leeds: Northern Universities Press, 1999). Among the most challenging of recent interpretations is Manfredo Tafuri, "'The Wicked Architect': G. B. Piranesi, Heterotopia, and the Voyage," in idem, *The Sphere and the Labyrinth: Avant-Gardes and Architecture from Piranesi to the 1970s,* trans. Pellegrino d'Acierno and Robert Connolly (Cambridge: MIT Press, 1987), 25–40.

19. Tafuri, "'The Wicked Architect'" (note 18), 26.

20. Giovanni Battista Piranesi, *Trofei di Ottaviano Augusto innalzati per la Vittoria ad Actium e conquista dell'Egitto con varj altri ornamenti diligentemente ricavati dagli avanzi più preziosi delle fabbriche antiche di Roma, utili a pittori, scultori ed architetti* (Rome: Stamperia di Giovanni Generoso Salomoni, 1753). See Wilton-Ely, *Complete Etchings* (note 6), 1:314–26.

21. The significance of *Le antichità romane* is considered by John Wilton-Ely, "Piranesi and the Role of Archaeological Illustration," in Anna Lo Bianco, ed., *Piranesi e la cultura antiquaria, gli antecedenti e il contesto: Atti del convegno, 14–17 novembre 1979* (Rome: Multigrafica, 1983), 317–37.

22. For the circumstances behind the *Lettere di giustificazione* and the quarrel with Charlemont, see Lamberto Donati, "Giovan Battista Piranesi e Lord Charlemont," *English Miscellany* (Rome) 1 (1950): 231–42; Scott, *Piranesi* (note 14), 108–10; and Wilton-Ely, *Complete Etchings* (note 6), 2:802–19. The full text and plates of the *Lettere* are reproduced in Giovanni Battista Piranesi, *The Polemical Works, Rome 1757, 1761, 1765, 1769,* ed. John Wilton-Ely (Farnborough, England: Gregg, 1972).

23. For a list of the recipients of the *Lettere di giustificazione,* see [Robert O. Parks et al.], *Piranesi,* exh. cat. (Northampton, Mass.: Smith College Museum of Art, 1961), 65–66 (cat. no. 176).

24. Quoted from the excerpts from the letter of 25 August 1756 (the first of the three published in the *Lettere di giustificazione*) translated in Lorenz Eitner, *Neoclassicism and Romanticism, 1750–1850: Sources and Documents,* vol. 1, *Enlightenment/Revolution* (Englewood Cliffs, N.J.: Prentice-Hall, 1970), 106. See also Giovanni Battista Piranesi, *Lettere di giustificazione scritte a Milord Charlemont e à di lui agenti di Roma* (Rome: n.p., 1757), xi–xii:

> ardisco credere.... d'aver finita un'Opera, che passerà alla posterità, e che durerà fin tanto che vi saranno de' curiosi di conoscere ciò, chè rimaneva nel nostro secolo delle rovine della più famosa Città dell'universo.... questa Opera non è del genere di quelle che si confondono nella folla de' libri d'un Biblioteca, ma ch'è composta di quattro Volumi in foglio; che abbraccia un nuovo sistema su i monumenti dell'antica Roma; che sarà depositata in molte Biblioteche pubbliche d'Europa.

25. Chambers's relationship to Piranesi and the history of the design of Somerset House, London, is discussed in John Harris, *Sir William Chambers: Knight of the Polar Star* (London: A. Zwemmer, 1970). For more recent coverage of these themes, see John Newman, *Somerset House: Splendour and Order* (London: Scala, 1990); and John

Harris and Michael Snodin, eds., *Sir William Chambers: Architect to George III,* exh. cat. (New Haven: Yale Univ. Press, 1996). For Piranesi's impact on Chambers's Somerset House, see John Wilton-Ely, "'Sognare il sublime': L'influenza di Piranesi e della sua scuola sul Grand Tour," in Cesare de Seta, ed., *Grand Tour: Viaggi narrati e dipinti* (Naples: Electa Napoli, 2001), 108–11.

In 1791 Chambers published this criticism of Piranesi's *Collegio magnifico* in the introduction to his *Treatise on the Decorative Part of Civil Architecture,* 3d ed. (London: printed by Joseph Smeeton, 1791), 10:

> A celebrated Italian artist, whose taste and luxuriance of fancy were unusually great, and the effect of whose compositions, on paper, has seldom been equalled; knew little of construction or calculation, yet less of the contrivance of habitable structures, or the modes of carrying real works into execution; though styling himself an architect. And when some pensioners of the French academy at Rome, in the Author's hearing, charged him with ignorance of plans, he composed a very complicated one, since published in his work; which sufficiently proves, that the charge was not altogether groundless.

However, Chambers had something more favorable to say about Piranesi when advising his pupil Edward Stevens, then on the point of leaving for Rome, in 1774: "Seek for those who have most reputation, young or old, amongst which forget not Piranesi, who you may see in my name; he is full of matter, extravagant 'tis true, often absurd, but from his overflowings you may gather much information"; quoted in Harris, *Sir William Chambers,* 22. In the early nineteenth century, Sir John Soane was to echo both Chambers's stricture and his praise in his Royal Academy lectures; see David Watkin, *Sir John Soane: Enlightenment Thought and the Royal Academy Lectures* (Cambridge: Cambridge Univ. Press, 1996), 531, 603, 605.

26. Mylne's relationship with Piranesi in Rome and after is examined in Christopher Gotch, "The Missing Years of Robert Mylne," *Architectural Review,* September 1951, 179–82. Therein Gotch translates a letter, dated 11 November 1760, from Piranesi to Mylne in which Piranesi refers to, among other things, their association in Rome; the complete Italian text of this letter (now in the collection of the Royal Institute of British Architects, London) appears in Georges Teyssot, *Città e utopia nell'illuminismo inglese: George Dance il giovane* (Rome: Officina, 1974), app. B, 188–92; see also Wilton-Ely, *Piranesi* (note 10), 95 (cat. nos. 236–38). For Piranesi's etched plate—dated 1764—of Blackfriars Bridge under construction, see Wilton-Ely, *Complete Etchings* (note 6), 2:1106–7; and Wilton-Ely, "'Sognare il sublime'"(note 25), 108. A significant new study of Mylne, both as architect and engineer, is provided in Roger J. Woodley, "Robert Mylne (1733–1811): The Bridge between Architecture and Engineering," 2 vols. (Ph.D. diss., University of London, 1999).

27. For Dance the Younger's relationship to Piranesi and the impact of the *Carceri* on Newgate Prison, see Dorothy Stroud, *George Dance, Architect, 1741–1825* (London: Faber & Faber, 1971), 98; as well as Harold D. Kalman, "Newgate Prison," *Architectural History* 12 (1969): 55. Dance the Younger is mentioned in Piranesi's letter to Mylne of 11 November 1760; see Gotch, "The Missing Years" (note 26), 182.

28. Piranesi's relationship with Robert Adam—by far the most significant of his

contacts with foreign designers—is discussed in John Fleming, *Robert Adam and His Circle in Edinburgh and Rome* (London: John Murray, 1962); see also Damie Stillman, "Robert Adam and Piranesi," in Douglas Fraser, Howard Hibbard, and Milton J. Lewine, eds., *Essays in the History of Architecture Presented to Rudolf Wittkower* (London: Phaidon, 1967), 197–206; A. A. Tait, *Robert Adam: Drawings and Imagination* (Cambridge: Cambridge Univ. Press, 1993); John Wilton-Ely, "Antiquity Applied: Piranesi, Clérisseau and the Adam Brothers," *Bulletin de l'Association des historiens de l'art italien* (Paris), no. 2 (1995–96): 15–24; and John Wilton-Ely, "'Amazing and Ingenious Fancies': Piranesi and Robert Adam" (paper presented at the conference "Piranesi: Nuovi contributi," American Academy in Rome, Centro di Studi sulla Cultura e l'Immagine di Roma, Bibliotheca Hertziana, and Accademia Nazionale dei Lincei, Rome, 6 April 2001).

29. Fleming, *Adam and His Circle* (note 28), 167.

30. The two Piranesi drawings from Sir John Soane's Adam collection are discussed in John Wilton-Ely, *Piranesi, Paestum and Soane* (London: Sir John Soane's Museum, 2002), 62 n. 9.

31. The range of Adam's executed works has been covered most recently in David King, *The Complete Works of Robert and James Adam* and *Unbuilt Adam* (Oxford: Architectural Press, 2001). A summary of these achievements can be found in Howard Colvin, *A Biographical Dictionary of British Architects, 1660–1840,* 3d ed. (New Haven: Yale Univ. Press, 1995), 51–62. See also Geoffrey Beard, *The Work of Robert Adam* (Edinburgh: John Bartholomew, 1978); and Joseph Rykwert and Anne Rykwert, *The Brothers Adam: The Men and the Style* (London: Collins, 1985). The interior designs of the Adams have been examined in Damie Stillman, *The Decorative Work of Robert Adam* (London: Alec Tiranti, 1966); and, most recently, Eileen Harris, *The Genius of Robert Adam: His Interiors* (New Haven: Yale Univ. Press, 2001).

32. For a discussion of the fantasy frontispieces in *Le antichità,* see Wilton-Ely, *Mind and Art* (note 6), 52–53.

33. According to Adam, writing in April 1756, "In one of the frontispieces representing the Appian Way in all its ancient splendour, with all the mausoleums of the Consuls, Emperors &ca., he [Piranesi] has taken the occasion to put in Ramsay's name and mine, with our Elogiums, as if buried in these tombs"; quoted in Fleming, *Adam and His Circle* (note 28), 207.

34. Giovanni Battista Piranesi, *Della magnificenza ed architettura de' romani = De Romanorum Magnificentia et Architectura* (Rome: n.p., 1761); the text and plates of *Della magnificenza* are reproduced in Piranesi, *Polemical Works* (note 22).

35. For Stuart and Revett, see Lesley Lewis, "Stuart and Revett: Their Literary and Architectural Careers," *Journal of the Warburg Institute* 2 (1938–39): 128–46; Dora Wiebenson, *Sources of Greek Revival Architecture* (London: A. Zwemmer, 1969); and David Watkin, *Athenian Stuart: Pioneer of the Greek Revival* (London: George Allen & Unwin, 1982). A more recent study of Stuart is to be found in Kerry A. C. Bristol, "James 'Athenian' Stuart (1713–1788) and the Genesis of the Greek Revival in British Architecture," 2 vols. (Ph.D. diss., University of London, 1997).

36. The critical role of Laugier in the Greek Revival, and his relationship to Lodoli's teachings, is discussed in Wolfgang Herrmann, *Laugier and Eighteenth Century French*

Theory (London: A. Zwemmer, 1962). For a modern translation into English of this key text, see Marc-Antoine Laugier, *An Essay on Architecture,* trans. Wolfgang Herrmann and Anni Herrmann (Los Angeles: Hennessey & Ingalls, 1977).

37. See Michel de Frémin, *Mémoires critiques d'architecture: Contenans l'idée de la vraye et de la fausse architecture... et sur d'autres matieres non encore éclaircies* (Paris: Charles Saugrain, 1702); and Jean-Louis de Cordemoy, *Nouveau traité de toute l'architecture; ou, L'art de bastir; avec un dictionnaire des termes* (Paris: Coignard, 1706). For the earlier concerns with Greek architecture, see Robin Middleton, "The Abbé de Cordemoy and the Graeco-Gothic Ideal: A Prelude to Romantic Classicism," *Journal of the Warburg and Courtauld Institutes* 25 (1962): 278–320; 26 (1963): 90–123.

38. Piranesi's relationship with Ramsay and the complex history of the latter's anonymous publication of "A Dialogue on Taste," which first appeared as *The Investigator, Number 332,* around 1755 and was reissued in 1762, are discussed in Alastair Smart, *The Life and Art of Allan Ramsay* (London: Routledge & Kegan Paul, 1952), 86–95; see also Alastair Smart, *Allan Ramsay: Painter, Essayist and Man of the Enlightenment* (New Haven: Yale Univ. Press, 1992); and Bernard D. Frischer and Iain Gordon Brown, eds., *Allan Ramsay and the Search for Horace's Villa* (Burlington, Vt.: Ashgate, 2001). Writing to Sir Alexander Dick in 1762, Ramsay believed that his dialogue had "become remarkable by a large folio which it has given rise to by Piranesi at Rome, and of which some copies are already come to London by land"; quoted in Smart, *Life and Art of Allan Ramsay,* 91. For a broader discussion of the opening exchanges of the Graeco-Roman quarrel, see Wiebenson, *Sources of Greek Revival* (note 35), 47–61; and J. Mordaunt Crook, *The Greek Revival: Neo-Classical Attitudes in British Architecture, 1760–1870,* rev. ed. (London: John Murray, 1995).

39. See Piranesi's letter to Mylne of 11 November 1760, translated in Gotch, "Missing Years" (note 26), 182.

40. Julien-David Le Roy, *Les ruines des plus beaux monuments de la Grèce* (Paris: H. L. Guerin & L. F. Delatour [etc.], 1758), 1:xiii:

> il parôit que les Romains manquérent de ce génie créateur qui avoit fait faire tant de découvertes aux Grecs: ils n'imaginérent rien de considérable dans les Ordres; celui dont ils s'attribuoient l'invention, que l'on nomme *Composite,* n'est qu'un mêlange assez imparfait de l'Ionique et du Corinthien; et à force d'élever la proportion des colonnes de l'Ordre Dorique, et de multiplier les moulures de son entablement, ils lui ont peut-être fait perdre beaucoup de ce caractere mâle qui le distinguoit dans la Grece.

41. Giovanni Lodovico Bianconi (a close friend of Winckelmann's) in his obituary of Piranesi observed, in pointing out the artist's lack of scholarly background and ignorance of Latin and Greek:

> Cattivossi egli destramente vari insigni letterati, i quali innamorati del suo ingegno, e del suo bulino non isdegnarono di lavorare per lui, componendo insigni trattati corrispondenti a sì bei rami, ed ebbero la generosità di permettergli fino, che li pubblicasse col suo nome. Non si dubiti di mettere in tale numero Monsig. Bottari, il dotto Padre Contucci Gesuita, e vari altri, che crediamo inutile di qui nominare.

(He cleverly enrolled some eminent men of letters who, in admiration for his genius and his etchings, were not above working for him, composing texts to fit his excellent prints, and generously permitting him to publish them under his own name. These writers included Monsignore Bottari, the learned Jesuit father Contucci and various others [whom we believe it useless to name here].)

For the Italian original, see Giovanni Lodovico Bianconi, "Elogio storico del cavaliere Giambattista Piranesi," *Antologia romana,* no. 34 (1779): 274; the entire Italian original is reprinted in Giovanni Lodovico Bianconi, *Opere,* vol. 2, *Lettere al marchese Filippo Hercolani* (Milan: Tipografia de' Classici Italiani, 1802), 125–40; and in "L'*Elogio* di Bianconi," *Grafica grafica* 2 (1976): 127–35. Up to the last phrase, the English translation is from Scott, *Piranesi* (note 14), 154.

42. For discussions on eighteenth-century Etruscan studies in Italy, see Mauro Cristofani, *La scoperta degli etruschi: Archeologia e antiquaria nel '700* (Rome: Consiglio Nazionale delle Ricerche, 1983); Franco Borsi, ed., *Fortuna degli etruschi,* exh. cat. (Milan: Electa, 1985); and Nancy Thomson de Grummond, "Rediscovery," in Larissa Bonfante, ed., *Etruscan Life and Afterlife: A Handbook of Etruscan Studies* (Detroit: Wayne State Univ. Press, 1986), 37–40. For Piranesi's direct involvement and intellectual response, see Mauro Cristofani, "Le opere teoriche di G. B. Piranesi e l'etruscheria," in Anna Lo Bianco, ed., *Piranesi e la cultura antiquaria, gli antecedenti e il contesto: Atti del convegno, 14–17 novembre 1979* (Rome: Multigrafica, 1983), 211–20.

43. For Maffei's concern with Etruscan studies, see Nancy Thomson de Grummond, ed., *An Encyclopedia of the History of Classical Archaeology,* s.v. "Maffei, Francesco Scipione."

44. See Paola Barocchi and Daniela Gallo, eds., *L'Accademia etrusca,* exh. cat. (Milan: Electa, 1985). The exhibition was held in 1985 at the Palazzo Casali, Cortona.

45. Jenkins, who was elected a Fellow of the Society of Antiquaries of London in 1757, sent regular reports of excavations in and around Rome to the society, and a letter of May 1761 describes his first excavation at Corneto (Tarquinia). See S. Rowland Pierce, "Thomas Jenkins in Rome in the Light of Letters, Records and Drawings at the Society of Antiquaries of London," *Antiquaries Journal* 45 (1965): 200–209. See also Thomas Ashby, "Thomas Jenkins in Rome," *Papers of the British School at Rome* 6 (1913): 487–511; and Brinsley Ford, "Thomas Jenkins: Banker, Dealer and Unofficial English Agent," *Apollo* 99 (1974): 416–25.

46. In 1765 Byres, in the company of Piranesi and John Wilbraham, explored the subterranean Etruscan tombs of Corneto (Tarquinia), including the reopened Tomba del Cardinale. An account of this expedition is given in George Dennis, *Cities and Cemeteries of Etruria* (London: John Murray, 1848), 1:316–17. Piranesi mentions in the trilingual text of his *Diverse maniere* of 1769 that "the very learned M. James Byres, architect, and antiquarian from Scotland, who is about publishing the designs of [the tomb wall paintings] in a work, in which will appear his extraordinary knowledge"; see Giovanni Battista Piranesi, *Diverse maniere d'adornare i cammini ed ogni altra parte degli edifizj, desunte dall'architettura egizia, etrusca, e greca, con un ragionamento apologetico in difesa dell'architettura egizia e toscana = Divers Manners of Orna-*

menting Chimneys and All Other Parts of Houses, Taken from the Egyptian, Tuscan, and Grecian Architecture, with an Apologetical Essay in Defence of the Egyptian and Tuscan Architecture = Differentes manieres d'orner les cheminées et toute autre partie des edifices, tirées de l'architecture egyptienne, etrusque, et greque, avec un discours apologetique en faveur de l'architecture egyptienne, et toscane (Rome: Stamperia Generoso Salomoni, 1769), 22 (English). The text and plates of *Diverse maniere* are reproduced in Piranesi, *Polemical Works* (note 22).

The engraved plates for Byres's work, etched by Christopher Norton (fl. 1760s) after drawings by Franciszek Smuglewicz (1745–1807), were eventually published without a text in 1842; see James Byres, *Hypogaei; or, Sepulchral Caverns of Tarquinia, the Capital of Antient Etruria*, ed. Frank Howard, 5 pts. in 1 vol. (London: Frank Howard, 1842). On the plates for Byres's publication, see David Ridgway, "James Byres and the Ancient State of Italy: Unpublished Documents in Edinburgh," in Guglielmo Maetzke, ed., *Secondo Congresso internazionale etrusco: Firenze, 26 maggio–2 giugno 1985: Atti* (Rome: Giorgio Bretschneider, 1989), 1:213–29. See also Brinsley Ford, "James Byres: Principal Antiquarian for the English Visitors to Rome," *Apollo* 99 (1974): 452–53; and Hans Möbius, "Zeichnungen etruskischer Kammergräber und Einzelfunde von James Byres," *Mitteilungen des Deutschen Archaeologischen Instituts, Roemische Abteilung* 73–74 (1966–67): 53–71, pls. 19–31.

47. For Sir William Hamilton and his concern with Etruscan culture, see Ian Jenkins and Kim Sloan, *Vases and Volcanoes: Sir William Hamilton and His Collection*, exh. cat. (London: British Museum Press, 1996).

48. According to Lodoli's disciple Andrea Memmo (who sided with Piranesi against Le Roy), Piranesi sent a copy of *Della magnificenza*, which was published only a few months before the Franciscan died in 1769, to Lodoli in Venice as a present; see Andrea Memmo, *Elementi d'architettura Lodoliana; ossia, L'arte del fabbricare con solidità scientifica e con eleganza non capricciosa* (Zara, Italy: Tipi dei Fratelli Battara, 1833; reprint, Milan: G. Mazzotta, 1973), 2:139. See also Rykwert, *First Moderns* (note 5), 335 n. 111.

49. Memmo, *Elementi* (note 48), 1:296–97.

50. In this quotation from Le Roy's *Les ruines* incorporated into plate XX of Piranesi's *Della magnificenza* (note 34) (see fig. 11), Piranesi has extracted two phrases from the section of Le Roy's text that is headed "Du Chapiteau Ionique du Temple d'Érecthée" and accompanies plate XIX of volume 2; see Le Roy, *Les ruines* (note 40), 2:18:

> un chapiteau Ionique dont on n'a eu jusqu'ici aucune idée. Ce chapiteau que j'ai représenté en grand, Planche XIX, figure I, est, selon mon sentiment, d'une très-grande beauté, et supérieur à plusieurs égards aux plus beaux chapiteaux de cet ordre que l'on voit encore aux Monuments antiques des Romains, et à celui dont Vitruve nous a donné la description.
> (an Ionic capital not previously known to exist. This capital, which I have illustrated on a large scale in figure 1, is, to my mind, an extremely beautiful one and is superior in several respects to the most beautiful capitals of the same order still to be seen on Roman monuments, and also to the one described by Vitruvius.)

While Le Roy shows only half of the capital in question in plate XIX, he reproduces the full capital in plate XX, which Piranesi uses.

51. Piranesi's impressive sequence of polemical-archaeological treatises of the 1760s are considered in Wilton-Ely, *Mind and Art* (note 6), 65–73. The entire range of plates is illustrated in Wilton-Ely, *Complete Etchings* (note 6).

52. Piranesi's relationship with Adam in the production of *Il Campo Marzio,* and the remarkable character of the book, is examined in John Wilton-Ely, "Utopia or Megalopolis? The *Ichnographia* of Piranesi's *Campus Martius* Reconsidered," in Alessandro Bettagno, ed., *Piranesi tra Venezia e l'Europa* (Florence: Leo S. Olschki, 1983), 293–304. See also Wilton-Ely, *Mind and Art* (note 6), 73–77. For a contrary view of the *Ichnographia,* see Manfredo Tafuri, "Borromini e Piranesi: La città come 'ordine infranto,'" in Alessandro Bettagno, ed., *Piranesi tra Venezia e l'Europa* (Florence: Leo S. Olschki, 1983), 89–101.

53. See Isaiah Berlin, *Vico and Herder: Two Studies in the History of Ideas* (London: Hogarth, 1976). Giambattista Vico's *Principj di una scienza nuova intorno alla natura della nazioni* (Principles of a new science concerning the nature of nations) was first published in Naples in 1725, revised in 1730, and considerably changed and expanded for the third edition published in 1744. For a modern edition of Vico's key work, see Giambattista Vico, *Principj di scienza nuova,* in idem, *Opere,* ed. Fausto Nicolini (Milan: R. Ricciardi, 1953). Lodoli corresponded with Vico, attempted unsuccessfully to have the second edition of the *Principj di una scienza nuova* printed in Venice, and was involved in persuading the philosopher to write his autobiography in 1725, which was first published in Venice in 1728; see Rykwert, *First Moderns* (note 5), 280–82, 288.

54. In about 191, the Templum Pacis (Temple of Peace) and its library were destroyed by fire. Sometime between 203 and 211, it was restored by Lucius Septimius Severus, who had a plan of the city of Rome incised on 151 rectangular slabs of marble and affixed in eleven rows to one wall of the Bibliotheca Templi Pacis. Drawn to a scale of approximately 1:240, the Severan Marble Plan, or Forma Urbis Romae, shows details of buildings and landmarks that otherwise would be unknown; about 10 percent of the original survives today.

55. While Piranesi had initiated this complex system of planning by aggregates of geometric forms in such visionary compositions as the *Pianta di ampio magnifico collegio* (see fig. 4), published in the *Opere varie* of 1750, the impact of his ideas on Peyre and de Wailly during their student years in Rome and on their later designs continues to resonate in later neoclassical French architecture in, for example, the executed works and projects by Etienne-Louis Boullée and Claude-Nicolas Ledoux. See Braham, *Architecture of the French Enlightenment* (note 17).

56. The creative value of Piranesi's *Ichnographia* in *Il Campo Marzio* was recognized with considerable percipience by his acquaintance Andrew Lumisden (1720–1802), Scottish lawyer, antiquarian, and secretary to the exiled Stuarts in Rome. His book, *Remarks on the Antiquities of Rome and Its Environs: Being a Classical and Topographical Survey of the Ruins of That Celebrated City* (London: printed by W. Bulmer, 1797; 2d ed., London: printed by W. Bulmer, 1812), frequently refers to Piranesi's works and cites many of his etched plates. While critical of the archaeological merits of

the Venetian's observations in *Il Campo Marzio*, he recognized the wider implications of the visionary plan as follows: "Piranesi, in his elegant plan of the Campus Martius, has completely traced all the buildings, which the Roman writers have mentioned to have stood there, as if he had seen and measured them; though, of the greatest part of them, no vestige remains. But this magnificent work, which is a proof of the fertile invention of its ingenious author, will be apt to mislead strangers and future antiquaries, whilst it must afford many noble ideas and useful hints to artists"; see Lumisden, *Remarks on the Antiquities*, 252. See Michael McCarthy, "Andrew Lumisden and Giovanni Battista Piranesi," in Clare Hornsby, ed., *The Impact of Italy: The Grand Tour and Beyond* (London: British School at Rome, 2000), 65–81.

57. Giovanni Battista Piranesi, "Al chiarissimo signore, Sig. Roberto Adam," in idem, *Il Campo Marzio dell'antica Roma = Campus Martius Antiquae Urbis* (Rome: n.p., 1762), [xi]:

> Sebbene ciò di che io piuttosto temer debbo, si è, che non sembrino inventate a capriccio, più che prese dal vero, alcune cose di questa delineazione del Campo; le quali se taluno confronta coll'antica maniera di architettare, comprenderà, che molto da essa si discostano, e s'avvicinano all'usanza de' nostri tempi. Ma chiunque egli sia, prima di condannare alcuno d'impostura, osservi di grazia l'antica pianta di Roma . . . osservi le antiche ville del Lazio, quella d'Adriano in Tivoli, le terme, i sepolcri, e gli altri edifizj di Roma, che rimangono, in ispezie poi fuori di porta Capena: non ritroverà inventate più cose dai moderni, che dagli antichi contra le più rigide leggi dell'architettura. O derivi pertanto dalla natura e condizione delle arti, che quando sono giunte al sommo, vanno a poco a poco in decadenza e in rovina, o così porti l'indole degli uomini, che nelle professioni ancora reputansi lecita qualsisia cosa; non è da maravigliarsi, se troviamo eziandio dagli architetti antichi usate quelle cose, che nelle fabbriche nostrali talvolta biasimiamo.

Piranesi was particularly influenced by the ingenious planning forms of surviving structures at Hadrian's Villa. As a result of his many expeditions there from the 1740s onward (including those made with Robert Adam and Charles-Louis Clérisseau in the 1750s), apart from producing a series of impressive *vedute*, he prepared a highly detailed site plan. This was posthumously published in six contiguous plates by his son Francesco as *Pianta delle fabbriche esistenti nella Villa Adriana* (Rome: Francesco Piranesi, 1781). See Wilton-Ely, *Complete Etchings* (note 6), 2:1098–100, 1125–30; John A. Pinto, "Piranesi at Hadrian's Villa," in Russell T. Scott and Ann Reynolds Scott, eds., *Eius Virtutis Studiosi: Classical and Postclassical Studies in Memory of Frank Edward Brown (1908–1988)*, Studies in the history of art, 43 (Washington, D.C.: National Gallery of Art, 1993), 465–77; and William L. MacDonald and John A. Pinto, *Hadrian's Villa and Its Legacy* (New Haven: Yale Univ. Press, 1995), 246–65.

58. Winckelmann's *Gedanken über die Nachahmung der griechischen Wercke in der Mahlerey und Bildhauer-Kunst* (Friedrichstadt, Germany: gedruckt bey Christian Heinrich Hagenmüller, 1755) was widely translated; the earliest published English translation, entitled *Reflections on the Painting and Sculpture of the Greeks* (London: printed by A. Millar, 1765), was by the painter Henry Fuseli. For a discussion of the

German scholar's revolutionary aesthetic theories, see David Irwin, "Introduction," in Johann Joachim Winckelmann, *Writings on Art,* selected and ed. David Irwin (London: Phaidon, 1972), 3–57. A major new study examining Winckelmann's significance in the historiography of art is Alex Potts, *Flesh and the Ideal: Winckelmann and the Origins of Art History* (New Haven: Yale Univ. Press, 1994). For a discussion of the circle of Cardinal Albani and Winckelmann, see Lesley Lewis, *Connoisseurs and Secret Agents in Eighteenth-Century Rome* (London: Chatto & Windus, 1961).

59. Winckelmann's *Anmerkungen über die Baukunst der alten Tempel zu Girgenti in Sicilien* (Leipzig: Johann Gottfried Dyck, 1762) was based on drawings of the Greek temples at Agrigento, Sicily, carried out for him by the Scottish architect Robert Mylne. These drawings may well have been one of the sources Piranesi used in formulating his discussion and etching of the Temple of Concord in Agrigento; see Piranesi, *Della magnificenza* (note 34), xxvii–xxix, pl. XXII. *The Ruins of Palmyra, Otherwise Tedmor, in the Desart* (London: n.p., 1753) and *The Ruins of Balbec, Otherwise Heliopolis in Coelosyria* (London: n.p., 1757), both produced by the English scholar Robert Wood, with the assistance of the architect James Dawkins, had a major impact upon the Graeco-Roman debate in illustrating and discussing a wide range of late Imperial Roman classicism outside the Vitruvian canon. See David Constantine, *Early Greek Travellers and the Hellenic Ideal* (Cambridge: Cambridge Univ. Press, 1984), 66–84; and Robert Eisner, *Travelers to an Antique Land: The History and Literature of Travel to Greece* (Ann Arbor: Univ. of Michigan Press, 1991), 72–73.

60. Johann Joachim Winckelmann, *Abhandlung von der Fähigkeit der Empfindung des Schönen in der Kunst, und dem Unterrichte in Derselben* (Dresden: in der Waltherischen Buchhandlung, 1763). See Johann Joachim Winckelmann, *Winckelmann's Werke,* ed. C. L. Fernow (Dresden: in der Waltherschen Hofbuchhandlung, 1808–25), 2:410: "In der Baukunst ist das Schöne... in der Proportion besteht: denn ein Gebäude kann durch dieselbe allein, ohne Zierrathen, schön werden und seyn"; English translation from Johann Joachim Winckelmann, *Writings on Art,* selected and ed. David Irwin (London: Phaidon, 1972), 97.

61. Johann Joachim Winckelmann, *Anmerkungen über die Baukunst der Alten* (Leipzig: verlegts Johann Gottfried Dyck, 1762; reprint, Baden-Baden: Heitz, 1964). See Winckelmann, *Winckelmann's Werke* (note 60), 1:407: "Der Baukunst ergieng es, wie den alten Sprachen; diese wurden reicher, da sie von ihrer Schönheit abfielen, welches so wohl von der Griechischen als Römischen zu beweisen ist, und da die Baumeister ihre Vorgänger in der Schönheit entweder nicht erreichen, oder nicht übertreffen konnten, suchten sie sich reicher als jene zu zeigen"; English translation from Winckelmann, *Writings on Art* (note 60), 87. It is interesting to note the excessively rich and complex interiors created by Carlo Marchionni (1702–86) for Winckelmann's patron, Cardinal Albani, at Albani's celebrated villa on the Via Salaria in Rome at the time when Winckelmann's influence—and his austere aesthetic standpoint—was at its height. See Rykwert, *First Moderns* (note 5), 342–51; W. O. Collier, "The Villa of Cardinal Alessandro Albani, Hon. F.S.A.," *Antiquaries Journal* 67 (1987): 338–47; and Carlo Gasparri, "Piranesi a Villa Albani," in *Committenze della famiglia Albani—Note sulla Villa Albani Torlonia* (Rome: Multigrafica, 1985), 211–19. For the Albani circle, see Lewis, *Connoisseurs* (note 58).

62. For these small fantasies added to the *Opere varie,* see Wilton-Ely, *Complete Etchings* (note 6), 1:84–87.

63. Giovanni Battista Piranesi, *Différentes vues de quelques restes de trois grands edifices qui subsistent encore dans le milieu de l'ancienne ville de Pesto autrement Posidonia qui est située dans la Lucanie* (Rome: n.p., 1778). See Wilton-Ely, *Complete Etchings* (note 6), 2:777–800; Roberto Pane, *Paestum nelle acqueforti di Piranesi* (Milan: Edizioni di Comunità, 1980); Roberto Pane, "Piranesi a Paestum," in Alessandro Bettagno, ed., *Piranesi tra Venezia e l'Europa* (Florence: Leo S. Olschki, 1983), 377–88; and Wilton-Ely, *Piranesi, Paestum and Soane* (note 30).

64. Pierre-Jean Mariette, "Lettre de M. Mariette aux auteurs de la *Gazette littéraire de l'Europe,*" *Gazette littéraire de l'Europe,* Supplément, 4 November 1764, 232–47 (note that Mariette's letter ends on page 241; six pages of commentary by the "auteurs de la *Gazette littéraire*" follow). According to correspondence with Giovanni Bottari, the letter was issued without Mariette's knowledge; see Giovanni Bottari, *Raccolta di lettere sulla pittura, scultura ed architettura scritte da' più celebri professori che in dette arti fiorirono dal secolo XV al XVII,* vol. 5 (Rome: Stamperia di Marco Pagliarini, 1766), nos. 157, 162, 167. As a print connoisseur, Mariette had great admiration for Piranesi's etchings and did a great deal to make them more known in France. Following Piranesi's rejoinder, Mariette told Bottari, in a letter dated "30 del 1766," that "la diversità del suo parere non m' ha fatto diminuir punto la stima, che io debbo avere de' suoi talenti" (the difference in our opinions does not diminish one bit the esteem that I have for his talents); see Bottari, *Raccolta di lettere,* 5:292 (no. 157). Recent sources on Mariette include *Le cabinet d'un grand amateur, P.-J. Mariette, 1694–1774: Dessins du XVe siècle au XVIIIe siècle,* exh. cat. (Paris: Réunion des Musées Nationaux, 1967); Barbara Scott, "Pierre-Jean Mariette: Scholar and Connoisseur," *Apollo* 97 (1973): 57; and Kate T. Steinitz, *Pierre-Jean Mariette and le Comte de Caylus and Their Concept of Leonardo da Vinci in the Eighteenth Century* (Los Angeles: Zeitlin & Ver Brugge, 1974).

65. Mariette, "Lettre" (note 64), 239: "Il n'est alors aucune production qui ne se charge d'ornemens superflus et absolument hors d'oeuvre. On sacrifie tout au luxe, et l'on se rend à la fin partisan d'une maniere qui ne tarde pas à devenir ridicule et barbare."

66. Piranesi's exceptional range of activities as a practicing designer during the 1760s is described in Wilton-Ely, *Piranesi as Architect* (note 1). Piranesi's biographer, Jacques Guillaume Legrand, comments on the artist's friendly relationship with Clement XIII and members of the Rezzonico family. Among other things, Legrand mentions that Piranesi taught the pope's nephews to draw but does not specify which of the four were involved; see Jacques Guillaume Legrand, "Notice historique sur la vie et les ouvrages de J. B. Piranesi.... Rédigée sur les notes et les pièces communiquées per ses fils, les compagnons et les continuateurs de ses nombreaux travaux [Paris, 1799]," nouv. acq. franç. 5968, Département des Manuscrits, Bibliothèque Nationale de France, Paris; transcribed in Gilbert Erouart and Monique Mosser, "À propos de la 'Notice historique sur la vie et les ouvrages de J.-B. Piranesi': Origine et fortune d'une biographie," in Georges Brunel, ed., *Piranèse et les Français: Colloque tenu à la Villa Médicis, 12–14 mai 1976* (Rome: Edizioni dell'Elefante, 1978), 227. See also Bruno

Contardi, "Piranesi e la corte Rezzonico," in Barbara Jatta, ed., *Piranesi e l'Aventino,* exh. cat. (Milan: Electa, 1998), 49–55.

67. The earliest reference to the Lateran commission appears in a letter, dated 21 September 1763, from Charles-Joseph Natoire, director of the Académie de France à Rome, to the marquis de Marigny, surintendant des bâtiments; see Anatole de Montaiglon and Jules Guiffrey, eds., *Correspondance des directeurs de l'Académie de France à Rome avec les surintendants des bâtiments,* vol. 11, *1754–1763* (Paris: Noël Charavay, 1901), 489 (no. 5696, "Nouvelles de Rome"): "Sa Sainteté, voulant orner la basilique de Saint-Jean-Latran d'un maître-autel qui répond à la magnificence de cette église, elle a ordonné au sieur Piranesi, célèbre architecte-sculpteur, de composer un dessein propre à l'exécution de ce projet" (His Holiness, wishing to embellish the basilica of St. John Lateran with a high altar appropriate to the magnificence of this church, has commissioned Signor Piranesi, a celebrated architect-engraver, to produce a design specially for this project).

The drawing of the papal altar and baldachino illustrated here (see fig. 17) is discussed in [Dorothea Nyberg and Herbert Mitchell], *Piranesi: Drawings and Etchings at the Avery Architectural Library, Columbia University, New York: The Arthur M. Sackler Collection,* exh. cat. (New York: Arthur M. Sackler Foundation, 1975), 63, 290 (cat. no. 19 by Dorothea Nyberg); and John Wilton-Ely, with Joseph Connors, *Piranesi architetto,* exh. cat. (Rome: Edizioni dell'Elefante, 1992), 59 (cat. no. 25), pl. 25.

68. The eighteenth century's strongly negative reactions to Borromini are briefly discussed in Anthony Blunt, *Borromini* (London: Allen Lane, 1979), 218–19. For a modern appraisal of Borromini in relation to Piranesi, see Tafuri, "Borromini e Piranesi" (note 52), 89–101. Borromini's surviving designs for the Lateran Basilica, now in the Biblioteca Apostolica Vaticana, are discussed and illustrated in Joseph Connors, "Borromini at the Lateran / Borromini al Laterano," in John Wilton-Ely, with Joseph Connors, *Piranesi architetto,* exh. cat. (Rome: Edizioni dell'Elefante, 1992), 97–123.

69. In the *Prima parte,* Piranesi uses the plan and stepped roof of Borromini's Sant'Ivo della Sapienza, Rome (1642–50), as ingredients in the *Mausoleo antico,* while its spiral cupola appears twice in the background of the *Prospetto d'un regio cortile;* see Robison, *Piranesi* (note 7), 75, 86. The plan of two matching vaulted rooms at the lower angles of the *Pianta di ampio magnifico collegio* in the *Opere varie* also owes much to Borromini's church; see Robison, *Piranesi* (note 7), 126.

70. It is interesting to find that Borromini also appears to have planned to build a half-dome at the end of the Lateran Basilica and to construct the tribune with an ambulatory around it, according to the early-eighteenth-century architect Giuseppe Antonio Bianchi who had seen the seventeenth-century master's original designs, then in possession of Borromini's heirs, for the complete transformation of the Lateran Basilica; see Paolo Portoghesi, *Borromini, architettura come linguaggio* (Rome: Ugo Bozzi, 1967), 160, drawing CXXVII. There is no evidence that Piranesi was aware of this precedent for his own solution.

71. The twenty-three presentation drawings for the Lateran tribune, which came to light in 1972, are discussed in detail and reproduced in [Nyberg and Mitchell], *Piranesi . . . Sackler Collection* (note 67). More recently, the Avery Architectural Library's drawings have been discussed and illustrated in Wilton-Ely, with Connors,

Piranesi architetto (note 67). A pioneering study of Piranesi's project for the Lateran tribune, mainly based on the then only known drawings in the Pierpont Morgan Library, New York, is to be found in Manfred F. Fischer, "Die Umbaupläne des Giovanni Battista Piranesi für den Chor von S. Giovanni in Laterano," *Münchner Jahrbuch der bildenden Kunst,* 3d ser., 19 (1968): 207–28. Two of the Avery Architectural Library's studies for the papal altar, probably rendered by a studio assistant, pursue the Borrominian idiom to a point where the drawings are actually inscribed "inventato sul gusto [su lo stile] del Boromino" (devised in the taste [in the style] of Borromini); see [Nyberg and Mitchell], *Piranesi... Sackler Collection* (note 67), 67, 71, 291 (cat. nos. 20, 22 by Dorothea Nyberg).

72. The letter of 11 February 1764 is quoted in Giulio Pane, "Vanvitelli e la grafica," in *Luigi Vanvitelli e il '700 Europeo: Congresso internazionale di studi: Atti* (Naples: Arte Tipografica, 1979), 2:382–83: "È un fenomeno particolare che il Pazzo Piranesi ardisca far l'Architetto; solo dirò che non è mestiere da Pazzi." See also Jörg Garms, "Die Briefe des Luigi Vanvitelli an seinen Bruder Urbano in Rom: Kunsthistorisches Material," *Römische historische Mitteilungen* 13 (1971): 225, 260, 263. For comparisons between the two architects, see John Wilton-Ely, "The Relationship between Giambattista Piranesi and Luigi Vanvitelli in Eighteenth-Century Architectural Theory and Practice," in *Luigi Vanvitelli e il '700 Europeo: Congresso internazionale di studi: Atti* (Naples: Arte Tipografica, 1979), 2:83–99; and Cesare de Seta, "Luigi Vanvitelli e Giovan Battista Piranesi*:* Un'ipotesi integrativa del ruolo sociale dell'artista a metà Settecento," in Alessandro Bettagno, ed., *Piranesi tra Venezia e l'Europa* (Florence: Leo S. Olschki, 1983), 103–25.

73. Contemporary references to the vanished interior schemes for the Rezzonico family are tantalizingly scant. According to Legrand, "La faveur du Pape le mit à même de décorer avec magnificence plusieurs appartemens du Palais pontifical, à la ville et à la campagne et de vivre avec familiarité dans la maison de *Rezzonico*" (Having won the pope's favor he was set to magnificently decorating several suites in the papal palace, both in town and in the country, and became a regular guest of the Rezzonicos, who treated him as one of their own); see Erouart and Mosser, "À propos de la 'Notice'" (note 66), 234.

In dedicating the *Diverse maniere* of 1769 to Cardinal Giovanni Battista Rezzonico, Piranesi reminded his patron of the work he has done for him and his brother, Senator Abbondio Rezzonico; and in the "Apologetical Essay," Piranesi notes, "these ornaments which serve to make the whole uniform may be executed in painting, as I have done... those in the apartments of the Senator of Rome after the Grecian and Tuscan manners"; see Piranesi, *Diverse maniere* (note 46), 8 (English).

For a description of what actually survives of Senator Rezzonico's apartments in the Palazzo Senatorio on the Campidoglio (although nothing appears to remain of Piranesi's scheme), see Carlo Pietrangeli, "La 'Sala nuova' di Don Abbondio Rezzonico," *Capitolium* 38 (1963): 244–46. One of two surviving side tables for Cardinal Rezzonico's Lateran apartments is discussed in Francis J. B. Watson, "A Masterpiece of Neo-Classic Furniture: A Side-Table Designed by Piranesi," *Burlington Magazine* 107 (1965): 101–2, figs. 55–57. See also John Wilton-Ely, "Piranesi: Designer e antiquario," in Barbara Jatta, ed., *Piranesi e l'Aventino*, exh. cat. (Milan: Electa, 1998), 95–104.

74. A detailed discussion of the design and execution of Piranesi's complex of buildings for Santa Maria del Priorato has been provided by Barbara Jatta, ed., *Piranesi e l'Aventino*, exh. cat. (Milan: Electa, 1998), which includes my essay, "Piranesi architetto" (pp. 63–78), and the related catalog entries (nos. 36–48) in the section entitled "L'intervento di Piranesi per il Priorato" (pp. 171–89). See also Wilton-Ely, with Connors, *Piranesi architetto* (note 67). The major part of the surviving drawings, which were shown in both Rome exhibitions, are now in the Pierpont Morgan Library, New York, and are discussed in Felice Stampfle, *Giovanni Battista Piranesi: Drawings in the Pierpont Morgan Library* (New York: Dover, 1978).

75. For a detailed discussion of Piranesi's iconographic program and its sources, see John Wilton-Ely, "Piranesian Symbols on the Aventine," *Apollo* 103 (1976): 214–27. Wittkower, "Piranesi as Architect" (note 1), first directed attention to the significance of the detailed account book that was compiled by the foreman (*capomastro muratore*), Giuseppe Pelosini, throughout the church's construction; this book is now in the Avery Architectural Library, Columbia University, New York. For a more recent assessment of this account book, see Joseph Connors, "Il Libro dei conti della Avery Architectural Library della Columbia University," in Barbara Jatta, ed., *Piranesi e l'Aventino*, exh. cat. (Milan: Electa, 1998), 86–94.

76. Piranesi's use of his drawn architectural fantasies to develop a concept that was eventually the basis of the Aventine altar is discussed in John Wilton-Ely, "Design through Fantasy: Piranesi as Architect," in Corinna Höper, Jeannette Stoschek, and Elisabeth Kieven, eds., *Giovanni Battista Piranesi—Die Wahrnehmung von Raum und Zeit* (Marburg: Jonas, 2002), 65–88.

77. For a comparison of the incorporation of ancient tombs within a modern decorative scheme by Borromini at the Lateran Basilica and by Piranesi at Santa Maria del Priorato, see Wilton-Ely, *Piranesi as Architect* (note 1), 114, figs. 111, 112.

78. The sole record of Piranesi's decorations for the Caffè degli Inglesi are two plates published in 1769 in his *Diverse maniere* (note 46). The Welsh painter Thomas Jones, in December 1776, described the Caffè degli Inglesi as "a filthy vaulted room, the walls of which were painted with Sphinxes, Obelisks and Pyramids, from capricious designs of *Piranesi*, and fitter to adorn the inside of an Egyptian-Sepulchre, than a room of social conversation"; see A. P. Oppé, ed., "The Memoirs of Thomas Jones," *Walpole Society* 32 (1946–48): 54.

79. See Piranesi, *Diverse maniere* (note 46), 3.

80. Robert Adam and James Adam, *The Works in Architecture of Robert and James Adam = Les ouvrages d'architecture de Robert et Jaques Adam, Vol. 1* (London: printed for the authors, 1773), pt. 2, 4.

81. Giovanni Battista Piranesi, *Osservazioni di Gio. Battista Piranesi sopra la lettre de M. Mariette aux auteurs de la* Gazette littéraire de l'Europe, *inserita nel supplemento dell'istessa gazzetta stampata dimanche 4. novembre MDCCLIV; e Parere su l'architettura, con una prefazione ad un nuovo trattato Della introduzione e del progresso delle belle arti in Europa ne' tempi antichi* (Rome: Generoso Salomoni, 1765). The text and plates of the *Osservazioni* are reproduced in Piranesi, *Polemical Works* (note 22).

The significance of the "Parere su l'architettura" was first explored in Rudolf

Wittkower, "Piranesi's *Parere su l'architettura*," *Journal of the Warburg Institute* 2 (1938–39): 147–58.

82. Piranesi, *Osservazioni* (note 81), 10: "quella pazza libertà di lavorare a capriccio." It is interesting to find that in the preface to his *Opus architectonicum* (Rome: Sebastianus Gianninus, 1725), Borromini asserted, "io al certo non mi sarei posto a questa professione, col fine d'esser solo copista" (I would never have given myself to this profession [architecture] with the idea of being merely a copyist).

83. Tafuri, "'The Wicked Architect'" (note 18), 43.

84. Piranesi, *Osservazioni* (note 81), 11:

> Osserviamo le pareti d'un edifizio sì di dentro, che di fuori. Queste in cima terminano con gli architravi, e col resto, che vi va sopra; e sotto questi architravi per lo più vi si dispongono delle colonne semidiametrali, o de' pilastri. Or domando, che cosa regge, il tetto dell'edifizio? Se la parete, questa non ha bisogno d'architravi; se le colonne, o i pilastri, la parete che vi fa ella? Via scegliete, Signor Protopiro, che cosa volete abbattere? le pareti, o i pilastri? Non rispondete? E io distruggerò tutto. Mettete da parte, *Edifizi senza pareti, senza colonne, senza pilastri, senza fregi, senza cornici, senza volte, senza tetti;* piazza, piazza, campagna rasa.

85. Piranesi, *Osservazioni* (note 81), 14:

> Ma ammettiamo l'impossibile; supponghiamo, che il Mondo, sebben è ristucco, di tutto quel che non varia di giorno in giorno, facesse alla vostra monotonia la grazia di sosserirla, l'Architettura a che sarebb'ella ridotta? *À un vil métier où l'on ne feroit que copier,* ha detto un certo Signore: talchè voi altri non solamente sareste Architetti ordinari ordinarissimi, com' io v' ho detto poc'anzi, ma da meno de' muratori. Imperocchè questi dal porre in opera sempre una cosa, oltre che, la imparerebbono a mente, avrebbono di più di voi altri il vantaggio del meccanismo: anzi finireste affato di essere Architetti; imperocchè i padroni, qualora volessero fabbricare, sarebbero sciocchi a chieder anche dall'Architetto quel che con tanto meno di spesa potrebbono avere dal muratore.

86. The genesis and reception of James Adam's design for a British order in his project for a new Houses of Parliament in London are described in Fleming, *Adam and His Circle* (note 28), 303–6; and Tait, *Robert Adam* (note 28), 56–70. A portrait of James Adam by Pompeo Batoni of 1763 shows the Scottish architect's newly devised capital in the foreground; see Fleming, *Adam and His Circle* (note 28), pl. 88. An engraving of the order, as later reused for the projected gateway to Carlton House, London, is included in Robert and James Adam's *Works in Architecture* (note 80), pt. 5, pl. II. See also Wilton-Ely, *Piranesi* (note 10), 71 (cat. no. 173).

87. Piranesi, *Osservazioni* (note 81), 11:

> mostratemi de' disegni fatti da qualsivoglia rigorista, da chiunque si crede d'aver conceputo un progetto de' più maravigliosi per far un'opera; e se non sarà più sciocco costui di chi opera da libero, mio danno: più sciocco sì; imperciocchè potrà idearsi un edifizio senza irregolarità, quando quattro pali ritti con un coperto soprappostovi, che sono tutto il prototipo dell'Architettura, potan sussistere interi ed uniti

nell'atto medesimo che saran dimezzati, distratti, e disposti per mille versi; in somma, quando il semplice sarà un composto, e l'uno sarà quella moltitudine che si vuole.

88. Giovanni Battista Piranesi, *Trofeo o sia magnifica colonna coclide di marmo composta di grossi macigni ove si veggono scopite le due guerre daciche fatte da Traiano inalzata nel mezzo del Gran Foro eretto al medesimo imperadore per ordine del senato e popolo romano doppo i suoi trionfi* (Rome: n.p., 1774–79). The publication history of this folio, which also includes the monumental relief columns of Marcus Aurelius (the Antonine Column) and of Antoninus and Faustina, is particularly complex and is discussed in Wilton-Ely, *Complete Etchings* (note 6), 2:743. Piranesi, who took enormous pains to record every ornamental aspect of these works (including, in some editions, a contiguous image of Trajan's Column in joined plates from top to bottom), may just possibly have had an opportunity to record the reliefs by using a suspended cradle, lowered down the side of the shaft. Alternatively, some form of scaffolding may have been employed, as used when surveying the surviving columns of the Temple of Castor and Pollux in the Forum Romanum, according to Piranesi's letter to Mylne of 11 November 1760; see Gotch, "Missing Years" (note 26), 182.

89. Matthew Nulty (ca. 1716–78), an Irish artist, antiquarian, and agent, was a member of Piranesi's circle; see John Ingamells, ed., *A Dictionary of British and Irish Travellers in Italy, 1701–1800, Compiled from the Brinsley Ford Archive* (New Haven: Yale Univ. Press, 1997), 717–18.

90. Piranesi had been elected an Honorary Fellow of the Society of Antiquaries of London on the strength of his services to scholarship with the recently published *Le antichità romane,* 4 vols. (Rome: Stamperia di Angelo Rotilj [etc.], 1756). According to Peter Murray, "The Minute Book of the Society of Antiquaries records, on 24 February 1757, 'Il Signor Giovanne Battista Piranesi, a Venetian, resident at Rome, a most ingenious architect, and Author of the Antiquities in Rome and its Neighbourhood in V Vols. Folio, and desirous of being admitted an honorary Member of this Society. . . .'"; see Peter Murray, *Piranesi and the Grandeur of Ancient Rome* (London: Thames & Hudson, 1971), 46; and Joan Evans, *A History of the Society of Antiquaries* (Oxford: printed at the University Press by Charles Batey for the Society of Antiquaries, 1956), 118, 126. Winckelmann was accorded the same honor on 9 April 1761; see Collier, "Villa of Cardinal Alessandro Albani" (note 61), 346 n. 1. Piranesi had proudly drawn attention to his recent election to this august institution on the title page to the *Lettere di giustificazione* of 1757 (note 24) but wrongly added "Real" (royal) to "Società degli Antiquari di Londra"; he was to repeat this error in other citations, including the headpiece to the second part of the *Osservazioni* (note 81).

91. An inscribed stela (no. 47), a panpipe (no. 94), and a serpent motif (no. 84) are included in Piranesi's chart of "Etruscan inventions" in the etched plate accompanying the prefatory essay in the *Diverse maniere* (note 46), pl. 1 (after p. 30).

92. The engraving of the demolished Palazzo Branconio dell'Aquila by Raphael was published in Pietro Ferrerio, *Palazzi di Roma de piu celebri architetti* (Rome: Gio. Iacomo Rossi, [1655]); reproduced in Peter Murray, *The Architecture of the Italian Renaissance,* new rev. ed. (London: Thames & Hudson, 1969), fig. 96.

93. Initially, these six plates were unnumbered and were published in at least three

different sequences (the first and the last plates are the same in all three, but the positions of the others vary); the Roman numerals were added at some later date. The numbered version used here is in Special Collections at the Getty Research Institute, and it matches the numbered sequence followed by Henri Focillon in his pioneering *Giovanni-Battista Piranesi: Essai de catalogue raisonné de son oeuvre* (Paris: Libraire Renouard/Henri Laurens, 1918), nos. 977–82. These variations make it harder to substantiate Rykwert's fascinating theory that the images were intended by Piranesi to convey a formal and theoretical progression; see Rykwert, *First Moderns* (note 5), 379–81. His theory is based on the order of one of the unnumbered versions, as reproduced in Piranesi, *Polemical Works* (note 22).

94. The six surviving drawings for the additional "Parere" plates, including two recently discovered at Sledmere House, Yorkshire, England (now in the collection of the National Gallery of Art, Washington, D.C.), are discussed in John Wilton-Ely, "The Art of Polemic: Piranesi and the Graeco-Roman Controversy," in Philippe Boutry et al., eds., *La Grecia antica: Mito e simbolo per l'età della grande rivoluzione: Genesi e crisi di un modello nella cultura del Settecento* (Milan: Guerini, 1991), 121–30. The two signed drawings in Washington, D.C., are full-scale studies in pen, ink, and wash with chalk for GRI *Osservazioni* pls. V, VII. According to inscriptions on one, it was purchased from the artist in Rome by the Adams' famous plasterworker, Joseph Rose the Younger, in March 1770; see Christie's, *Old Master Drawings,* London, 4 July 1989, lots 104, 105.

Although less likely, another possible rejected design for the large "Parere" plates is an architectural composition in the Egyptian style drawn in red crayon, on a scale comparable to the others, on the verso of Piranesi's prepartory study for *Altra veduta del tempio della Sibilla in Tivoli* (circa 1764) of the *Veduta di Roma.* See Wilton Ely, *Complete Etchings* (note 6), 1:239; and Alessandro Bettagno, ed., *Disegni di Giambattista Piranesi,* exh. cat. (Venice: Neri Pozza, 1978), 63 (cat. no. 72), fig. 72 verso.

95. See Antonio Francesco Gori, with Girolamo Francesco Zanetti di Alessandro, *Le gemme antiche di Anton-Maria Zanetti di Girolamo (Dactyliotheca Zanettiana)* (Venice: Stamperia di Giambatista Albrizzi, 1750), pls. XXXIII (giant), XXXVII (Minerva), LXV (tiger), LXVII (two dolphins). The source from gemstones was first indicated in Diana Scarisbrick, "Piranesi and the *Dactyliotheca Zanettiana,*" *Burlington Magazine* 132 (1990): 413–14.

96. See Wittkower, "Piranesi's *Parere*" (note 81), 155, where Wittkower renders this excerpt from the prologue of *Eunuchus* (40–43) as "It is reasonable to know yourself, and not to search into what the ancients have made if the moderns can make it" and observes that "Conclusions as to Piranesi's knowledge of Latin seem to be allowed from the fact that he engraved 'vas' instead of 'vos.'" See also Rykwert, *First Moderns* (note 5), 379–80, who translates the lines as "Wherefore it is but just that you should know this, and make allowance if the moderns do what the ancients used to do" and points out that the "this" in the quotation "refers to Terence's justification of his cribbing characters from Menander rather than translating him into literary Latin."

97. The composition's resemblance to the sixteenth-century tomb of Pietro Bernardo by Tullio Lombardo in Santa Maria Gloriosa dei Frari, Venice, is suggested in Andrew Robison, "Piranesi's Later Drawings of Architectural Fantasies," in Corinna

Höper, Jeannette Stoschek, and Elisabeth Kieven, eds., *Giovanni Battista Piranesi—Die Wahrnehmung von Raum und Zeit* (Marburg: Jonas, 2002), 49–64. I thank James Wilton-Ely for examining and photographing the tomb on my behalf.

98. See Wittkower, "Piranesi's *Parere*" (note 81), 155, where Wittkower renders this quotation from the *Metamorphoses* (15.252–53) as "Nature renews herself constantly—to create the new out of the old is, therefore, also proper to man." See also Rykwert, *First Moderns* (note 5), 379, who translates the passage as "the great renewer, Nature, makes form from form" and describes it as "the introduction to Pythagoras' teaching on transmigration."

99. See Rykwert, *First Moderns* (note 5), 380, who translates the quotation from the *Bellum Igurthinum* (85.14) as "They despise my humble birth [or: my originality] and I their cowardice." See also Wittkower, "Piranesi's *Parere*" (note 81), 155, where the quotation is rendered as "They despise my novelty, I their timidity."

100. The Masonic symbol of clasped hands had appeared previously, in Piranesi's early fantasy etching, entitled by Robison *The Tomb of Nero,* the third (usually) of a suite of four untitled works dating from the period 1747–49, known subsequently as the *Grotteschi;* see Robison, *Piranesi* (note 7), 115–22. In this work, the motif can be seen in a small circular relief on the front of a sarcophagus, based on the so-called Tomb of Nero, an antique monument near Rome. Maurizio Calvesi was among the first scholars to suggest Piranesi's membership in the Masonic Order on the basis of this particular work as well as other associated signs and emblems in his designs; see [Maurizio Calvesi], *Giovanni Battista e Francesco Piranesi,* exh. cat. (Rome: De Luca, 1967), 22–24, figs. 19a–24. While this matter has continued to be explored by Calvesi in subsequent writings—especially in his "Saggio introduttivo" (note 14)—and by other scholars, as yet no hard evidence has come to light to support the suggestion in the way that, for example, Mozart's membership is reliably documented (see H. C. Robbins Landon, *Mozart and the Masons: New Light on the Lodge "Crowned Hope"* [London: Thames & Hudson, 1982]). Moreover, since Freemasonry had been banned by Clement XII and the interdict had been repeated by Benedict XIV in 1751 and other subsequent papal patrons of Piranesi, it is extremely unlikely the artist would have risked jeopardizing such important favor by joining the brotherhood.

101. Kunstbibliothek, Berlin, Hdz 134r; see Sabine Jacob, ed., *Italienische Zeichnungen der Kunstbibliothek Berlin: Architektur und Dekoration 16. bis 18. Jahrhundert* (Berlin: Staatliche Museen Preussischer Kulturbesitz, 1975), 171 (cat. no. 867 by Marianne Fischer).

102. Prints and Drawings Collection, British Museum, London, inv. no. 1908-6-16-44; see [Georges Brunel and Pierre Arizzoli, eds.], *Piranèse et les Français, 1740–1790,* exh. cat. (Rome: Edizioni dell'Elefante, 1976), 279 (cat. no. 152 by Jean-François Méjanès).

103. The original Sphinx capital, as used both on the Aventine facade and in this unexecuted study in the British Museum (see fig. 23), was at the Villa Borghese in Rome and engraved in *Della magnificenza* (note 34), pl. XIII. Piranesi states in the *Diverse maniere* (note 46), 12, that Robert Adam owned another version of this capital.

104. For Piranesi's theoretical attitude toward the Etruscans, see Cristofani, "Le opere teoriche" (note 42), 211–20.

105. See GRI *Osservazioni* pl. I: "Problême historique à l'avantage des Tailleurs. Qui des Etrusques ou des Grecs a été l'inventeur de ces espèces de gallons qui out été decouvertes par Piranesi en Toscane dans les cavernes de Corneto et de Chiusi." On *Osservazioni* pls. I–III, see Nancy H. Ramage, "Piranesi's Decorative Friezes: A Source for Neoclassical Border Patterns," *Ars Ceramica,* no. 8 (1991): 14–19.

106. The theoretical and artistic character of Piranesi's *Diverse maniere* (note 46), and especially the "Apologetical Essay," are discussed in John Wilton-Ely, "Vision and Design: Piranesi's 'Fantasia' and the Graeco-Roman Controversy," in Georges Brunel, ed., *Piranèse et les Français: Colloque tenu à la Villa Médicis, 12–14 mai 1976* (Rome: Edizioni dell'Elefante, 1978), 543–44; and Wilton-Ely, *Piranesi as Architect* (note 1), 54–60. A detailed bibliography on this key work is included in Wilton-Ely, *Complete Etchings* (note 6), 2:886–962. See also William Rieder, "Piranesi's *Diverse maniere,*" *Burlington Magazine* 115 (1973): 309–17; John Wilton-Ely, "Nature and Antiquity: Reflections on Piranesi as a Furniture Designer," *Furniture History* 26 (1990): 191–97; and Susan M. Dixon, "Giovanni Battista Piranesi's *Diverse maniere d'adornare i cammini* and Chimneypiece Design as a Vehicle for Polemic," *Studies in the Decorative Arts* 1, no. 1 (1993): 76–98.

107. For the impact of the *Diverse maniere* plates on the Adam brothers' designs for chimneypieces, see Stillman, "Robert Adam and Piranesi" (note 28), 203–6. Executed examples particularly closely related to Piranesi's plates include those at 20 St. James's Square, London, 1772 (see King, *Complete Works* [note 31], 284, fig. 398); Apsley House, London, 1774 (see Simon Jervis and Maurice Tomlin, *Apsley House, Wellington Museum,* 2d rev. ed. [London: Victoria & Albert Museum, 1995], 33); and the former Drummond's Bank, London, 1777 (see King, *Complete Works* [note 31], 52, fig. 57). An unexecuted chimneypiece, more indirectly related to Piranesi's Egyptian manner, appears in a design (now at Sir John Soane's Museum) by George Dance the Younger for Lansdowne House, London; see Damie Stillman, "The Gallery for Lansdowne House: International Neoclassical Architecture and Decoration in Microcosm," *Art Bulletin* 52 (1970): 79–80, fig. 14.

For the *Diverse maniere*'s more indirect influence on French designers, see [Brunel and Arizzoli], *Piranèse et les Français* (note 102); Wilton-Ely, *Mind and Art* (note 6), 123; and Wilton-Ely, *Piranesi* (note 10), 106–7 (cat. nos. 273–75). Piranesi's achievements and influence on contemporary Italian design in the applied arts in general are discussed in the section entitled "Piranesiana" included in the "Roma" part of Alvar González-Palacios, *Il tempio del gusto: Roma e il Regno delle Due Sicilie: Le arti decorative in Italia fra classicismi e barocco* (Milan: Longanesi, 1984), 1:113–48.

108. Piranesi's source material for his Egyptian designs, chimneypieces, and interiors, and his contributions to the Egyptian Revival are discussed in Rudolf Wittkower, "Piranesi e il gusto egiziano," in Vittore Branca, ed., *Sensibilità e razionalità nel Settecento* (Florence: Sansoni, 1967), 659–74; and Rudolf Wittkower, "Piranesi and Eighteenth-Century Egyptomania," in idem, *Studies in the Italian Baroque* (London: Thames & Hudson, 1975), 260–73. See also James Stevens Curl, *The Egyptian Revival: An Introductory Study of a Recurring Theme in the History of Taste* (London: George Allen & Unwin, 1982), 79–81; and Jean-Marcel Humbert, Michael Pantazzi, and Christiane Ziegler, *Egyptomania: Egypt in Western Art, 1730–1930,* exh. cat.

(Paris: Réunion des Musées Nationaux; Ottawa: National Gallery of Canada, 1994).

109. Giovanni Battista Piranesi to Thomas Hollis, 18 November 1768; as quoted in Nikolaus Pevsner and Susanne Lang, "The Egyptian Revival," in Nikolaus Pevsner, *Studies in Art, Architecture and Design,* vol. 1, *From Mannerism to Romanticism* (London: Thames & Hudson, 1968), 216: "Vederete in quest' Opera usato cio che peranche in questo genere non era conosciuto. L'Architettura Egiziana, per la prima volta apparisce; la prima volta, dico, perchè in ora il mondo ha sempre creduto non esservi altro che piramidi, guglie, e giganti, escludendo non esservi parti sufficenti per adornare e sostenere questo sistema d'architettura." Piranesi's letter to Hollis, whom Piranesi had met in Rome during the latter's second Grand Tour trip, is attached to the copy of the *Diverse maniere* in the Society of Antiquaries' library. Hollis presented this copy of Piranesi's work to the society at a meeting on 25 May 1769; see Evans, *History of the Society* (note 90), 126.

110. Piranesi, *Diverse maniere* (note 46), 18–19 (English). See also Niccolo Gualtieri, *Index Testarum Conchyliorum quae Adservantur in Museo Nicolai Gualtieri* (Florence: Typographia Caietani Albizzini, 1742).

111. The two drawings concerned (a design for sconces in the Pierpont Morgan Library, New York; and a study for a cabriole table leg in the Victoria and Albert Museum, London) are discussed and reproduced in Wilton-Ely, "Nature and Antiquity" (note 106), 191–97, figs. 6, 9.

112. Piranesi, *Diverse maniere* (note 46), 33 (English).

113. For examples of the impact of the *Diverse maniere* on designers other than the Adam brothers, see Wilton-Ely, *Piranesi* (note 10), 106–7 (cat. nos. 273–75); and [Brunel and Arizzoli], *Piranèse et les Français* (note 102).

114. Adam's Etruscan rooms are examined within the remarkable development of such painted interiors *all'antica* in John Wilton-Ely, "Pompeian and Etruscan Tastes in the Neo-Classical Country-House Interior," in Gervase Jackson-Stops et al., eds., *The Fashioning and Functioning of the British Country House* (Washington, D.C.: National Gallery of Art, 1989), 51–73. See also Stillman, "Robert Adam and Piranesi" (note 28), 197–206; and Harris, *The Genius* (note 31), 177–79.

115. The background to the influential publication of Hamilton's first collection of painted vases (and other antiquities) by d'Hancarville is provided in Jenkins and Sloan, *Vases and Volcanoes* (note 47), 139–59.

116. James Barry to Edmund Burke, 8 April 1769; quoted in James Barry, *The Works of James Barry, Esq., Historical Painter . . . Containing His Correspondence from France and Italy with Mr. Burke . . . To Which Is Prefixed Some Account of the Life and Writings of the Author* (London: T. Cadell & W. Davies, 1809), 1:163.

117. "Advertisement [dated 1 October 1780]," in Horace Walpole, *Anecdotes of Painting in England; with Some Account of the Principal Artists and Incidental Notes on Other Arts,* vol. 4 (Strawberry Hill, London: printed by Thomas Kirgate, 1771), vi. Walpole's changing attitudes toward the Adam revolution in design are discussed in John Wilton-Ely, "'Gingerbread and Sippets of Embroidery': Horace Walpole and Robert Adam," *Eighteenth-Century Life* 25, no. 2 (2001): 147–69.

118. Francesco Milizia, *Roma, delle belle arti del disegno: Parte prima: Dell'architettura civile* (Bassano, Vicenza, Italy: [G. Remondini], 1787), 197. Bianconi, "Elogio

storico" (note 41), 275: "Oh quanto è diverso *Il disegnar dall'eseguir le imprese!* L'opera riuscì troppo carica d'ornamenti, e questi pure, benchè presi dall'antico, non sono tutti d'accordo fra di loro. La Chiesa del Priorato piacerà certo a molti, come piaceva sommamente al Piranesi, che la riguardò mai sempre per un capo d'opera, ma non piacerebbe nè a Vitruvio, nè al Palladio, se tornassero in Roma."

119. Donatien Alphonse François, marquis de Sade, *Voyage d'Italie; ou, Dissertations critiques, historiques et philosophiques sur les villes de Florence, Rome...*, ed. Maurice Lever (Paris: Fayard, 1995), 113: "cette église est nouvellement ornée par l'architecte Piranesi, qui a chargé ce temple d'ornements pris de l'antique, mais placés avec une confusion et traités avec une dureté qui fatigue les yeux et déplaira certainement toujours." Another negative comment of a foreign visitor is found in the manuscript diary of Prince Stanislas Poniatowski from Poland, where in the entry for 1 January 1786, he remarked on both Piranesi's church and the designer's funerary monument within it: "Près de la, sur la même Mont Aventin, il Priorato, defiguré par la mauvaise église de Piranesi, ou il se trouve un Candelabre, compose de belles pièces de sculture, qui sont assemblées avec peu de goût et placées meme hors de la perpendiculaire" (Close to there, also on the the Aventine, [is] the priory, defigured by Piranesi's ugly church, in which there is a candelabra made up of beautiful pieces of sculpture assembled quite tastelessly and not even set up at a perpendicular). I am extremely grateful both to Dr. Elżbieta Büdzinska, who is editing Prince Poniatowski's manuscript diary (now in the Gabinet Rycin, Warsaw) and to Gertrud Seidmann for drawing my attention to this source.

120. Antoine-Chrysostome Quatremère de Quincy, *Encyclopédie méthodique: Architecture* (Paris: Panckoucke, 1788–1825), s.v. "Composé ou Composite (Ordre)": "Le recueil des fragmens antiques de Piran[e]si, pourroit nous fournir encore bien d'autres exemples de cette fertilité des anciens, dans la composition de leurs chapiteaux, et dans la décoration du corinthien" (2:31).

121. Sylvia Lavin, *Quatremère de Quincy and the Invention of a Modern Language of Architecture* (Cambridge: MIT Press, 1992), 133. Quatremère de Quincy, *Encyclopédie* (note 120), 1:614, s.v. "Charpente":

> On s'imagine souvent que ce systême de l'imitation de la *charpente*, sur lequel on fait reposer celui de toute l'architecture, consiste plus en supposition de ce qui auroit pu être, qu'en réalité. Les fig. 2, 3, 4, 5, 6, et 7, tirées de Piranesi, vont détruire toute espèce de soupçon de ce genre. Cet illustre dessinateur n'eut en vue, dans les figures en question, que d'expliquer la formation et la disposition de la frise et du plafond de l'ordre dorique; mais rien n'est plus propre à la démonstration du systême générale de l'architecture. Que le lecteur jette les yeux sur ces planches, et il y verra que rien n'existe dans les plus beaux temples grecs qui ne soit le résultat exact de la *charpente*, et qu'on ne puisse exécuter en bois.
>
> (One often wonders whether this system of imitating *carpentry*, said to be the basis for all of architecture, rests more on the supposition of what could have been than on reality. Figs. 2, 3, 4, 5, 6, and 7, taken from Piranesi, will demolish every sort of suspicion of this kind. This illustrious draftsman hoped only to explain the form and arrangement of the Doric frieze and ceiling through the figures in question, but

nothing is better suited to demonstrating architecture's general system. If the reader should cast an eye over these illustrations, he will see there that nothing exists in the most beautiful Greek temples that is not the precise result of *carpentry* and that cannot be wrought in wood.)

122. For the impact of Piranesi, see John Wilton-Ely, "Soane and Piranesi," in Roger White and Caroline Lightburn, eds., *Late Georgian Classicism: Papers Given at the Georgian Group Symposium, 1987* (London: Georgian Group, 1988), 45–57; and Wilton-Ely, *Piranesi, Paestum and Soane* (note 30).

123. Watkin, *Sir John Soane* (note 25), 605. In an earlier passage of censure from the same lecture, Soane went even further; see Watkin, *Sir John Soane* (note 25), 603:

> That men unacquainted with the remains of ancient buildings should indulge in licentious and whimsical combinations is not matter of surprise, but that a man who had passed all his life in the bosom of classic art, and in the contemplation of the majestic ruins of ancient Rome, observing their sublime effects and grand combinations, a man who had given innumerable examples how truly he felt the value of the noble simplicity of those buildings, that such a man, with such examples before his eyes, should have mistaken confusion for intricacy, and undefined lines and forms for classical variety, is scarcely to be believed; yet such was Piranesi.

124. The reception of Piranesi—specifically the influence of the visionary architecture of the *Carceri d'invenzione* on Romanticism and on the world of literature as well as twentieth-century film-set design and music—was explored in John Wilton-Ely, "The Voices of the Imagination: Creative and Critical Responses to Piranesi from His Contemporaries and from Posterity" (Getty Lecture Series in Art and Art History, University of Southern California, Los Angeles, 1, 2, and 7 March 1995). For a detailed study of the impact of the *Carceri d'invenzione* on French literature, see Luzius Keller, *Piranèse et les Romantiques français: Le mythe des escaliers en spirale* (Paris: José Corti, 1966).

125. Key contributions to the interpretation of Piranesi's arcane language, formal as well as symbolic, include Calvesi, "Saggio introduttivo" (note 14); [Calvesi], *Giovanni Battista e Francesco* (note 99); Maurizio Calvesi, "Ideologia e referimenti delle *Carceri,*" in Alessandro Bettagno, ed., *Piranesi tra Venezia e l'Europa* (Florence: Leo S. Olschki, 1983), 339–60; and Maurizio Calvesi, "Nota ai 'grotteschi' o capricci di Piranesi," in Anna Lo Bianco, ed., *Piranesi e la cultura antiquaria, gli antecedenti e il contesto: Atti del convegno, 14–17 novembre 1979* (Rome: Multigrafica, 1983), 135–40.

Manfredo Tafuri's most significant contributions on Piranesi include the following: "Giovan Battista Piranesi: L'architettura come 'utopia negativa,'" *Angelus novus: Trimestrale di estetica e critica,* no. 20 (1971): 89–127; "Il complesso di Santa Maria del Priorato sull'Aventino," in Alessandro Bettagno, ed., *Piranesi: Incisioni, rami, legature, architetture,* exh. cat. (Venice: Neri Pozza, 1978), 78–87; "Borromini e Piranesi" (note 52); "'The Wicked Architect'" (note 18); and "The Historicity of the Avant-Garde: Piranesi and Eisenstein," in Manfredo Tafuri, *The Sphere and the Labyrinth: Avant-Gardes and Architecture from Piranesi to the 1970s,* trans. Pellegrino d'Acierno and Robert Connolly (Cambridge: MIT Press, 1987), 55–64.

An important reassessment is also to be found in Rykwert, *First Moderns* (note 5). Recent contributions that widen the discussion to literary construction (and deconstruction) as well as architectural theory and design include Joseph Rosa, ed., *The Imagined and Real Landscapes of Piranesi: Critical Writings in America*, exh. cat. (New York: Columbia Books of Architecture, 1992); and Jennifer Bloomer, *Architecture and the Text: The (S)crypts of Joyce and Piranesi* (New Haven: Yale Univ. Press, 1993).

Observations on the Letter of Monsieur Mariette

with

Opinions on Architecture, and a Preface to a New Treatise on the Introduction and Progress of the Fine Arts in Europe in Ancient Times

Observations

by Giovanni Battista Piranesi on the Letter of Monsieur Mariette to the Authors of the *Gazette littéraire de l'Europe*

Included in the Supplement of the *Gazette* Published Sunday, 4 November 1764

Monsieur Mariette's Letter

Dear Messieurs, Monsieur Piranesi, the author of a number of works on Roman antiquities that have been reviewed in your pages, has recently published another,[1] which may perhaps be unknown to us,[†A] in which he sets out to write a defense of the Romans and to show—contrary to your opinion, which I share—that in the arts, and in architecture in particular, not only does that nation owe nothing to the Greeks[B] but also it is greatly superior to them by virtue of the solidity, the size, and the magnificence of the buildings that formerly adorned its capital city. He contrasts these buildings with those properly pertaining to the Greeks, some vestiges of which are still to be seen in Athens and elsewhere in Greece.[C] He finds none that can bear comparison, in either solidity or size, with the Cloaca Maxima [(sewer system)] of Rome, the foundations of the ancient Capitolium, and the emissarium [(drainage outlet)][2] of Lago Albano—not to mention

Observations

A

To Signor Mariette this work is unknown, no *perhaps* about it.

B

To my mind, there is a difference between saying *As far as architecture is concerned, the Romans owe nothing to the Greeks* and saying, as one reads in Piranesi's preface to the published edition of his work, *In the matter of architecture, the Romans owed little or nothing to the Greeks.* Italians understand that the phrase *poco o nulla* [(little or nothing)] is intended to belittle the nature of the debt incurred by the Romans, not to deny that there was any such debt; anyone who has read Piranesi's book knows whether this is true. On *page 93* he demonstrates that Greek architecture conferred no advantage, public or private, on Rome, which had long taken its lead from Etruscan architecture; and that Greek architecture had been preferred to Etruscan not on merit but out of caprice. There is the *little or nothing* that came to Rome from Greece.

[1] *Della magnificenza e[d] architettura de' romani* (Rome, 1761).

†A dagger indicates an editorial note; see pp. 142–53. —ED.

[2] The fear of disastrous flooding caused the Romans to interrupt the siege of Veii to carry out this engineering work, which, although complex in the extreme, did not take very long. They nevertheless had to bore through a mountain and build a canal of some considerable length, lined with stone masonry.* We today would think twice before embarking on such an enterprise. It is mentioned in Livy.†

*Neither Livy nor any other ancient author, of all the many who speak of this canal, says that it was lined with stone; there was no need for this, since, as Piranesi has shown in a detailed treatise on the emissarium, the tunnel through the mountain was cut through the living rock. —PIRANESI

C

In his book, Piranesi makes no comparison with *the buildings properly pertaining to the Greeks, some vestiges of which are still to be seen in Athens and in other parts of Greece.* He does make a comparison with those vestiges, because he has seen them, not *the buildings* of which they formed part.

D

And, in comparing those vestiges with those of ancient Rome, he draws no distinction whatever between what was constructed in that city in *the earliest days of the republic* and what was done later.

E

Which are the plates in Piranesi's work in which he has collected *a considerable number of capitals, bases, column shafts, entablatures, . . . , all varying in shape as well as in the ornaments with which they are laden?* Plates VI, VII, VIII, IX, X, XI, XII, XIII, XIV, XV, XVI, XVII, XVIII, XIX, and XX, I imagine. Now, what does he have to say about all this? *That, these being the things brought into Latium by the Greeks, this would seem to indicate the methods of construction used by the Tuscans* (page 129), *and consequently by the Romans, before they knew the Greeks.* How is it, then, that *these diverse fragments, all varying in shape as well as in the ornaments with which they are laden* are claimed by Piranesi as *convincing proof of the fecundity of the genius of the Romans?* Listen to what he has to say about these architectural members elsewhere in the same work: *Many of these things are likewise to be seen in Rome, either because they were transported there from Greece, or because they were the work of Greek architects; some of these have been collected by me in plates VI, VII, VIII, IX, X, and so on.* So Piranesi, after having made this concession to the Greeks, avails himself of it as convincing proof of the fecundity *of the genius of the Romans?* But on what page, on what line? May Signor Mariette excuse me for saying that by writing such a review of Piranesi's book, he has insulted the public even more than he has offended the author.

How does Piranesi describe the building methods handed on by the Etruscans to the Romans? He says that the Etruscans thought wisely and used little adornment on their architecture. And what does he say of the Greeks? That by dividing their architectural members too much by carving, they achieved too much vain prettiness and too little gravity, *page 101*. That the

sundry other ancient structures built of huge ashlars from the earliest days of the republic onward[D] that still serve the purpose for which they were first built. The same Monsieur Piranesi has collected a considerable number of capitals, bases, column shafts, entablatures, and so forth. These diverse fragments, which vary in shape as well as in the ornament with which they are laden, furnish him—or so he claims—with convincing proof of the fecundity of the genius of the Romans.[E] That genius, in the opinion of this author, also manifests itself in the size and the scale of the spacious edifices that, though now in ruins, cover vast tracts of land in Rome today. His argument is as follows.

ornaments in their architecture are for the most part monstrous and run counter to the truth, *ibid*. All which would entitle us to say that the reviewer has not read one word of Piranesi's book. But let us continue.

F

What chicanery! Where exactly, in his book, does Piranesi state that *the more recent buildings of the Romans, laden with ornaments, can be recognized by architectural members of bizarre shape that in no way resemble the same members as invented by the Greeks?* How could he assert such a thing, after having attributed not to the taste of the Romans but to that of the Greeks these same *architectural members of bizarre shape*, and after having said, as I mentioned above, that these things *are to be seen in Rome, either because they were transported there from Greece, or because they were the work of Greek architects?* It is quite true that Piranesi draws a comparison between the ruins of ancient Greece and the monuments (including the most recent) of ancient Rome, including *the buildings laden with ornament, a considerable number of capitals, bases, column shafts, entablatures, . . . , all varying in their shapes as well as in the ornamentation upon them;* but to what purpose? Here it is: *If anyone,* he says on *page 195, travels to Greece for the purpose of study, what will Greece provide for his instruction? It will not teach him about capitals, because, aside from those of the Erechthion, there are none that bear comparison with Roman capitals; it will not teach him about columns, because there are so many more in Rome of every sort and size; it will not teach him about statues or bas-reliefs—one finds these in Rome in the greatest abundance and elegance, in comparison to those of the Greeks; finally, it will not teach him about work of any other kind, Italy being so chock-full that—as can well be said—to find Greece we should look no further than Italy. Let no one object, at this point, that many of these monuments were taken from the Greeks, or else made by the Romans in the Greek manner; we are trying not to establish the makers of the works in question, whether Greek or Roman, but to determine which is the most appropriate place to learn these arts, Rome or Greece. We have already seen what Rome has to offer to foreign visitors; but what will Greece have to teach those who make their way there, exhausted by the sea crossing, by travel, and by architectural campaigning, if neither the things adduced by us nor ancient or modern architecture can teach them?* Now, such being his

The earliest buildings of the Romans were built before any communication took place between their nation and that of the Greeks. The more recent buildings are laden with ornaments and can be recognized by architectural members of bizarre shape that in no way resemble the same members as invented by the Greeks.[F] Therefore the Romans borrowed nothing and learned nothing from the Greeks; they owe them neither the science of construction and good building practice nor taste in ornamentation.

premises, how could Piranesi ever have asserted *that the Romans borrowed nothing and learned nothing from the Greeks?* He certainly did say—and demonstrate, too—that the Romans *did not owe them the science of construction and good building practice;* but he did not say *that they did not owe them taste in ornamentation:* they certainly did, as is shown by all those features of *architecture of bizarre shape.*

G

True enough; the statement that *when the first Romans wished to erect buildings, they enlisted the aid of the Etruscan architects who were their neighbors, does not prove that they derived the manner that they used from their own resources.* But where has Piranesi ever undertaken to prove that the Romans derived that manner *from their own resources?* In his book, Piranesi lumped together the later Greeks, Rome, Etruria—in other words, Italy—as being different from Greece; since for his purposes, it did not matter in the slightest whether they were different from each other; not that he would have been unable to show that those Etruscans who practiced the arts in Rome before the Greek arts were ever introduced there were more Roman than Terence, Horace, Cicero, Virgil, or any of the many other celebrated writers whom scholars (and Signor Mariette himself at the end of his letter) have not the slightest difficulty in admitting to Roman citizenship. He wished to reserve this, however, for another time and a more appropriate place, as we shall hear in these pages.

I would like Signor Mariette to tell me whether we are to take his word for it that *the Etruscans were Greek by origin;* or are we to rely on such evidence as he might be able to supply. If on the evidence, he must have read [Theodore] Ryckius, [Antonio Francesco] Gori,[†] or some other writer who shares his interpretation of a lengthy Etruscan tablet such as one of those found at Gubbio and—even without knowing the alphabet—concludes that the Etruscan language is a dialect of Greek. No ancient writer ever dreamed of such a thing. Herodotus[†] conjectured that the Etruscans were from Lydia; Strabo[†] and Patrocles[†] said the same. Dionysius[†] [of Halicarnassus] rejected this, on the grounds that their language and customs differed from those of any other nation. Now, Signor Mariette, if you did not get this from Ryckius or from Gori, tell us from where you did get it? You who, at the end of your letter, for fear of being disbelieved when you state that Horace was a lyric poet, quote two lines of that poet's work to demonstrate

But this argument does not prove that the Romans derived either from their own resources. Monsieur Piranesi himself concedes that when the first Romans wished to erect the massive buildings whose solidity astounds us, they were obliged to enlist the aid of the Etruscan architects who were their neighbors. One might as well say the aid of the Greeks, because the Etruscans, who were Greek by origin, knew and practiced no arts except those that had been taught to their forefathers in the country from which they came.[G]

Here we have them, these Romans, who, persuaded of the excellent constitution of their government, which they believed would last forever, came up with the idea of erecting buildings that would last as long as their empire; but they possessed only the courage to ordain them, not the talent to execute them.

the fact. Here is my source, replies Signor Mariette: *The Etruscans knew, and practiced, no arts except those that had been taught to their forefathers in the country from which they came.* Now, what do you mean by that? Perhaps you mean that the arts practiced by the Etruscans in Italy, and recognized to be the same arts that were in use among the Greeks, demonstrate that the Etruscans *were Greek by origin?* That would be an excellent proof indeed; but have you thought to inquire whether, by the time the Etruscans had begun—or by the time the Etruscans had ceased—to practice those arts; whether, by the time (I shall find words for this if I persist) the Etruscans had ceased to rule, the Greeks had even yet begun to learn them?

Eventually they extended their conquests beyond the confines of Italy. They subjugated Greece, and there they found the arts in a flourishing condition; they were dazzled by the brilliance of those arts, much as a man rich and powerful but lacking in taste might be dazzled by the sight of an imposing object that he planned to praise to connoisseurs;[H]

H

Brilliance is made for the eyes; and, if the eyes are *dazzled by the brilliance of the arts,* this does not reflect the praise *that they heard from connoisseurs*—it reflects taste. And so, if the Romans had no such eyes, Signor Mariette, how did they ever contrive to be *dazzled by that brilliance?* And where did you ever learn that the Romans were such dolts when it came to the arts? In his book, Piranesi proves that they cultivated Etruscan architecture from the moment Rome was first built, *page 7.* That the Tuscans taught them the arts of peace, *pages 15, 17.* That they were excellent mathematicians before they knew anything of the Greek arts, *pages 19, 21.* That they practiced sculpture long before they encountered the Greeks, *ibid.* That, until they conquered Greece, they never built in imitation of the manners or the magnificence of the Greeks, *pages 49, 51.* That in the earliest times they were as magnificent as the Egyptians and the Greeks, *page 53,* and, as time passed, more magnificent than any other nation, *page 71.* That in construction they followed their own customs, not the customs of the Greeks, *page 67, 69.* That they were admirably inventive, *page 91.* That, by applying the rules of architecture as hitherto practiced in Rome, *those dazzled by the brilliance of the arts of Greece* were able to correct very many of the defects of Greek architecture, *page 181.* And, on *page 197,* he shows with what rashness—or rather with what sheer want of knowledge on the part of some persons who have not the first idea about the fine arts or about Roman history—the Romans have been branded as vulgarians and regarded as men *lacking in taste.*

and, in a most singular reversal, the victors subordinated their taste to that of the vanquished.[3] The fruit of their victory was the introduction of the fine arts into Rome.[I]

I

How do you make out, Signor Mariette, that the Romans *who were lacking in taste, subordinated their taste to that of the vanquished?* Whereas Piranesi, in his book, has challenged all present and future champions of the Greeks to produce evidence that the Romans ever felt this alleged admiration or that they preferred the buildings of the Greeks to those of the Italians. He has said that the Romans adopted the architecture of the Greeks not on its merits but for the splendor of the marbles, *pages 61, 69.* That this architecture brought the Romans no benefit or advantage, public or private, *page 93,* since Tuscan architecture had already provided for everything. And, despite the fine passage from Horace, *Graecia capta forum . . .*,[3] which he, too, quotes, he dared to assert that no praise of Greek architecture is to be found in the work of any writer, Greek or Latin.

From the moment that they set foot in the houses of the Greeks, recognized their comforts, and admired the majesty of their temples and public buildings, the Romans could think of nothing but the means of procuring such things for their own country.[K]

K

On page 63 of his book, Piranesi says: *Desist, therefore, not from admiring things Greek (I am not averse to them) but rather from proclaiming that the Romans were stunned by the magnificence of their works when they saw them.* Piranesi says *therefore* because he has replied to all the arguments that have been advanced against the Romans, as to the comfort and elegance of the buildings of the Greeks and their own desire to have something similar. Have you, Signor Mariette, nothing to say to those replies? What? Would an account of them not have suited your version of the introduction of Greek art into Rome?

It certainly was not through any superiority of genius that they came to this resolution.[L] They consulted only that instinct, so natural in men, to procure their own well-being—and, above all, a sense of vanity that would not permit them to see themselves outdone in magnificence by a subject people.[M]

L

This should read as follows: *It certainly was not due to the sight of an imposing object*—as Piranesi proves in his book.

M

Pliny [the Elder]—but this author, Signor Mariette remarks at the end of this letter, *was bound to be interested in the glory of his own nation.* Be that as it may, Pliny,[†] who so irritates Signor Mariette, says on this same subject: *ships are built for the sake of these marbles, and here and there sections of mountains are transported across the sea* (by the Greeks? No, by the

[3] *Graecia capta ferum victorem cepit, et artes / intulit agresti Latio* [(Conquered Greece her conqueror subdued, and into rustic Latium brought the arts)]. Horat. lib. 1. ep. 1. [Horace, *Epistles,* bk. 2, epistle 1, ll. 156–57.]

Romans). *Consider the cost paid for each load and the huge bulk that is hauled away — and for what use and for what pleasure other than that of falling asleep among different colored marbles?* After studying the subject in great detail, Piranesi has reached the same conclusion as Pliny concerning the instinct *so natural in men to procure their own well-being.* As for the vanity that made the Romans unwilling *to see themselves outdone in magnificence,* he said and he has shown that the object of their desire was marble alone; as for architecture, their own was as good as, or better than, that of the Greeks, for anyone who espouses (as Signor Mariette does) the principle that buildings should not be created *from fragments that vary in shape as well as in the ornament with which they are laden.* As for marble, Piranesi goes on to say, *page 57: It will be objected that the temples of the Greeks and their public buildings were of marble; but I ascribe this detail to the nature of the country, not to the magnificence of its inhabitants. What is so unusual about building with the stone that abounds in a country, as marble abounds in Greece? Like Cicero, I would have been amazed if they had used travertine, which would have cost so much to transport to Greece from a distant country.* Before firing off exaggerated accounts of the splendor of the Romans and the intelligence of the Greeks — as he does throughout his letter — Signor Mariette would have done well to pay heed to these and to all Piranesi's other arguments on this subject. Before celebrating his triumph, he should first have made sure of victory.

The sooner to enter into full possession, they shamelessly stripped the Greek buildings of their principal ornaments and made off with them. The consul [Lucius] Mummius set the example after taking Corinth. He transported countless masterpieces of art to Rome. The private houses and public buildings where these masterpieces were installed, although formerly modest and unassuming, were thus transformed into opulent and magnificent palaces and monuments.[N]

N

To all the protests concerning the sack of Corinth, the spoils removed to Rome by Mummius, and all the other thefts supposed to have been committed by the Romans here and there, Piranesi in his book replies by wondering if perhaps the victors did not have every right to do so — seeing that on occasion the most pious and merciful princes in all Christendom have sacked cities without violating the precepts of justice. Why, therefore, does Signor Mariette condemn the Romans for these acts of plunder? Because he considers that, since Greece was then stripped of all its finest possessions, persons of good sense will expect it to be still more denuded today. And also because men who were *lacking in taste* — as he would have it — nevertheless appear to have had sense enough to pick out *countless masterpieces of art,* and to leave behind them a lantern,** later known to the world as the Magic Lantern.†

As for the other contention, that *the buildings in Rome where these masterpieces were installed, though formerly modest and unassuming, were thus transformed into opulent and magnificent palaces and monuments*, Piranesi repeats that he has proved that, in the early days of Rome, its inhabitants were as magnificent as the Egyptians and the Greeks; that in construction they did not follow Greek practice but rather their own; and that the architectural rules already applied in Rome corrected many defects in Greek architecture... But is it my business to discuss what is contained in Piranesi's book, or is it the business of the person who has undertaken to review it?

The Romans were quite content to shine at so little cost, and there was no Roman who was not of the opinion that the practice of the arts was beneath the dignity of men devoted to the conquest of the entire universe.O

O

The person who shines *at little cost* is Signor Mariette, who in telling us the story of the introduction of Greek art into Italy has not even taken the minimal trouble to find the facts that might have spared him a number of assertions revealed for what they are worth by Piranesi in his book. You have said, Signor Mariette, that the Romans were unwilling *to be outdone in magnificence by a subject people;* and yet, according to you, they are entirely lacking in taste and they shine *at little cost* because they are neither architects nor sculptors nor painters? Therefore, in your opinion, anyone wishing to win praise for the fine arts must practice them himself. So remove all the names and all the inscriptions of princes and peoples from every building and from every work of art that they have commissioned, because they themselves were neither architects nor sculptors nor painters. As for yourself, Signor Mariette, what are you, who in your letter bestow and refuse credit for the possession of taste and talent in the fine arts? Neither a painter nor a sculptor nor an architect. Now, might not the Romans have had an ability of the same kind as yours? Might it not have been possessed by those princes and those peoples who, although they never published a letter denouncing a book *which is unknown to you* (no *perhaps* about it), have nevertheless promoted the building of all those grand and beautiful works that were and are the admiration of the universe?

**See the work [by Julien-David Le Roy] entitled *Les ruines des plus beaux monuments de la Grèce* [(Paris, 1758), 1:24–26, pl. XIII].

P

In his book, Piranesi has asserted (and this I repeat for the last time) that the Romans had already been instructed in the arts of peace by the Tuscans. That they (that is, they, the citizens) cultivated those arts after building Rome. That they (the citizens) were excellent in mathematics before they ever came into contact with the Greek arts. That they (they, the citizens) had practiced sculpture and painting before they ever became acquainted with the Greeks. That in matters of construction, once acquainted with the Greeks, they did not adopt the practices of the latter but persevered with their own; that in architecture they (they, the citizens) built things that it had never crossed the minds of the Greeks could be built by a living soul. That very many Romans (that is, of the citizens) were from time to time able architects. That they corrected many of the innumerable defects that they found in the architecture of the Greeks. That they achieved a magnificence equal to that of the Egyptians and the Greeks, and thereafter greater than that of any other nation. What more could the Romans have done to honor the fine arts? What more could they have done, to relieve Signor Mariette of the need to say *that they never had either the leisure or the inclination to distinguish between these arts and the purely mechanical trades?* Did not their emperors, and many illustrious citizens before them, condescend to cultivate the arts and to become practitioners? Nero was a talented painter and sculptor; Hadrian, besides having been an architect, was a painter, as were Severus Alexander, Valentinian, and others, and in Rome they left behind public evidence of their condescension. What more could they have done *to distinguish between these arts and the purely mechanical trades?* Was it their duty *to speak in praise of those who had cultivated* those arts, as [Claude] Perrault[†] says in the preface to his Vitruvius, *giving them a place among the illustrious.* If anyone ventures to deny that they did so, I appeal to the authority of Cossutius,[†] Varro, Pliny, Vitruvius himself, and many other Roman authors. At the same time, the greater part of the practitioners of the fine arts in Rome were slaves. Without wasting time in the attempt to disabuse Signor Mariette of this hasty supposition, I have this to say: Were they slaves because the Romans had decreed that the fine arts were to be practiced only by slaves? Or were they slaves because the slaves were poor and this was a way in which they sought to become rich? Now, in our own time—a time when the fine arts are separated from the purely mechanical trades—who

They never had either the leisure or the inclination to distinguish between these arts and the purely mechanical trades;[P] they left the cultivation of the arts to mercenary Greeks who, attracted by the promise of gain, did not hesitate to expatriate themselves and to quit a country where, after the Roman conquest, there were undoubtedly fewer opportunities to establish and maintain a reputation. Before long, the arts came to be practiced in Rome exclusively by slaves. People rich enough to keep a large number of slaves purchased them with both profit and utility in mind; they therefore sought out, by preference, slaves with artistic talent.

are most of their practitioners? The poor who seek to become rich, or grandees who condescend to practice the arts? If the laws of slavery had not been abolished, even now that these arts are flourishing once more, and have been separated from the purely mechanical trades, how many practitioners would be counted among the slaves! So many that a person who shared Signor Mariette's opinions would say that *the arts are practiced only by slaves.*

Furthermore, if in a country full of persons of taste—as was Greece—*after the Roman conquest, there were undoubtedly fewer opportunities to establish and maintain a reputation,* how could such opportunities have arisen in a country or in a city of men *lacking in taste?* And these men, ignorant and *lacking in taste,* how were they able to choose *slaves with artistic talent?* Perhaps they relied on the praises *that they heard from connoisseurs?* And were those *connoisseurs* Greek or Roman? They were Greek; Signor Mariette has already given us to understand as much. So the Romans purchased Greek slaves, and had them practice the fine arts, not because they knew the value of such slaves or of the works that they created but because those works were appreciated by the Greeks? So they attributed none of the genius to themselves, but to the Greeks? So the Romans *stripped the Greek buildings of their principal ornaments, transported to Rome countless masterpieces of art,* obliged all Greeks *with artistic talent to expatriate themselves,* made slaves of them all, and reduced Greece to a desert, not in order to please themselves but to please the Greeks? If this was the case, why does Signor Mariette say that the Romans *shamelessly stripped the Greek buildings of their principal ornaments?* This was no cause for shame; it was a boon.

Q

If these practitioners of the fine arts were *a class of men necessary to the state,* how did the Romans manage to survive for five or six centuries without them? Piranesi has demonstrated that they survived with another body of men who were equally talented; or, if he has failed to prove his point, Signor Mariette ought to have signaled the omission in his review of the book. But to return to the slaves. So are we to take it that *the slave dealers would quickly inquire into the natural aptitudes of those they were planning to offer for sale? That if they found signs of talent, they would urge them to cultivate it? And that to encourage them further, they would inform*

For their part, the slave dealers, guided purely by self-interest, would promptly inquire into the natural aptitudes of those they were planning to offer for sale. If they found signs of talent, they would urge them to cultivate it; to encourage them further, they would inform them (quite truthfully) that the more skilled they became, the better would be the treatment that they could expect from their future masters. The Greeks, the most industrious of all the nations subject to the Romans, furnished them with the greatest abundance of these artist slaves—a class of men necessary to the state[Q] but nevertheless relegated to a separate and lowly status and considered, for all their talents, far inferior to the lowliest Roman citizen. Thus Virgil represents them in the beautiful lines he puts into the mouth of the hero Anchises, when, consulted by Aeneas, he foretells the destiny of the Roman people.

them (quite truthfully) that the more skilled they became, the better would be the treatment that they could expect from their future masters? My question is this: Where did those dealers send the slaves to learn the fine arts? Where were the masters to teach them? Not in Greece, where *after the Roman conquest, opportunities to establish and maintain a reputation* had disappeared; where there was supposedly not one Greek left who could commission a building or a painting or a statue in his own honor. So the dealers had to send their talented merchandise to study in Rome. And where has Signor Mariette found that there existed these schools for marketable slaves?

R

As for Virgil, I ask Signor Mariette where we are to place him: among the Greeks or among the Romans? *The Romans,* he answers† at the end of his letter, *also borrowed from the Greeks all the mechanics of their versification, and their poetry offered little feeling and few images for which models or seeds had not been found in the poetry of the Greeks.... Virgil's* Aeneid *is nothing but a felicitous combination of the* Iliad *and the* Odyssey. So Virgil was a Roman; which in other words means that he was one of those men who in architecture, sculpture, and painting were *lacking in taste.* So how could he, this man without taste, distinguish the finer from the cruder of the bronze statues, or vivacity from stupidity in those of marble? Who dictated to him *spirantia mollius aera* [(more finely a breathing likeness from the bronze)] or *ducent de marmore vivos vultus* [(coax from marble living faces)]?

Excudent alii spirantia mollius aera;
Credo equidem, vivos ducent de
marmore vultus.
—lib. 6, vv. 847 f.[R]

[(Others, I well believe, will strike
more finely
A breathing likeness from the bronze,
and coax
From marble living faces.
—Virgil, *Aeneid* 6.847–48)]

These beautiful lines are beautiful indeed; but neither they nor those other lines by Horace have prevented Piranesi from demonstrating that in Italy there were sculptors as fine as the Greeks, and architects far better than the Greeks, long before the Greeks arrived. I do not know how the gentlemen who collect the various articles to compile the *Gazette littéraire* could have suffered Signor Mariette to use these passages from Virgil and Horace as illustrations of the blockheadedness of the Romans: are not these the editors who once said that *poetry is well known to rely on exaggeration and hyperbole?****

****Gazette littéraire de l'Europe,* vol. 1, [no. 1 (7 March 1764):] 10, at the end.

S

Piranesi having demonstrated in his book that the Romans corrected innumerable defects in the architecture of the Greeks, it follows that in the arts the latter were more concerned with pride than the former with taste.

T

You say, Signor Mariette, *it was enough for the Romans to have among them and in their employ men who would do their bidding and who were always ready to assist them with their projects.* Therefore architects want to have about them these men who are *always ready to assist them in their projects.* Now hear what Cicero[†] says to his brother Quintus about a villa that he had engaged one of these slaves to build for him: *Columnas, neque rectas, neque e regione Diphilus collocarat: eas scilicet demolietur; aliquando perpendiculo, et linea discet uti* [(The columns Diphilus had placed were neither perpendicular nor opposite each other; he will, of course, have to pull them down. Some day or other he will learn the use of the plumb-line and the tape)]. Would you have believed that Cicero himself was an architect?

V

I fail to understand, Signor Mariette, how payment comes into this. Did you not say that all these practitioners were slaves, sold by dealers to the Romans? So they were not to receive a fee, and even less could they have hoped to be paid for their works, which had all been paid for in advance in the price handed over to the dealers.

X

I do not know what *men are ashamed to follow in the footsteps of others* and *men want to surpass their models* have to do with one another. After all, have you not already said, Signor Mariette, *that the arts in Rome were practiced only by slaves? That this was no way to foster emulation? That it is honor that gives life to the arts?* Then how did these slaves come to feel *ashamed to follow in the footsteps of others* or keen *to surpass their models,* if not from ambition and the hope of gaining personal glory?

Y

Listen, Signor Mariette, to what Piranesi has to say in his book *concerning this profusion of ornament and these liberties that disgust you.* He says: *The Greeks, by*

This sentiment, dictated by pride, inevitably stifled in the Romans all love and propensity for the arts.[S] They must have considered it enough to have among them, and in their employ, men who would do their bidding and who were always ready to assist with their projects.[T] This was, of course, no way to foster emulation or to bring the arts to the degree of perfection that had been attained in Greece in those days when only free men were permitted to make art their profession. Honor, even more than financial reward, gives life to the arts.[V] Thus, while the number of projects grew and the projects became more ambitious, taste tended to degenerate rather than improve. At the moment when the arts first passed from Greece to Rome, taste had attained all the perfection that could ever have been hoped for: in other words, it was still governed by rules that ordained a beautiful and noble simplicity. Experience teaches us that matters never remain in the same state for long; everything goes in cycles in this world: fashion holds sway and exerts its sovereign and tyrannical rule; men are ashamed to follow in the footsteps of others;[X] love of novelty reigns supreme; men want to surpass their models, and this is always at the expense of good taste. At such times, nothing is produced that is not laden with superfluous and gratuitous ornament. All is sacrificed to luxury, and the result is a manner that rapidly becomes ridiculous and barbaric. So it was with the Romans in architecture; the examples given by Piranesi are proof enough. There is a profusion of ornament and disgusting liberties that, whatever he may say,[Y] prove the total decadence of genius in the architects who made the designs.

concentrating on ornamentation, on the subdivision of parts, and on carvings have been perhaps too successful in achieving a kind of vain prettiness, at the expense of gravity. It could truthfully be said that no shrub nor tree exists from which they have not borrowed little stems or fronds to embellish their architecture; there are no apples, flowers, or animal figurines that they have not imported into their friezes; no animal skins or moldings or caprices of any kind that have not been carved by them on pedestals or architraves. But, though all these are taken from nature, and formed as nature makes them, I still think it necessary to consider whether placing such things on cornices, friezes, or architraves is any more natural than, for example (as Horace† *says), painting a cypress tree in the midst of the sea when depicting a shipwreck. Such things are as contrary to what is usually done—and thus as contrary to the truth of architecture, and for that matter decorum—as placing a cypress in the middle of the sea. In which case, how is it possible that such things have ever been used on real buildings? Who would think of adorning architraves, friezes, facades, or courtyards of houses with garlands interwoven with apples and bunches of grapes, with walnuts, acorns, pines, small birds, and heads of oxen—more or less as the* cuccagna† *is offered to the populace in Naples, high up on platforms and adorned with laurel branches?* That is what Piranesi says *concerning this profusion of ornament and the liberties that disgust you.* He says this on *page 101.* Listen to what he adds on *page 179: If anyone were to ask after the origin of these incongruous additions, I am certain that the answer would be that the Greeks thought of the ornamentation first and the architecture afterward*... But what? Signor Mariette, do you really expect me to tell you everything that Piranesi said in his book? You ought to have read it yourself, Signor Book Critic, reviewing books you have not read or understood. All the same, since, on the subject of the proliferation of ornament *and the liberties that disgust you,* you remarked: *this is exactly what happened to the Romans in architecture,* I shall tell you a little more about the book. Listen to what he adds on *page 101,* after his words about the *cuccagna: Saint Mark's in Venice, built in the tenth century of our era, can provide a comprehensive specimen of such inventions to anyone visiting its interior. It is adorned with an almost infinite number of columns, capitals, cornices, and marble panels that were formerly in Greece. From these it is easy to observe how erratic was the Greeks' invention in architecture; they gradually assumed an almost total freedom to do exactly as they pleased. Many of these things are likewise to be seen in Rome, either because they were transported there from Greece or because they were the work of Greek architects; some are illustrated in my book on Roman antiquities, already published,*[†] *and others may be seen in plates VI, VII, VIII,* . . . But these are things that I have told you before.

Z

Once again, Signor Mariette, I am confused by what you say. Please reconcile these propositions for me: *The pride of the Romans stifled all love and all propensity for the arts. The arts came to be practiced in Rome exclusively by slaves. It was the Greeks, the most industrious of all the nations subject to the Romans, who furnished them with the greatest abundance of these artist slaves. They must have considered it enough to have among them and in their employ men who would do their bidding.* To which I say that if pride prevented the Romans from viewing the arts from a particular angle; if the arts were practiced in Rome only by slaves; if these slaves were for the most part Greeks; if the Romans could satisfy any need for art they might have had by having these slaves and telling them to create such and such a work, how then can you contend that *it comes as a surprise that the constant sight of so many excellent works that had been transported from Greece to Rome could not germinate some taste among the Romans, or set them on the right path?* Why did you not say: *could not cause taste to germinate among these slaves whom the Romans had in their employ?* Why this contradiction and this volley of blame directed at the Romans?

AA

Here, Signor Mariette, I am more at a loss than ever. Did you not say that good taste *had attained all the perfection that could ever have been hoped for at the moment when the arts first passed from Greece to Rome, and that it was still governed by rules that ordained a beautiful and noble simplicity?* Did you not say *that the constant sight of so many excellent works* ought *to have germinated some taste among the Romans and set them on the right path?* And that for guidance *they had only to imitate the beauties that constantly offered themselves to their gaze?* How, then, can you reconcile these principles with these others, that *too great an abundance of beautiful things, and particularly of works*

As I have said, all the most beautiful objects in Greece were transported to Rome; and it comes, no doubt, as a surprise that the constant sight of so many excellent works could not germinate some taste among the Romans or set them on the right path.[Z] They had, or so it seems, only to imitate the beauties that constantly offered themselves to their gaze. But it is only human to want to make one's own way; and even the most admired objects must eventually pall. Furthermore, I maintain that too great an abundance of beautiful things, and particularly of works that seem to be beyond the powers of mere mortals, is often harmful to those who take them as their models: we look upon them with a sense of respect and admiration that fetters the soul and the talent.[AA] And so we see that the modern artists who have shown the greatest genius are not those whom chance has most plentifully provided with such aid. Correggio, Raphael, and Michelangelo rose to such heights because nature alone was at work within them and because nature had endowed them with creative genius. If they had had masters of their own stature as predecessors, they might have been tempted to follow them and remain no more than faithful and mediocre disciples. For any imitator, whoever he may be, is inferior to his model. Anyone who merely follows in the footsteps of those who have already won the race will take only timid and clumsy strides. To this point I have concerned myself only with the taste of the Romans in architecture. Monsieur Piranesi's erroneous opinion, which I have been only too pleased to controvert, has caused me to concentrate on this topic to the exclusion of others. *The rest does not concern Piranesi.*

that seem to be beyond the powers of mere mortals, is often harmful to those who take them as their models? Why do you say that their contemplation gives rise to *a sense of respect and admiration that fetters the soul and the talent? That any imitator, whosoever he may be, is inferior to his model?* Therefore the Romans, in your opinion, were obliged to imitate, for fear of falling into a manner *that speedily became ridiculous and barbaric;* but they were obliged not to imitate, for fear of finding something that would fetter *the soul and the talent,* and lest they succumb to the desire to *surpass their models,* which always manifests itself, as you say, *at the expense of good taste?* Then you say that the Romans fell into this barbaric and ridiculous manner because they refused to follow the rules *that ordained a beautiful and noble simplicity,* because they were *ashamed to follow in the footsteps of others?* Because they were carried away by the love *of the new.* But how exactly were they to avoid all this, since you subsequently say that those *who have shown the greatest genius are not those whom chance has most plentifully provided with such aid?* Or that *Correggio, Raphael, and Michelangelo rose to such heights simply because nature alone was at work within them?* Now I understand. You are one of those Frenchmen *who,* as Signor [Francesco] Algarotti notes, *now regard the journey to Italy as utterly useless for young artists.*† I will not insist on trying to convince you that Correggio, Raphael, and Michelangelo were the imitators of a great number of dead artists (and living ones too); for these controversies, I refer you to what Signor Algarotti† has to say on the subject. For the rest, may I repeat that if you intend to write a review of the books of others, it is first necessary to read them; it is necessary to do as I have done with your letter. If you want to know the reason why not the Romans, as you say, but the Greeks, and the Greeks not in Rome but in Greece, began to decline from *beautiful and noble simplicity* to a manner that *speedily became ridiculous and barbaric,* lend an ear to a conversation that recently took place between a friend of Piranesi's and a certain Protopiro—who had, for his part, read Piranesi's book—on the subject of those drawings that Piranesi is now producing in a *ridiculous and barbaric manner.*

Opinions on Architecture: A Dialogue

Protopiro. So, Didascalo! You have plenty of experience in architecture; and yet, having learned to know good from bad, instead of making good use of your knowledge, you too are asking to be thought of as one of those who the more expert they think themselves, the less they really know?

Didascalo. Why, Protopiro?

Protopiro. Why, just look at these drawings that you try to defend! You remind me of Montesquieu's axiom: *A building laden with ornament is an enigma to the eyes, as a confused poem is an enigma to the mind.*† I said as much to Piranesi himself, when he showed the drawings to me as an example of something good that he has produced.

Didascalo. Good heavens! You don't mince your words.

Protopiro. Well, I love truth.

Didascalo. So do I; and because I love it more than you do, because I know it better than you do, I will tell you that Montesquieu knew more about poetry than he did about architecture. He understood that a poet has many ways of making his name without having to confuse his readers; but he did not know how little can be done with architecture (in terms of ornament) as soon as architects are forbidden to dress it up with anything not pertaining to architecture itself. Besides, a confused poem achieves nothing but mental confusion, whereas a building laden with ornament is a thing that has been popular for centuries and is now more so than ever. Believe me, buildings are made to please the public, not the critics. How can Montesquieu compare a work that is confused so that everyone rejects it, with a work rich in ornament that over the years has given and still gives delight to the greater part of humanity? My dear friend, be more circumspect in adopting some of these new proverbs; weigh them carefully, and you will find that nothing is good about them but the shell. Follow this old one: *L'uso fa legge*† [(Use makes law)].

Protopiro. Use may make law, but abuse does not. Tell me what right-minded architect or admirer of architecture has ever failed to condemn those irrelevant attributes that you could define no better than as *anything not pertaining to architecture itself?*

Didascalo. You force me to say something I did not want to say. You do not know what you're saying; and I will show you why. Tell me, on what grounds do you use the word "abuse" to describe the current practice of architecture?

Protopiro. Ask your friend Piranesi. He is the author of all those invectives, which can be read in his book *Della magnificenza ed architettura de' romani*, against the craze for constructing and decorating buildings with such things as are not supplied by truth, that is to say, by the nature of architecture.

Didascalo. Answer my question, and you will see that Piranesi is not so inconsistent as you make him out to be. On what grounds, I repeat, do you use the word "abuse" to describe the current practice of architecture?

Protopiro. You are trying to make me say what you already know as well as I do. Proving that current practice does not pertain to architecture at all, that it constitutes abuse, would require us to discuss the nature of architecture—and that would go on forever. Has not Piranesi already told us more than enough in his book? However, rather than have you claim that you reduced me to silence, I will answer Piranesi with some of the conclusions that he himself has drawn from his lengthy examination of the origins of architecture.

Didascalo. Please go on.

Protopiro. I may not remember it all; but I shall not be too far from the mark. In the first place, since the walls of a building are erected, if for nothing else, to give shelter at the sides and to support the roof, I would like to know, Why do they carry so much decoration—tympana, rustications (as they are called), modillions, cornices, and all the other appendages? What is the point of the festoons, fillets, masks, paterae, heads of stags and oxen, and all the other clutter to be found around doors, windows, arches, and other openings in the walls? And the festoons, the labyrinth frets, the arabesques, the hippogriffs, the sphinxes—why not send them all back to the realms of poetry? Why not send the dolphins back to the sea and the lions and other wild beasts to Libya? The oval, triangular, and octagonal columns—why not make them round again? Why not straighten out those that are twisted or distorted or bent? The former certainly fail to reproduce the roundness of the tree trunks that were their origin, and the latter reveal a structural weakness of the buildings. Let the triglyphs show that they derive from a well-set beam, and the modillions from a regular arrangement of joists in the roof of a building. Let the dentils be put in their place...

Didascalo. All these should be removed from the pediments of buildings, where they bear no relation to joists or rafters. On a facade, none of these things has any business on the cornice beneath the pediment, and they should be omitted.

Protopiro. Yes, sir. Let the broken pediments be put together again, and let us cease to pretend that a roof can be split along its length...

Didascalo. Making it rain indoors.

Protopiro. Take down all the *episkēnia*†...

Didascalo. So they do not crush the roof, and no one will say that one house has been built on top of another. And volutes and foliage must be ordered to stay on the capitals, where they belong.

Protopiro. That's right. Architects must recover from the obsession that has led them into all this and many other extravagances; then everything will go as it ought to go.

Didascalo. Do you have anything else to say?

Protopiro. I could go on for a hundred years. But if only the things I have mentioned were done, that would be a start: architecture would begin to revive.

Didascalo. What do you mean?

Protopiro. To revert to what it was in the days of its greatest glory.

Didascalo. By which you mean that the Greeks raised it to perfection—isn't that true? And that anyone who fails to do as you say demonstrates his ignorance? And so Piranesi, who has not done so, but who, in these designs of his, has taken the crazy liberty of following his own caprice...

Protopiro. Without good reason...

Didascalo. Yes, without good reason, like most present-day architects—is he too showing his ignorance?

Protopiro. Certainly!

Didascalo. With these maxims in mind, my dear Protopiro, you would have us all grazing herds!

Protopiro. I don't follow you.

Didascalo. You would have us live in huts such as those some say the Greeks took as the source for their architectural ornament.[4]

Protopiro. Didascalo, let us not descend into sophistry.

Didascalo. You are the sophist, you who impose on architecture rules that it has never possessed. What will you say, if I prove to you that austerity, reason, and imitation of huts are all incompatible with architecture? That architecture, far from requiring decorative features derived from the parts necessary for constructing and holding up a building, consists of ornaments that are all extraneous?

Protopiro. That is quite a tall order!

Didascalo. But, before we come to my proofs, tell me this: Where would you expect to find austerity, reason, and imitation? I imagine that it would be in the styles bequeathed to us by Vitruvius and implemented by [Andrea] Palladio, and by those other architects who were the first to revive this kind of architecture. Or perhaps in the styles lately imported from Greece and presented to us with more pomp than they initially seemed to warrant.

Protopiro. From both those sources, but without those errors and liberties that even the architects who revived them saw fit to add.

Didascalo. Make whatever stipulations you like. The more stipulations there are, the more you will shorten my way to a conclusive proof; the fewer there are, the more concessions you make to those architects who work without consenting to be held back by any such rules.

---

[4] See the work [by Julien-David Le Roy] entitled *Les ruines des plus beaux monuments de la Grèce* [(Paris, 1758), esp. 1:ix–xiv].

Protopiro. I have given you my opinion.

Didascalo. So it is Greece and Vitruvius? Very well: tell me, then, what do columns represent? Vitruvius says they are the forked uprights of huts;† others describe them as tree trunks placed to support the roof. And the flutes on the columns: what do they signify? Vitruvius thinks they are the pleats in a matron's gown.† So the columns stand neither for forked uprights nor for tree trunks but for women placed to support a roof. Now what do you think about flutes? It seems to me that columns ought to be smooth. Therefore, take note: *smooth columns.* The forked uprights and tree trunks should be planted in the earth, to keep them stable and straight. Indeed that is how the Dorians thought of their columns. Therefore they should have no bases. Take note: *no bases.* The tree trunks, if they were used to support the roof, would be smooth and flat on top; the forked props can look like anything you like, except capitals. If that is not definite enough, remember that the capitals must represent solid things, not heads of men, maidens, or matrons, or baskets with foliage around them, or baskets topped with a matron's wig. So take note: *no capitals.* Never fear; there are other rigorists who also call for *smooth columns, no bases, and no capitals.*

As for architraves, you want them to look either like tree trunks placed horizontally across the forked props or like beams laid out to span the tree trunks. So what is the point of the fasciae or of the band that projects from the surface? To catch the water and go rotten? Take note: *architraves with no fasciae and no band.*

What do the triglyphs stand for? Vitruvius says that they represent the ends of the joists of ceilings or soffits.† When they are placed at the corners of the building, however, not only do they belie this description but they can never be placed at regular intervals, because they have to be centered over the columns. If they are moved away from the corners, they can then be placed symmetrically only if the building is narrowed or widened with respect to the triglyphs. It is madness that a few small cuts on stone or mortar should dictate the proportions of a building, or that all or some of the due requirements of the building should be sacrificed to them. Thus, the ancient architects cited by Vitruvius[5] held that temples ought not to be built in the Doric manner;† better still, the Romans used the Doric without the added clutter. So take note: *friezes without triglyphs.* Now it is your turn, Signor Protopiro, to purge architecture of all the other ornaments that you disparaged just now.

Protopiro. What? Have you finished?

Didascalo. Finished? I have not even started. Let us go inside a temple, a palace, wherever you choose. Around the walls we shall observe architraves, friezes, and cornices adorned with those features that you just described as standing for the roof of a building—triglyphs, modillions, and dentils. And when those features are absent, and the friezes and cornices are smooth, even

[5] [*De architectura,*] bk. 4, chap. 3.

then the architraves and friezes will seem to support a roof and the cornices seem to be the eaves. These eaves, however, will drip rain inside the temple, the palace, or basilica. So the temple, the palace, or the basilica will be outside, and the outside inside, will they not? To rectify such anomalies, such travesties of architecture, take note: *internal walls of buildings with no architraves, friezes, and cornices.*

And then, on these cornices, which stand for eaves, vaults are erected. This is an even worse impropriety than those *episkēnia* on the roofs that we discussed a little while ago and that Vitruvius condemns.†

Therefore take note: *buildings with no vaults.*

Let us observe the walls of a building from inside and outside. These walls terminate in architraves and all that goes with them above; below these architraves, most often we find engaged columns or pilasters. I ask you, what holds up the roof of the building? If the wall, then it needs no architraves; if the columns or pilasters, what is the wall there for? Choose, Signor Protopiro, Which will you demolish? The walls or the pilasters? No answer? Then I will demolish the whole lot. Take note: *buildings with no walls, no columns, no pilasters, no friezes, no cornices, no vaults, no roofs.* A clean sweep.

You will say that I am imagining buildings in my own fashion. But just imagine one in your fashion. Show me designs by any of the rigorists, anyone who thinks he has conceived a wonderful design for a building; and I warrant he will look more foolish than the man who works to please himself—yes, more foolish—because the only way he could imagine a building without irregularities is when four upright poles with a roof—the very prototype of architecture—can remain entire and unified at the very moment of being halved, varied, and rearranged in a thousand ways; in short, when the simple becomes composite, and one becomes as many as you like.

Now, to return to what I was saying, isn't it true that you and your friends are making architecture subject to laws that have never really existed? Didn't I tell you that if you were to build according to the principles you have got into your heads—that is, to make everything in conformity with reason and truth—you would have us all go back to living in huts? The Scythians, the Goths, and other barbarous peoples, who all lived in those rational buildings of yours, made war upon those who lived in buildings that were designed more freely—or, as you would say, capriciously—in order to get themselves into those buildings. You can rest assured that no nation will ever go to war in order to occupy rational buildings.

This is the place to answer the objection you recently raised against Piranesi, that in his book *Della magnificenza ed architettura de' romani,* he denounced those whose work is marked by caprice. A rigorist had reproached the Romans for having corrupted Greek architecture; and Piranesi was obliged to show him that, on the contrary, the Romans, having adopted an architecture that was found to be infected to the core, and finding themselves consequently unable to cure its ills, attempted instead to mitigate them. Now, compare the spirit of that book with what I have just told you, and then judge whether Piranesi has changed his opinion. But what is this? Signor Protopiro, are you lost for words?

Protopiro. I am letting you have your say.

Didascalo. I can see that to you my criticisms seem unduly harsh. But, though I may have laid waste the rigorists' buildings with fire and sword, I did so with the same logic that they would use to lay waste the finest cities in the universe.

Protopiro. Have you finished? May I speak?

Didascalo. By all means.

Protopiro. Est modus in rebus [(There is moderation in all things)], says Horace;† all extremes are dangerous, as the saying goes. If you can bear this in mind in your arguments, then we will continue for a while. If not, goodbye.

Didascalo. You would like me to agree with you that the architectural manners laid down by Vitruvius are rational? That they imitate truth?

Protopiro. Rational—highly rational—by comparison with the unbridled license that prevails in construction today.

Didascalo. Aha! Rational by comparison with current practice? And so, if we leave current practice out of it, your rationality disappears at once. The critics, who never let up, will still want the last word; deprive them of the wide scope for indignation that present-day practice affords them, and they will soon turn against the little that you and your friends are prepared to accept. Then, go ahead and say that extremes are dangerous, that too much rigor is really abuse; all the same, the manners in which you build will be judged just as they were or might have been judged when first invented. You call me excessively severe, on the grounds that I am going too far by taking you back to huts in which people have no desire to live; but you would yourselves be condemned for monotonous buildings that people would detest just as much.

Protopiro. Monotonous?

Didascalo. Yes, monotonous, architecturally always exactly the same. As architects, you think yourselves extraordinary, but you would soon become utterly ordinary. When your simple manners of building were first established, why did the successors of those who established them soon begin to find different ways of decorating their buildings? Was it for want of the capacity to equal their predecessors? Surely not, since they had been trained as their pupils; and, all around them, they could see an architecture that was simple enough to be easy to reproduce.

Protopiro. I am not saying that we should do nothing but follow those early manners of building. I don't blame the successors of those first architects for wanting to innovate. But I do blame them for the quality of their innovations, and I blame all those architects who have vied with each other ever since in devising more and more of them.

Didascalo. I suppose you mean architects like [Gian Lorenzo] Bernini and [Francesco] Borromini, and all those others who have failed to bear in mind that ornament must derive from the components of architecture. But, in criticizing them, whom do you think you criticize? You criticize the greatest architect† who ever was or ever will be. You criticize the experience of all those many practitioners who from the moment when this kind of architecture was first invented until it was buried beneath the ruins always worked in this way; and the experience of those many who ever since this kind of architecture was first revived have been and are unable to work in any other way. You criticize the very spirit that invented the architecture that you praise; the spirit that, seeing the world still unsatisfied, has found itself obliged to seek variety by the very same ways and means that you dislike. Now if, over the centuries, among all those countless practitioners, the experience of the totality of architecture to date has failed to produce what you are looking for, then how can we avoid concluding that, if everything you dislike were removed from architecture, we would be left with buildings of unendurable monotony? What word other than foolish can we apply to those who flatter themselves that they are destined to find in this art something that has never been found in all these centuries? All the more foolish, in that they cannot even salve their own self-esteem by finding what they are looking for.

Protopiro. Prove to me that they set out deliberately to look for it.

Didascalo. Look for it yourself; give me an example of it. It is folly to try to teach without knowing what to teach. You say that what you would like to see has never yet been deliberately sought; yet there have been continual experiments and competitions. At one time, royal prizes were offered.[6] But what were the achievements of those enticed by such prizes? The undertaking was abandoned and the prize went unclaimed, because the task was impossible. And what was achieved by those who, not believing those pessimists, recently set out to scour Asia, Egypt, and Greece? To call people together to show them—what, exactly? Was it what they had been looking for? They say so, to those who walk in to see it; and when a person has seen it? They add, Please don't let us down by discouraging those who are still waiting outside. Someone goes off to inspect the antiquities and brings back the dimensions of a column, a frieze, or a cornice with the intention of enriching architecture with proportions different from those to which we have become accustomed to seeing, hoping that this will give as much pleasure as a new order or a new architectural manner that he cannot discover. But he has failed to understand, being a novice in this kind of work—or else, being an old hand, he has not yet wanted to understand—not only that no one ancient building has exactly the same proportions as another but also that there is not a single column, intercolumniation, arch, or whatever that has the same dimensions as another arch, intercolumniation, or column in the same structure. He refuses to see that an order, whatever it may be, whether Tuscan or Doric or Ionic or Corinthian or Composite, for all the diversity of dimensions and ornaments, is in appearance no different from another order. He refuses to see that we cultivate only

[6] See the aforementioned work [by Julien-David Le Roy,] *Les ruines des plus beaux monuments de la Grèce* [(Paris, 1758), 2:18].

one order or rather only one manner of architecture. Thinking of which, I cannot but laugh at the erroneous way in which the *Gazette littéraire* of France recently took issue with a design prepared in London by Signor [James] Adam, who as you know is one of the most judicious architects of our time. Wait, I have the *Gazette littéraire* in my pocket... Listen to this: *Monsieur Adam distinguishes himself as much by the grandeur of his ideas as by the manner in which he renders them. A short while ago, this artist exhibited a design that won the approval of all the connoisseurs. The design was for a magnificent building that would be suitable not only for the meetings of the London Parliament but also for those of the academies of sciences and letters. If executed, this vast undertaking would suit the magnificence of a great nation; it is particularly remarkable for the dignity and sobriety that prevail in all its parts. It is an imitation of the finest manner of the ancient Egyptians, Greeks, and Latins. The intelligence and orderliness with which Monsieur Adam has assigned scenes from the history of England wrought in bas-relief to the various parts of the building is beyond praise.*

Protopiro. So, what have you to say to all that?

Didascalo. Nothing. But, after all this well-deserved praise of the architect, listen to the thoughts of the critic and of those whom he admonishes. *However,* he continues, *it should not be imagined that this design presents a new order of architecture, as those who have termed it the "British order" have fancied. One does not create a new order just by putting new ornaments on the capitals and on the other parts of a building. If one were to consider examples of the Corinthian order, one would find so many different manners of ornamental detail that one could define as many orders as there are monuments; but if one examines the main proportions, one will find them to be almost all uniform.* Now, what do you make of that? The critic lavishes praise on Signor Adam, but at the same time he wants us to understand that to be truly excellent the design would have had to introduce a new order.

Protopiro. No, forgive me, but you accuse the critic of making the same mistake as those whom he takes to task for wanting to give the name "British order" to the design.

Didascalo. Do I attribute to the critic the faults that he finds in others? I would indeed be maligning him, as you say, except that he subscribes to their crazy belief in the possibility of creating a new Order, and consequently an infinite succession of new Orders. Does he not say that *if one examines the main proportions* of the so-called British order, *one will find them to be almost all uniform?* Is this not the same as saying that a new order requires proportions different from all the other orders—the Doric, the Ionic, and the Corinthian? Now, of course it is perfectly possible to devise such proportions; therefore, a new order can be invented. This is the reasoning of the critic. Do you believe it? Just consider the bizarre notions that he puts forward. He says that *one does not create a new order just by putting new ornaments on the capitals and on the other parts of the building.* And that *if one were to consider the orders composed in the Corinthian order, one would find so many different manners of ornamental detail that one could define as many orders as there are monuments.* My question to the critic (and this, as I said, is what makes me laugh) is whether he believes the Doric, the Ionic, and the Corinthian are all orders? Does he believe they are three different manners of architecture? He will say, Yes. Now, I am going to imagine that I am living in the times when first the Doric order, then the Ionic, and the Corinthian were invented; and, using the critic's words, I say to the men who invented them: *One does not create a new order, gentlemen, just by putting new ornaments on the capitals and on the other parts of the building.* My dear sirs, here we still have columns, architraves, friezes, and cornices, just as they are in the Doric: *If one were to consider the Doric order in all the temples, one would find so many different manners of ornamental detail that one could define as many orders as there are monuments.* What would the inventors of the Ionic and Corinthian orders reply? They, too, would say, borrowing our critic's words, *If one examines the main proportions of our orders, one will find them significantly different from those of the Doric,* and thus they would believe that they had silenced me. But I would once more borrow the critic's words, and against both them and the critic I would add: *If one were to consider the Doric order in all the temples of Greece, Asia, Italy, and so on, one would find so much variety in its main proportions that one could define as many orders as there are temples. Of this the examples furnished by Messieurs [Julien-David] Le Roy and [James] Stuart in their published surveys are proof enough.*† And so, to return to what I was saying, my dear Protopiro, we practice only one manner of architecture, though we are loath to admit that a diversity of ornamentation does not in itself constitute a diversity of orders. To be more precise, we cultivate three manners—or, if you prefer, orders—in architecture: one composed of columns, one composed of pilasters, and one composed of a continuous wall. To imagine that different proportions could produce a new species of architecture is, I repeat, sheer madness: the new proportions would be lost in the overall effect, since variations in the dimensions of buildings, whether ancient or modern, are indistinguishable. In any case, why look for different proportions? It is enough that the frieze does not collapse under the weight of the cornice, the architrave under the weight of the cornice and frieze, and the column under the weight of the cornice, frieze, and architrave: those are the proportions of architecture, and they have all been discovered. The variations in these proportions—whether they are slightly greater or slightly smaller, according to what is required for the stability of the building—are generally small or of little importance. They cannot represent visual differences but invariably result from the need to support the building. My dear Protopiro, since there is no possible way of creating new orders, and since altering the proportions makes little or no difference to the look of the building, how are we to reject current practice in architecture without running the risk of monotony? Let us imagine the impossible: let us imagine that the world—sickened though it is by everything that does not change from day to day—were gracefully to accept your monotony; what would architecture then become? *A low trade, in which one would do nothing but copy,* as a certain gentleman has said.† So that not only would you and your colleagues become extremely ordinary architects, as I said before, but further you would be something less than masons. By constant repetition, they learn to work by rote; and they have the advantage over you, because they have the mechanical skill. You would ultimately cease to be architects at all, because clients would be fools to use an architect to carry out work that could be done far more cheaply by a mason.

Protopiro. Yes, if architecture consisted in nothing but beauty and majesty.

Didascalo. Don't talk to me about the rest. You know as well as I do that masons are quite as good as architects when it comes to foundations, materials, the thickness and diminution of walls, and the springing of arches—in short, anything relating to the stability of a building. We would consider the works to be far more simple, and in keeping with tradition.

Protopiro. Would these master builders have any knowledge of siting and of the proper ways to locate one thing and another? Would they know about the economics of a building or the uses to which it is put? . . .

Didascalo. As for that, look at what is now being done, and what always has been done. One normally calls in an architect in order to build something beautiful; this can be said to be the definition of architecture nowadays. But, wherever such considerations do not apply, clients act as their own architects, and all they want is someone to put the walls up for them. Everything else in architecture, ornament aside, is so little regarded and so little likely to bring fame to the architects, that very few of them put much reliance on it.

Protopiro. But do you regard those people as architects? Are you in favor of the clients who build in this way?

Didascalo. As to that, I will tell you only that people have managed very well in countless buildings constructed under the supervision of clients, masons, or architects of this kind, and anyone who sees people living in those buildings, far from pitying them for living in squalor, is likely to reproach them for living in pampered luxury. But to return to our topic: take away every man's freedom to decorate as he sees fit, and you will very soon see the architectural sanctum open to all and sundry. When everyone knows how to practice architecture, everyone will despise it. As time goes by, buildings will grow worse, and the architectural manners that you gentlemen consider so rational will be destroyed by the very means whereby you seek to preserve them. You will lose the will to compete with and to stand out from all the other architects—since there will be no architects. That, for you, will be the greatest misfortune of all. And so, to set matters straight, I ask only this: by all means treasure the rationality that you proclaim, but at the same time respect the freedom of architectural creation that sustains it.

Please do not imagine that in defending this freedom I am suggesting that all buildings, no matter how adorned and no matter how planned, are to be considered beautiful and good. My view on ornament is this. Why does it sometimes happen that something that we have pictured mentally as beautiful fails to please us when it is built? Why has no one ever thought to blame poets for the imaginary buildings that they enrich with ornaments far more irrational and eccentric than those employed by architects? Montesquieu denounces a building laden with ornament; but he does not say that a poem that describes such a building is confused. Let us find out why this is. Is it perhaps because the imagination does not cause us to see as much as the eye reveals to us? This is what I think: the poet leads us from one ornament to another and leaves us there, without proving or making perceptible to us how they fit together. For example, in the poet's work, such and such ornaments please us—just as, in various statues by a good sculptor, we praise the feet of a Cupid, the legs of an Adonis, the face of a Venus, the arms of an Apollo, the chest of a Hercules, the nose of a giant, and so on. But collect the parts in question from all those diverse and differently sized statues, put them together; what is the result? A ridiculous statue, a repellent monstrosity. This is the kind of defect that I deplore in architecture. There are parts that are admirable in themselves but look unbearable when they are jumbled together; the effect of the whole is undermined by the part, of the serious by the trivial, of the majestic by the mean and petty. Now, so that all these parts that seem so admirable to us in isolation may seem equally admirable when put together, and so that incompatibility may not spoil our enjoyment, let us confer gravity and majesty on all that appears petty in them. Take statues, for example, since we have been speaking of them: inside a temple, when made in a variety of poses, they look like individuals who profane the temple's sanctity by unseemly behavior; but when they are beautifully upright and restrained in their gestures, they are among the temple's finest ornaments. That will never do, I hear you say; the niches in the temple looked better without the statues than with them. But how are we to take pleasure in a niche without a statue, when the niche itself was devised not with any idea of its being beautiful in itself but expressly to contain a statue? The eye, I hear you reply, is unable to enjoy more than one thing at a time; it enjoys the niche when there is nothing else to be seen, and the statue when it sees nothing but the statue. Hence Montesquieu's remark that a building laden with ornament is an enigma to the eyes, as a confused poem is to the mind.

The rigorists thus reason as Montesquieu reasons. But why should any reason prevail if, when weighed in the balance, it carries no more weight than another? Here is the other: the niches in the temple, the rigorists maintain, look better without the statues than with them because the eye cannot enjoy more than one thing at a time. But, I would ask, why should the niches not look well if the statues are the very ones for which they were made? The doors or windows of a house designed to a normal human scale would not match the scale of a race of giants. So what clashes with the architecture is not the statue itself but the large size of the statue or the small size of the niche; the temple becomes impossible to praise not because it is encumbered with statues but because of the scale of the statues and their lack of proportion with their niches, bases, and so on. Tell me, which of the two arguments carries more weight? Mine or that of the rigorists? You will say that both are true, and I agree; but might there ever be a way to reconcile them? To train the eye to look at a building laden with ornament and not find it an enigma? In Rome there are two columns with narrative sculptural reliefs on them, both designed in the same way: that of Trajan and that of Marcus Aurelius. If you had seen only that of Marcus Aurelius, I have no doubt that you would have adduced it as evidence of the truth of Montesquieu's axiom, for the column is encumbered from top to bottom with a rash of bas-reliefs. You would have told me such kind of work was calculated to mar the column rather than to adorn it. But I wonder, would you have said the same after seeing Trajan's column, which is also crammed with bas-reliefs from top to bottom and all over the pedestal as well? Did those carvings offend your eyes? Their low relief has reconciled my argument with yours. The architecture of the column is consistent in the definition of its parts and is in no way spoiled by the presence and the protuberance of its ornaments.

What if someone intends to adorn a building with ornaments bearing a high relief? Let him single out the main subject from the accompaniment; spectators should not be faced with a multitude of objects, all or most of them competing to be the main attraction. The decorations should be graded as things are in nature, some being more imposing and dignified than others. In such art, as in nature, the eyes will see not confusion but a beautiful and pleasing arrangement of things. And, in truth, if the ornaments used in architecture are beautiful in themselves, then the architecture will also be beautiful. Why choose to give the eyes a single pleasure, such as that of looking at a piece of architecture, when we can give them the twofold pleasure of seeing it clothed in ornament, since we can see our way to reconciling the two?

So much for some of the ways to secure a reconciliation of the parts with the whole: this, I believe, must be achieved and maintained not only in these attributes of architecture but also in all ornaments that one might someday see fit to combine with it. In the drawings that prompted this discussion of ours, Piranesi has found a way to convey information to us through a work of art, realizing that to do so in words would be difficult. This is because, if architects are to have a free hand in their work, it would take an eternity to discuss the constraints that will nevertheless apply to them, freedom or no freedom. Now, as to whether in his own work Piranesi has conformed to his own and my way of thinking, he himself will judge or the public will judge. Goodbye, my dear Protopiro. Stand by your own opinion—it would be whimsical to concede defeat to a madman like me.

Now, what do you make of all this chatter, Signor Mariette? How much did it take to make Didascalo admit to being what he is? As you will have seen by now, the arguments that he deploys to demonstrate that architecture, which once possessed a beautiful and noble simplicity, has now developed into something ridiculous and barbaric, were valid even in ancient times. If you do not like them, find some of your own. Demonstrate that without straying from *beautiful and noble simplicity* or without adopting a *ridiculous and barbaric* manner, and yet not wanting to reduce architecture to *a low trade, in which one would do nothing but copy,* there is nevertheless all possible scope for variation and for multiplying inventions. Even—what shall I say?—even without descending to a *ridiculous and barbaric* manner. By all means, show that this manner is so; but how can you describe as barbaric the work of the Greeks and the Romans, and indeed of all Europe today? How can you describe as ridiculous something that was admired, is admired, and, as Didascalo has just told you, always will be admired by all the Protopiri there are and ever will be?

As for the difference of opinion between yourself and Piranesi, the matter is by no means closed. Listen to what he is preparing for you to review, in addition to the drawings mentioned in the debate: a treatise, of greater length than *Della magnificenza ed architettura de' romani,* which will include a great number of Etruscan monuments and monuments from other ancient nations. See its title and preface in the pages that follow.

On the Introduction and Progress of the Fine Arts in Europe in Ancient Times

Preface

There is a mistaken but comparatively widespread belief that the Greeks were the inventors not only of the fine arts (the subject of this treatise) but also of eating, drinking, and clothing (which are attributed to their Ceres, their Bacchus, and their Minerva). The error is of no great consequence and, though foolish, has hitherto readily been tolerated. But now that it begins to become pernicious and make those who wish to distinguish themselves in the fine arts stray from—I would not say unappreciative of—the path to perfection in the fine arts, anyone who flatters himself that he has the ability to divert them from error must surely wish to make some public trial of his skill.

All Europe is aware of the great advances made in the fine arts by so many talented men, with the consequence that those arts have begun to revive; anyone who knows that human ingenuity has its boundaries set by nature must be aware that these advances could not have been greater. Since ancient times, the school of these arts has always been Italy; not, as some thoughtlessly suppose, because the Italians possess more aptitude than any other nation but because Italy, more than any other country, still possesses examples of those monuments that must be studied by any person who wishes to become a good painter, a good sculptor, or a good architect.

Nevertheless there are some, newcomers to the arts, who—although compatriots of those whose many beautiful works have shown and still show that foreigners can be as successful as Italians in the arts provided that they learn the lessons taught by the variety and great beauty of Italian monuments—have in their writings urged those who seek artistic distinction to go and study the fine arts in Greece. And why? Because Italy learned the arts from the Greeks, and because in Italy few of the many ancient monuments that once adorned the country are now extant. But who built those monuments? People who wanted to imitate the Greeks and yet could do no more than ape them. Poor exponents of the fine arts, with all their magnificent works, with all their glory, with all the great reputations they made for themselves, all derived from the study of those monuments!

Greece it must be, therefore; but, these teachers of ours, as they admonish us to make that journey, what guarantee do they give that, nearly two thousand years after the arts flourished in Greece, and after the country's finest possessions were plundered, we are likely to discover things there that are better than we find in Italy? A number of their recently published volumes contain a few drawings of architecture and sculpture, but these are so disfigured and deformed that if these were held up as models of all that is beautiful and good, they would give no encouragement to anyone required to prove his skill with a design for a public building. Such is their evidence! One of them, their self-appointed leader,† despite his great partiality for such fragments, dares not point to his own appreciation of them when called to testify on their behalf: instead of advising that they be studied through the drawings in his book, he refers the reader to those fragments from antiquity that still remain unrecorded in Greece—as if all that he has collected were merely a sample by comparison with what remains unrecorded. He knows full well that students have long since made their way in a steady stream to Greece, Asia Minor, Syria, and all those other lands where the Greeks sowed the seeds of their art; and every one of them has returned with the same things. All have brought back the same drawings of disfigured and deformed architecture and sculpture. In other words, his injunction to go to Greece, despite all the surveys made there by so many, is not motivated by a desire to see the fine arts flourish and prosper; it is a solemn mockery of anyone who might wish to distinguish himself in them.

Shall I nonetheless take up the pursuit of those miserable relics of ancient Greece? Oh, I have said quite enough on that topic in my recently published book *Della magnificenza ed architettura de' romani.* My present purpose is to discover what reason the world has, or has ever had, for believing that in the fine arts Italy is indebted to Greece rather than Greece to Italy. As far as I can see, some have heeded the advice to travel to Greece not because they hope to return with large fragments of ancient works far better than all that remains and is daily rediscovered in Italy but because almost everyone believes it to be an incontrovertible truth that the Greeks invented everything.

In my book I illustrated, for all to see, those magnificent works that were created by the Romans before they knew anything of the Greeks and in accordance with the precepts of the Etruscans. And yet listen to what has been said about them: *The Doric order, passing from Greece into Asia Minor, was there perfected and indeed produced a new order. Another, very different transformation also took place in those far-off times: when the order was transported by colonists to Magna Graecia and Tuscany, the latter nations impoverished it, whereas the Ionians had enriched it. They had not sufficient genius to make it into a new order.*

Here an attempt has been made to persuade the public that the Italians not only have never been good at imitation but also never invented anything; and that, if the Romans learned from the Etruscans before ever hearing of the Greeks, the Etruscans themselves had learned what little they knew from the Greeks. The writer is in error in assigning the transfer of the Doric order from Greece to Italy to such a late date (that of the colonies in Magna Graecia); he thereby assigns to the same late date all the arts practiced in Italy before the Romans knew of the Greeks. This has had the effect of making the public believe that among the earliest inhabitants of Italy were the Aborigines, the Pelasgians, the Arcadians, the Peloponnesians, and others—all from Greece. It remains for me to deal with this argument.

But what a labyrinth I must enter to expose such chicanery! I shall have to consider who the Etruscans were, when they arrived in Italy, and from where; and whether the Pelasgians, who have received more credit than anyone for introducing the arts into Italy, were a party of Etruscans who at some stage had gone to acquaint themselves with the Greeks or a party of Greeks who had settled in Italy; and, finally, whether at a time when Italy not only was inhabited but also possessed many great and splendid cities filled with men learned in those same arts and sciences that were later to adorn Greece, the Greeks themselves had any notion of what the fine arts were or had never yet guessed that it was better to live and comport themselves like the Italians than to lurk in caves like wild beasts.

I shall be obliged to consider whether not only the fine arts but also languages, literature, philosophy, religion, and politics—all those things, then current in Italy, on which a nation relies to differentiate itself from every other nation—were taught by the peoples of Asia to the Greeks and by the Greeks to the Italians, or by the Italians to the Greeks. The fine arts bring all these other issues along with them, but issues such as the fine arts demand to be discussed in turn, separately and thoroughly. No one has ever yet ventured into this tangled thicket: the reason being sheer mental indolence. I, for my part, now intend to make the attempt. "With what hope of success?" I hear you say. This is my answer.

The pagans, Eusebius† tells us,[7] at one time complained that those responsible for the eradication of idolatry showed scant respect for the local customs, laws, and ceremonies by which all nations and peoples were governed, and that they had deserted the gods who were the saviors and protectors of the world (and what gods they were, honored and worshiped with sacrifices, festivals, games, and ceremonies in every town, every city, every stretch of countryside, by all kings, tyrants, philosophers, and legislators, and by all nations, whether Greek or barbarian, and, in short, by the whole world!) in favor of certain Jewish fairy tales that defied both reason and all humankind. In which case, why blame me for declining to believe what all historians, scholars, and sages have to say concerning the origins of the fine arts, what all Europe believes and has believed since time immemorial? What arguments did the pagans use to dispute the truths unveiled by those great men? The same arguments as are used in support of the belief that the Greeks were the inventors of the fine arts: the arguments that are enshrined in the books of the Greeks, which are distributed throughout the world as the source of all wisdom, divine and human. But such was the force of truth on the lips of those

---

[7] *De praeparat. Evng.* lib. 1. [Eusebius of Caesarea, *Evangelica praeparatio* = *De evangelica praeparatione*, bk. 1.]

great men that the Greeks' books lost their strong allure; it was seen that their teaching in matters of religion was no better than a farrago of nonsense, fairy tale, and falsehood. Subsequently, people continued to read those books because they imparted literary learning and it was believed that they could also impart secular knowledge. But, if they have been exposed as a mass of impostures in relation to divine knowledge, can they be any less so in relation to secular knowledge? These two forms of knowledge are so closely allied in those books that as soon as the foundations of the one were undermined in the course of these controversies, the foundations of the other could not hold. If, in order to argue the pagans out of their religion, it had been necessary to prove to them that none of the arts then practiced (and now lately practiced in Europe once more) were invented in Greece, I have no doubt that the truth of this would have been discovered along with all the other truths. But this was never discussed, and was this not also a distortion? For them, at the time, it was enough. The world needed the books and fairy tales in question so that literature might be more pleasurably learned; and for the books to be read, they needed to retain some credit, at least on matters of indifference. In the schools, therefore, with the exception of those parts that embodied a false religion, all the rest—even where at first glance it appeared entirely incredible—was accepted, and is accepted still, as the truth. And so people were taught, and are still taught, from earliest childhood that the Greeks were the inventors of our fine arts; when we grow to an age at which we might differentiate good from bad in these authors, and distinguish contradiction from consistency, or sophistry from sound reasoning, instead of using our adult discernment we are kept in a state of unreasoning belief by our affection for the authors, whose books delight us, and by our own mental indolence. Therefore, by employing the means handed down to us by those illuminators of the universe—namely, the true number and order of the centuries—and by basing the history of the fine arts and of allied matters on centuries, not on indefinite periods of time as used to be the custom, I intend to try, as I have said, to disabuse those in authority in the arts, as well as the students whom they have started to lead astray, of their other argument for believing that the Greeks were the inventors of everything, which consists in the statement that the present, miserable remains of ancient Greece are superior to the antiquities of Italy. It may be—indeed, it will be—that my own arguments, and not the belief against which they are directed, will be considered false. But I mean to make the attempt.

Of one thing I am sure: that they will be dismissed as false by the authors of the Parisian *Gazette littéraire,* since those gentlemen are of the same mind as Signor Mariette. To judge by their response to my books, they—I said this first of Signor Mariette, and now I shall apply it to them all—do not read the books of which they write reviews. Listen to what they say on the subject of the treatise on the emissarium of Lago Albano, which I published recently, between the antiquities of Albano and those of Castel Gandolfo:[8]

The celebrated Monsieur Piranesi has recently published two books in which his talent for drawing and his knowledge of architecture take on still greater luster from his extraordinary erudition. The first of these books.... The second is a description of the aqueduct at Castel Gandolfo that transports the waters of the lake from one side of the mountain to the other. (In the treatise, Piranesi says that to transport these waters *the mountain was tunneled through*. In order to translate this detail, has the French language no more appropriate words than *from one side of the mountain to the other?*) *And distributes them across the countryside around Albano. Like the first, this second essay is full of erudition and shows an impressive knowledge of antiquity; the most interesting aspect of the essay, however, is a minutely detailed description of all parts of this structure—a work truly representative of the grandeur of Roman architecture. The author has recourse to these monuments in his attempt to prove that the Romans borrowed nothing from the Greeks in matters of architecture and that they nevertheless equaled or even surpassed them. Whatever the truth of this matter, which the author has discussed at length in another work, it appears to us that the ancient aqueducts are proof of the grandeur of the ideas and enterprises of the Romans, rather than appropriate points of comparison between their nation and that of Greece in respect of good taste in architecture.*[†]

Anyone who knows anything of taste in architecture will smile at the idea that Piranesi might lack sufficient judgment to distinguish good taste from grandeur or from the practical usefulness of the art in question. First hear what Piranesi says in the aforementioned treatise, and then decide whether the criticism is valid:

True, some have maintained that these two structures were not built when the water first flowed out, but much later. "It is not likely," I have heard them say, "that such a solid and well-planned construction should have been built in those early days in which the Romans, not yet having learned the Greek arts, were unacquainted with regular architecture. Domitian had a villa on Monte Albano (many vestiges of which still remain) and went there every year for amusement, as [Cassius] *Dio*[†] *and Suetonius*[†] *report. But what if it were suggested that those two structures were built by the same emperor?" But why? Where are we ever told that before they became acquainted with Greek art, the Romans had no regular architecture? Does the fact that Domitian had a villa on Monte Albano, where he was responsible for the construction of some (or many) buildings, really prove that he was responsible for the two structures at the inlet and outlet of the emissarium? Neither is it necessary nor is this the place for me to comment here on the frivolity of such*

---

[8] *Gazette littéraire,* 1765. "Italie." ["Italie II," *Gazette littéraire de l'Europe,* vol. 1, no. 3 (21 March 1764): 40–41.]

suppositions, which I sufficiently rebutted in my treatise Della magnificenza ed architettura de' romani; *nevertheless, I would ask anyone who makes such a contention, what feature of these structures would the Romans have been unable to construct without the assistance of Greek art? The walls, perhaps, because they consist of enormous blocks of stone? The arches, the channel, and the vault at the outlet of the emissarium? If this is the case, then the walls of the seven hills of Rome, the sewers, the substructure of the Campidoglio, and many of the other buildings mentioned in my aforementioned treatise, which resemble these in every respect, must also have been constructed either toward the end of the republic or by the Caesars—at a time when most of the writers who attribute them to the kings and consuls of early Rome were already dead. Although these walls, arches, and vaults resemble the works of the kings and earliest consuls, they also resemble many other structures built at the time of the Caesars. What does this resemblance indicate, if not that very many structures for which the Greeks are blindly thanked were in fact built by the Caesars in pursuit of the example of their own forefathers? Therefore, in architecture, as in many other matters, the Romans were not so dependent on the Greeks as so many suppose.*

Meanwhile, let us compare the criticism made by the *Gazette littéraire* with the argument put forward by Piranesi. *It appears to us,* says the *Gazette, that the ancient aqueducts are proof of the grandeur of the ideas and enterprises of the Romans, rather than appropriate points of comparison between their nation and that of Greece in respect of good taste in architecture.* But, I ask the *Gazette,* where in his discourse does Piranesi compare the taste of the Romans in design with that of the Greeks? You say that the emissarium is proof *of the grandeur of the ideas and enterprises of the Romans;* and Piranesi says the same. But, you will reply, Piranesi has not finished what he has to say. Let us hear him out.

Thus, Piranesi continues, *there is every reason to believe that such a solid and well-planned structure as the one in question was built in early times. But there are inventions, it is said, that are impossible to associate with the ignorance of those times: for example, the architrave (or wide lintel) made up of wedge-shaped stones that spans the inlet of the reservoir, and the stone columns, architraves, and beams of stone erected in the reservoir to support the bridge surely could not be said to have been in use among the Tuscans, since tradition has it that the Romans learned from the Tuscans how to build only in wood. On the subject of Tuscan temples, Vitruvius says: "Above the columns they place beams fastened together with clamps and bars."† So is the problem simply that of a lintel made up of wedge-shaped stones, on the one hand, and stone architraves, on the other? At this point I should first like to ask whether we are talking about a pronaos with widely spaced columns, as described by Vitruvius,† with main beams that are not flanked by any continuation of the walls of the building or subject to any great load from above (if these were made of stones cut in the way previously described, they would soon be dislodged); or are we talking about a [subterranean] reservoir?*

Second, where does Vitruvius deny that on other occasions the Tuscans used stone or any other material suitable for building—whether for architraves, beams, or any other architectural component? Visit the reservoir at Volterra, built not only long before the introduction of Greek practices into Latium but possibly even before the Greeks themselves had learned them from other nations—as I demonstrated many times over in my discussion of Etruscan art in the volume mentioned above. Look at the drawing in the Museum *of the learned Gori.*† *There you will see stone architraves of the same proportions as those in the reservoir of our emissarium; but these also span a wide gap and are composed of several pieces cut in a wedge shape, just like the lintels of the inlet already mentioned. The columns and pilasters are the same, although theirs vary from ours in that the pilasters are beveled to offer less resistance to the passage of the water into the channel. Is there anything else in our emissarium that cannot be attributed to the early Romans?*

Perhaps the walls of the structure at the inlet, because these were constructed (for stability's sake) with regular projections of one stone over another, so that the courses project like steps, breaking the line, as can be observed in some Roman works built after the spread of the arts of Greece? The very same projecting stones and jutting courses of masonry were used by [Lucius] Tarquinius Superbus, when he built the great embankment on the Tiber for the outfall of the sewers. The same projecting stones and jutting masonry can be seen in the ruins of an extremely ancient Tuscan temple at Alba degli Equi, near Lago Fucino, which I have visited and discussed in the aforementioned volume.†

Now, I ask the *Gazette:* has Piranesi ever yet compared the taste of the Romans in architectural ornament with that of the Greeks? Let us therefore proceed.

It is a principle constantly verified by experience that, in terms of grandeur, solidity, and elegance of construction, the Romans of later times owe nothing to the Greeks, though the latter can rightly lay claim to metopes, triglyphs, leaves, and the horns of Jupiter Ammon, none of which, by the way, are to be found on the beam-ends or capitals of the two buildings of the emissarium.

Is this, perhaps, the passage in which Piranesi is said to compare the Romans' taste in building with that of the Greeks? To say that *the Romans owe nothing to the Greeks, though the latter can rightly lay claim to metopes,* and so on, is not in my view a comparison; if it were, however, where does he make the error, imputed to him, of comparing dissimilar things? Where exactly does he fail to distinguish *the grandeur of the ideas and enterprises of the Romans* from *good taste in architecture?* When Piranesi states that *it is a principle constantly verified by experience,* he is recalling what the Romans produced on many other occasions and linking this to what we see in the emissarium (as he demonstrated in his book *Della magnificenza ...*); this is so that, all things considered, it may be determined whether he is right to conclude that *in terms of grandeur, solidity, and elegance of construction, the Romans of successive periods owe nothing to the Greeks, although the latter can rightly lay claim to the aforementioned foolish trifles.* It is true that he uses the word "elegance," which has to do with taste and would seem to have nothing to do with a tunnel in a mountain; but, aside from the fact that he associates the emissarium with so many other buildings that show eminent good taste, how does the *Gazette* know that in building the emissarium the Romans found no way of displaying their taste in architecture? Listen to what Piranesi adds:

And, truth to tell, what further arguments are required, beyond those supplied by Tuscan architecture, and by these two buildings, to demonstrate that the Romans, throughout their history, were not only perfectly acquainted with everything that pertains to the solidity of structures built for the public good, but possessed a complete knowledge of all those parts or devices that constitute regularity and symmetry in architecture? These consist of steps, columns, pilasters, capitals, architraves, beams, arches, lintels composed of wedge-shaped stones, simple and testudinal vaults. All these are to be found in the structures in question. This knowledge was supplemented by their knowledge of ornament. The task in hand was to build a structure at the mouth of a tunnel, to accord with the roughness of the latter. The architects considered that this roughness although it might not detract from the majesty of a building, would certainly do nothing to make it pleasing; they therefore reduced it by stages until they achieved elegance, leaving rustic the part of the architecture around the mouth of the tunnel itself, reducing the rustication on part L, *reducing it further between* L *and* K, *and fashioning the rest with all possible polish, an art that cannot be learned except with a taste refined through knowledge of ornamentation, and with long experience of all that relates to architectural decoration. The elegance of the interior of the reservoir is splendid, with its columns, capitals, beams, and ceiling, all composed of very large blocks, and all so neatly worked that it would have deserved to appear on a building exposed to public view, rather than be hidden away to serve the merely utilitarian purpose to which those great men of old, with no thought for personal vanity, devoted the most admirable efforts of their genius. From these examples alone, not to mention the many others that history sets before us, it is quite clear that, in order to determine what in architecture can be attributed to the Romans unassisted by the Greeks, we must take as our guide not some foolish prejudice as to the Romans' poverty and ignorance, but first the achievements of the Tuscans, their neighbors—that is to say the tradition, long established in Italy before the building of Rome, of working to achieve utility, permanence, and striking effects—and then their own sense of pride, which would not let them consent to be outdone by the Tuscans.*

Such is the conclusion of that part of Piranesi's essay on the emissarium of Lago Albano, for which he was censured by the gentlemen of the French *Gazette*. Of what does that part consist? Of the following. A certain gentleman[†] believed that the two structures, respectively at the inlet and outlet of the emissarium of Lago Albano, were the work of the later Romans: that is to say, of Romans who had received instruction from the Greeks. This was because, in his view, the structures in question displayed a knowledge of architecture that he did not believe the Romans of an earlier age, the builders of the emissarium itself, to have possessed. In his essay, Piranesi attempts to disabuse him of this false supposition. Now, the gentlemen of the *Gazette* take it upon themselves to inform the public not that Piranesi has proved (or failed to prove) that the early Romans were the excellent architects he takes them for but that he has attempted to prove *that the Romans borrowed nothing from the Greeks;* and that in those gentlemen's opinion *these ancient aqueducts are proof of the grandeur of the ideas and enterprises of the Romans, but they are not appropriate points of comparison between their nation and that of Greece in respect of good taste in architecture.* Well: *Quid lecytho cum strophio?*† [(What has a cruse to do with a breast band?)] What has the moon to do with crabs?

What exactly is it that these gentlemen say? *These ancient aqueducts are proof of the grandeur of the ideas and enterprises of the Romans, but they are not appropriate points of comparison between their nation and that of Greece in respect of good taste in architecture!* How backward you are, my dear sirs, in your knowledge of these antiquities! You ought to know that, for those who are knowledgeable about these antiquities, saying—as you now assert that Piranesi has said—that the ancient aqueducts are proof that the Romans had better taste than the Greeks in architectural design would be doing nothing but making a comparison between two dissimilar things; those other authorities would not say that—as you gentlemen believe—he equates the grandeur of the Romans' ideas and enterprises with good taste; since they well know that the Romans, while in their aqueducts they give proof of the grandeur of their ideas, have in many places clothed some of those aqueducts with all that is most beautiful and most tasteful in architecture; and Piranesi believes that in some of his books he has demonstrated this. Likewise, these authorities would say that many of those aqueducts were decorated by the Romans after the Greeks had introduced the fine arts into Rome; and they would require him [Piranesi] either to distinguish one set of aqueducts from another, those built before the moment of introduction from those built after, or to demonstrate that the elements of taste discovered in the aqueducts built subsequently were in use among the Romans before they ever knew the Greeks. Now, does he [Piranesi], in speaking of the above-mentioned aqueduct and castellum [(cistern)] of the Aqua Julia, both as to ornament and as to matters of architectural taste, draw any comparison between that aqueduct and its castellum, on the one hand, and Greek architecture on the other? Certainly not. Here are his words: *The remaining parts of the castellum, and especially the parts above the five outlets previously mentioned of which a plan is given . . . and several illustrations are made, together with all the rest of the structure . . . , since they pertain only to the ornament of which they have now been completely stripped, there is nothing about them that requires to be discussed apart from the aforementioned illustrations. Suffice it to say that this castellum was richly decorated, as is indicated first by some vestiges of the marble facing that remain in the niche shown in the plate ... and by the holes in which were fixed the metal clamps that supported the facing, all over the structure wherever it was exposed to view.... Second, the actual marble that was found, some of it still affixed to the walls of the castellum (those that were buried ...), and some excavated and lost when the surroundings of the castellum were excavated.... Third, the bases shown in the plate ... which ran along both sides and the front of the castellum, and upon which columns must have stood, placed there as ornament; we know this from a portion of a cipolin marble shaft, found during the aforesaid excavations.... Finally, the superb marble trophies ... that were discovered beneath the arches marked in the plate ... and transported to Piazza del Campidoglio, where they still are, on account of the excellence of their workmanship and of their ornament. The fact that the castellum was erected by Augustus should convince us that these trophies are related to his victories, and thus cut short the debate among antiquarians as to whether they refer to* [*Gaius*] *Marius (as I mentioned at the start), to Domitian, or to Trajan ...* But why dwell on this any further? For Signor Mariette, these things belong to another world. Why for Signor Mariette? Where does his name appear in the criticism? Yes, for Signor Mariette: the criticism is a preface to the letter from him that we have transcribed. I am therefore sorry to have said that the gentlemen of the *Gazette* do not read the books that they review: it is Signor Mariette who does not read them.

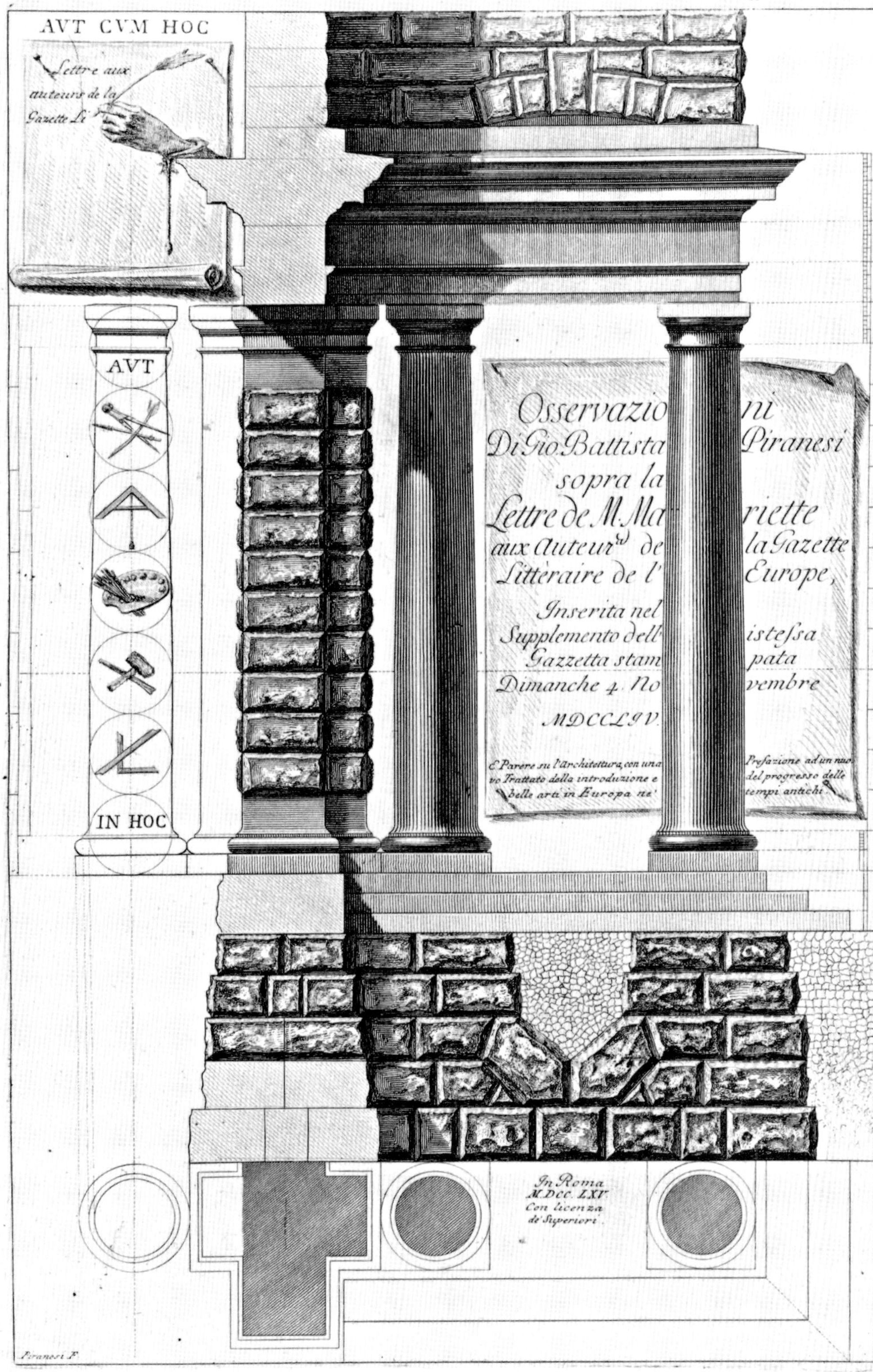

Title page 1765, etching, 40 × 25.2 cm (15¾ × 9⅞ in.)

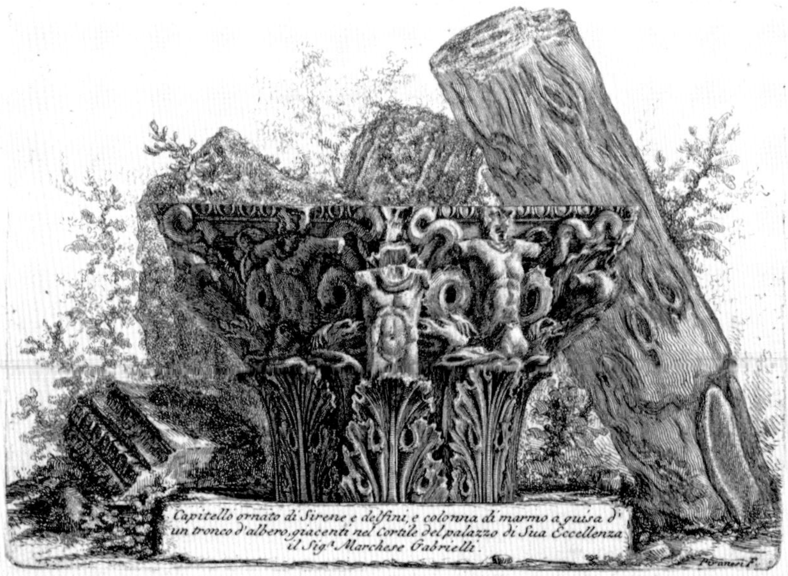

OSSERVAZIONI
DI GIO. BATTISTA PIRANESI
SOPRA LA
Lettre de Monſieur Mariette aux Auteurs de la Gazette Littéraire de l'Europe,

Inſerita nel ſupplemento dell' iſteſſa Gazzetta, ſtampata, *Dimanche* 4. *Novembre* 1764.

OSSERVAZIONI.

A
Queſt' Opera al Sig. Mariette è incognita ſenza quel *peut être*.

LETTRE
DE M. MARIETTE.

M. Piraneſi, auteur de pluſieurs ouvrages ſur les antiquités Romaines dont vous avez rendu compte, MM. en a publié un (1) depuis peu d'années qui A peut-être nous eſt inconnu, & dans lequel il s'eſt propoſé de faire l'apologie des Romains & de montrer, contre vôtre ſentiment qui eſt auſſi le mien, que par rapport aux arts, & pour ce qui concerne en particulier l'Architecture, non ſeule-

A ment

(1) *Della Magnificenza, e Architettura de' Romani*, in Roma 1761.

Chapter opening 1765, vignette: etching, 16 × 21 cm (6 1/4 × 8 1/4 in.)

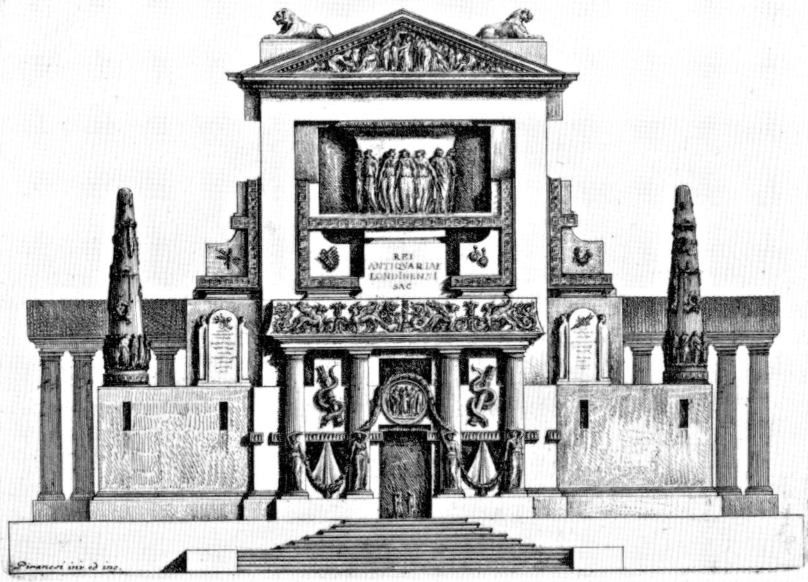

PARERE SU L' ARCHITETTURA.

DIALOGO.

Protopiro, e Didascalo.

Protop. Come, Didascalo! Dopo che, per la tanta pratica che avete dell'Architettura, eravate giunto a discernere il buono dal cattivo, in vece di approfittarvi del vostro sapere, anche voi volete farvi tenere per un di coloro che, quanto più credono d' intendersi di quest' arte, tanto meno ne sanno?

Didasc. Perchè, Protopiro?

Propop. Ma che disegni son quelli, che vi mettete a difendere? Mi fate ricordare di quell' assioma del Montesquieu: *Un edifizio carico d' ornamenti è un enimma per gli occhj, come un poema confuso lo è per la mente.* Così dissi al Piranesi medesimo, nell' atto ch' ei mi mostrava codesti disegni come per qualche cosa di buono, che fusse uscita dalle sue mani.

Didasc. Cappita! Oh voi sì, che non portate in groppa.

Protop. Oh, io amo la verità.

Didasc. Anch' io; e poichè l'amo più di voi, perchè meglio di voi la conosco, vuò dirvi, che il Montesquieu s' intendeva più di Poesìa, che d'Architettura. Comprendeva, che v'erano tanti altri ripieghi per un Poeta da distinguersi, senza star a confonder la mente a' leggitori; ma non sapeva, in genere d'ornamenti, quanto sono scarse le rendite dell'Architettura, se si proibisce agli Architetti di raffazzonarla con altro, che con quel ch'è suo. E poi ditemi: un poema confuso non ha fatto altro, che confonder la mente: all' incontro un edifizio carico d' ornamenti è quello, ch' è piaciuto per tanti secoli, e che or piace più che mai, credendomi, che gli edifizj non sieno fatti per dar nel gusto ai censori, ma al Pubblico. Or come pone egli, il Montesquieu, un'opera, ch'essendo confusa, si solleva tutti contro, con un' opera che, ricca d' ornamenti, ha allettato ed alletta la maggior parte degli uomini? Amico, siate più circospetto nell' adottare certi proverbj nuovi; poichè, a ben pesarli, non han di bello altro che la buccia. Attenetevi a quell' antico: *L'uso fa legge.*

C *Protop.*

Chapter opening 1765, vignette: etching, 16 × 21.5 cm (6¼ × 8½ in.)

16

„ quando uno non voglia ridurre l' Architettura a *un vil mètier où l' on ne feroit que* „ *copier*, vi ſia tutto il campo di variare, e di moltiplicar le invenzioni. Anzi, che „ dico io? ſenza dare in una maniera *ridicule & barbare*. Moſtrate, che queſta ma- „ niera ſia tale; imperocchè, come date voi di barbaro a quel che hanno fatto i Gre- „ ci e i Romani, e che oggidì ſi fa in tuttaquanta l' Europa? Come potete dire, che „ ſia ridicolo ciò che fu già apprezzato, ſi apprezza, e per quanto avete udito da „ quel Didaſcalo, ſi dovrà apprezzare da quanti Protopiri vi ſono, e ſaranno per „ eſſervi?

„ Per la diverſità poi del modo di penſare del Piraneſi dal voſtro, non finiſce qui la „ coſa. Udite quel, ch' egli ſta preparando, perchè ne rendiate conto, oltre i diſegni „ mentovati nella cicalata: un altro trattato più voluminoſo di quello della Magnifi- „ cenza, e dell' Architettura de' Romani, unito a un gran numero di monumenti Etruſchi, „ e di altre antiche nazioni. Vedetene il titolo, e la Prefazione nel ſeguente foglio.

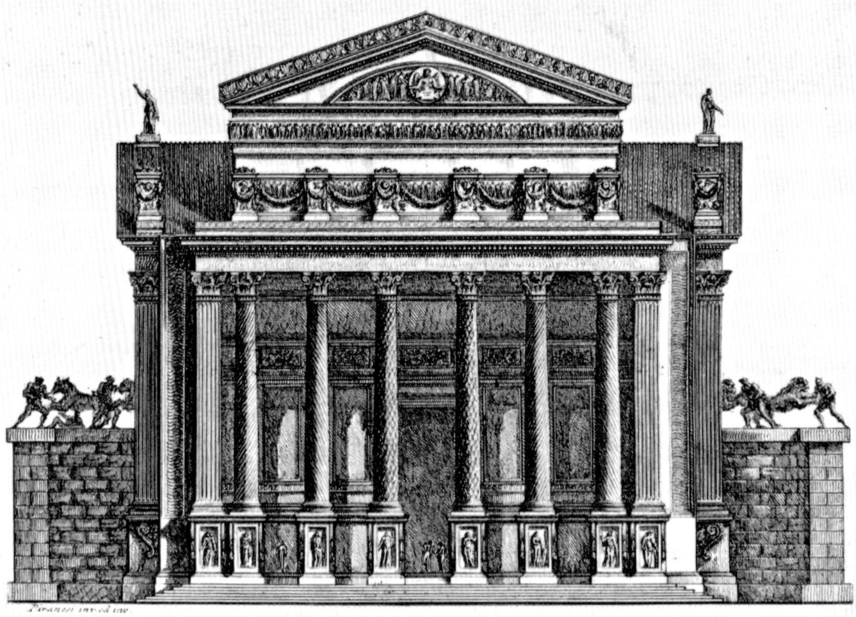

Chapter tailpiece 1765, etching, 16 × 20.5 cm (6¼ × 8⅛ in.)

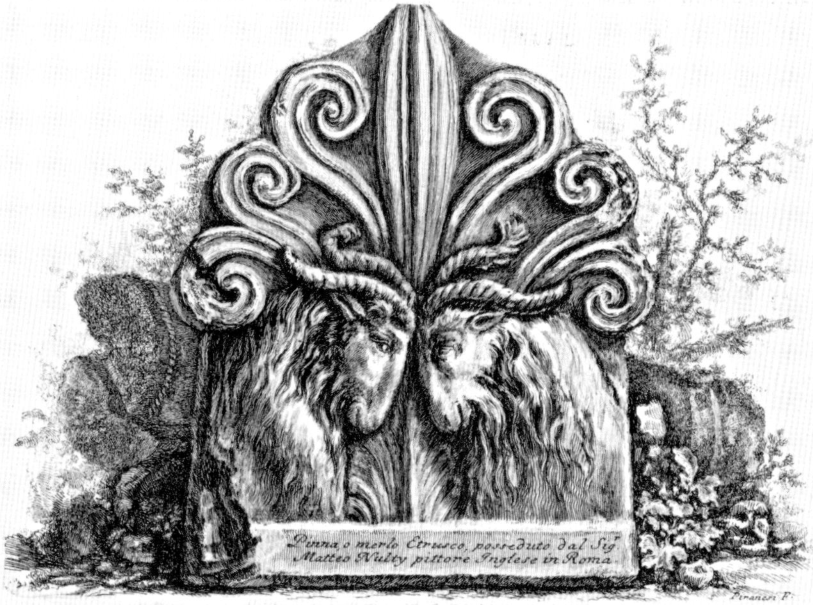

DELLA INTRODUZIONE
E DEL PROGRESSO DELLE BELLE ARTI
IN EUROPA
NE' TEMPI ANTICHI.

PREFAZIONE.

FInchè l'errore, poco men che comune, di credere, che i Greci ſiano ſtati gl' inventori non ſolamente delle belle arti, che ſono il ſoggetto del preſente Trattato, ma eziandio del mangiare, del bere, e del veſtire, attribuito alle lor Cereri, a' loro Bacchi, ed alle loro Minerve, non è ſtato errore di conſeguenza, l'inutile corſo ſuo ſi è potuto pacificamente tollerare: ma allor quando incomincia ad eſſer dannoſo, e a fare, non dico, ingrati, ma diſviati dal ſentiero della perfezione nelle preſate belle arti tanti e tanti, che deſiderano di diſtinguervisi; chi ſarà che, luſingandoſi di avere il modo di ritrarneli, non voglia moſtrare, ſe veramente lo abbia?

Tutta l' Europa vede il gran profitto fatto da tanti valent' uomini nelle belle arti, da che elle hanno incominciato a riſorgere; e chiunque ſa, che l'ingegno umano ha i ſuoi confini aſſegnatigli dalla natura, vede, che il profitto non poteva eſſer più grande. Or la ſcuola di queſte arti fin da quel tempo è ſtata ſempre l'Italia, non perchè, come s' immaginano certi inconſiderati, gl' Italiani per eſſe

E ſieno

Chapter opening 1765, vignette: etching, 15.8 × 21.5 cm (6¼ × 8½ in.)

arti ; ed obbligherebbon quel tale o a separare acquidotti da acquidotti, acquidotti fatti prima di questa introduzione da acquidotti fatti dopo, o a mostrare, che quelle tali cose di gusto, ritrovate negli acquidotti fatti dopo, fossero state in uso appo i Romani, prima che questi conoscessero i Greci. Quindi egli parlando dell' acquidotto e Castello dell' acqua Giulia da lui di sopra mentovato, quanto agli ornamenti ed a ciò che si appartiene al gusto dell' Architettura, fa egli verun paragone di tale acquidotto e Castello con l' Architettura de' Greci? Nò certamente. Ecco le sue parole: *Le rimanenti parti del Castello, ed in ispezie le superiori alle divisate cinque foci delle quali si dà la pianta ec. e si fanno più dimostrazioni assieme con tutto il restante dell' edifizio ec. siccome non appartenevano se non se all' ornato, di cui a' dì nostri sono affatto spogliate, non hanno perciò cosa che abbia di bisogno d' esser esposta oltre le predette dimostrazioni: basta soltanto dire, che questo Castello era ornatissimo, dandone un certo indizio primieramente alcuni residui delle incrostature di marmo, che tuttavia restano nel nicchio accennato nella Tavola ec., ed i forami in cui eran conficcate le grappe di metallo, che reggevano le incrostature medesime, disposte per tutto l' edifizio, per quanto rimaneva esposto alla vista ec. secondariamente gl' istessi marmi rinvenuti, parte ancor affissi alle pareti del Castello, per quanto queste sono interrate ec. e parte scavati e dispersi, allor che il Castello fu scavato d' intorno ec. in terzo luogo la base accennata nella Tavola ec., che ricorreva da ambo i lati, e dalla parte anteriore del Castello, e sopr' a cui certamente dovean posare le colonne appostevi per ornamento, come apparve da un tronco di marmo cipollino, ritrovato nello scavo predetto ec. finalmente i superbi trofei di marmo ec. che furon tolti di sotto gli archi notati nella Tavola ec. per trasferirli su la piazza del Campidoglio, di cui sono oggidì, per l' eccellenza del lavoro, il non minore ornamento. L' essersi veduto, che la fabbrica del Castello appartiene ad Augusto, debbe indurci a credere, che questi trofei appartengano altresì alle di lui vittorie, e toglie di mezzo le quistioni state finora fra gli antiquarj, se siano o di Mario, come ho accennato fin da principio, o di Domiziano, o di Trajano......* Mà a che dilungarmi? Pel Sig. Mariette queste son cose dell' altro Mondo. Come pel Sig. Mariette? Ov' è il suo nome in questa censura? Sì, pel Signor Mariette: la censura è una prefazione della Lettera, che abbiam trascritta. Spiacemi perciò d' aver detto, che i Signori Gazzettieri non leggono le Opere di cui rendon conto: è il Signor Mariette, che non le legge.

I M P R I M A T U R,
Si videbitur Reverendissimo Patri Magistro Sacri Palatii Apostolici.
D. Jordan. Archiep. Nicomed. Vicesg.

I M P R I M A T U R.
Fr. Thomas Augustinus Ricchinius Ord. Præd. Sac. Pal. Apost. Magister.

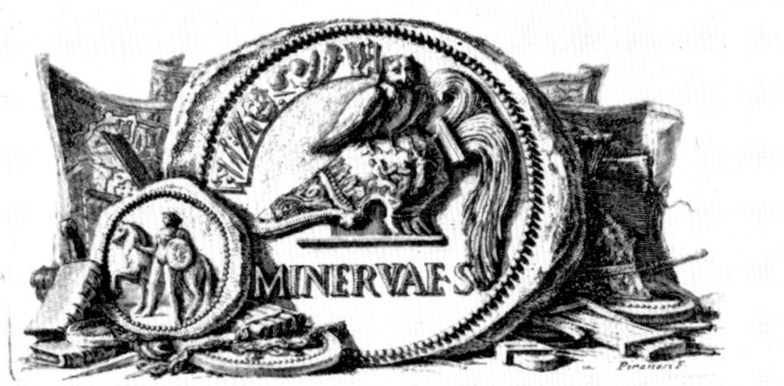

IN ROMA MDCCLXV.

PER GENEROSO SALOMONI.
Con licenza de' Superiori.

Colophon vignette 1765, etching, 7.5 × 14.5 cm (3 × 5¾ in.)

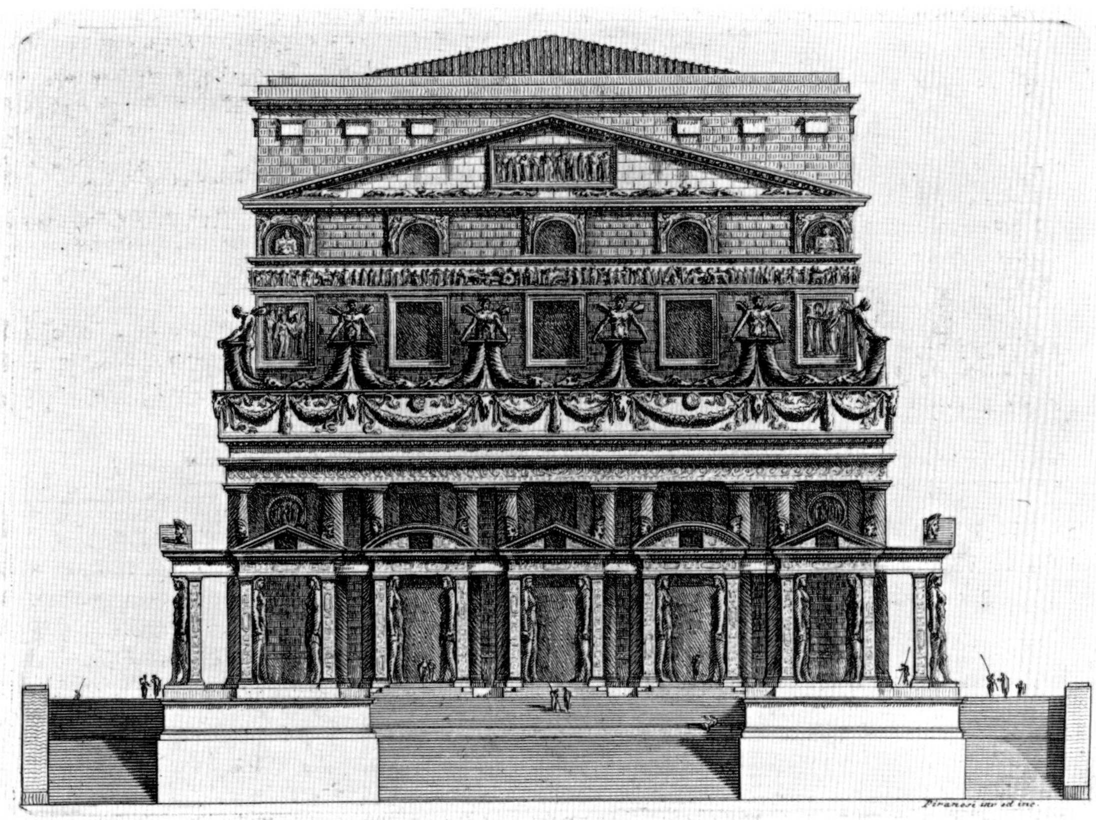

Vignette 1765, etching, 16 × 20.8 cm ($6\frac{1}{4}$ × $8\frac{1}{8}$ in.)

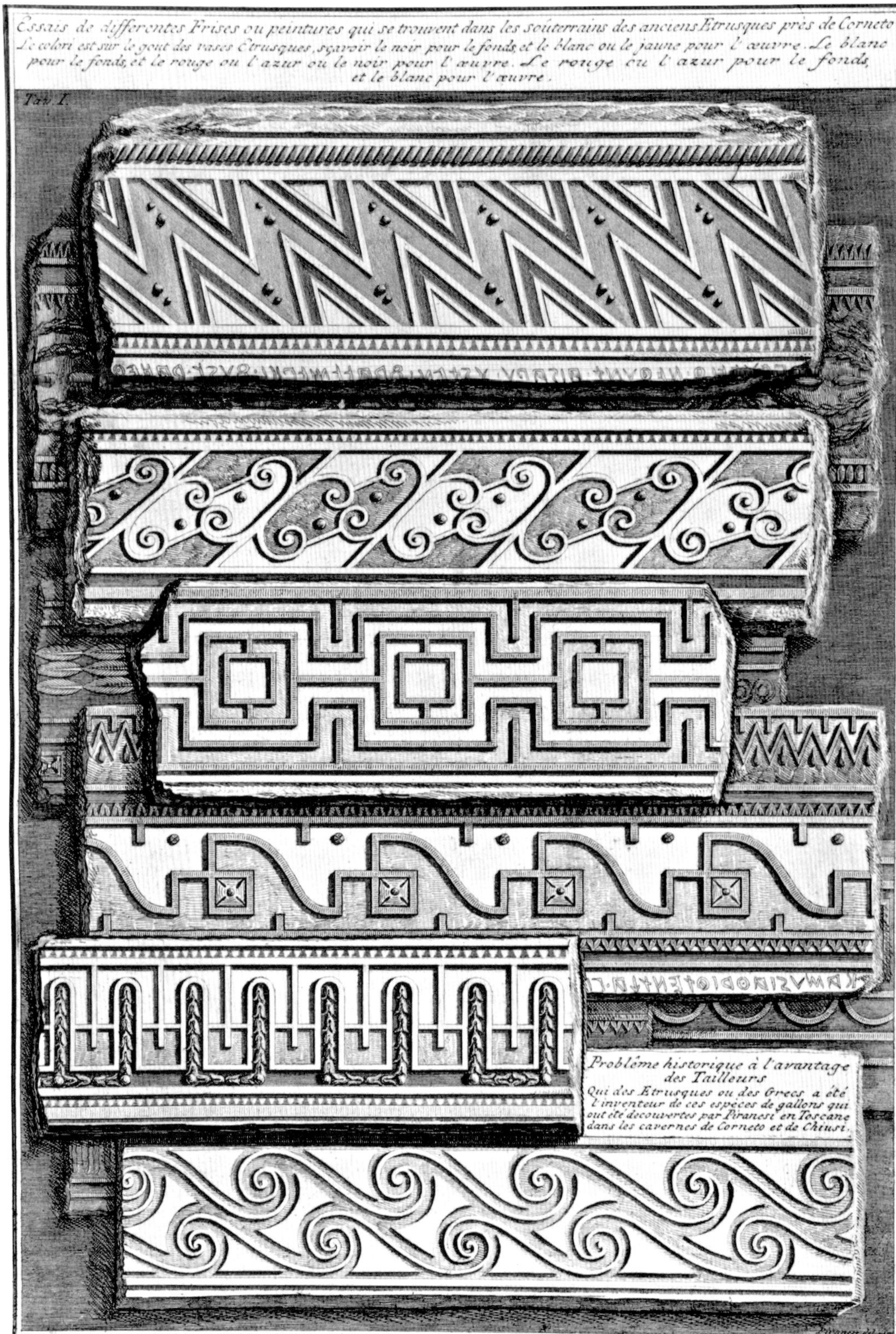

Plate I 1765, etching, 41 × 27 cm (16⅛ × 10⅝ in.)

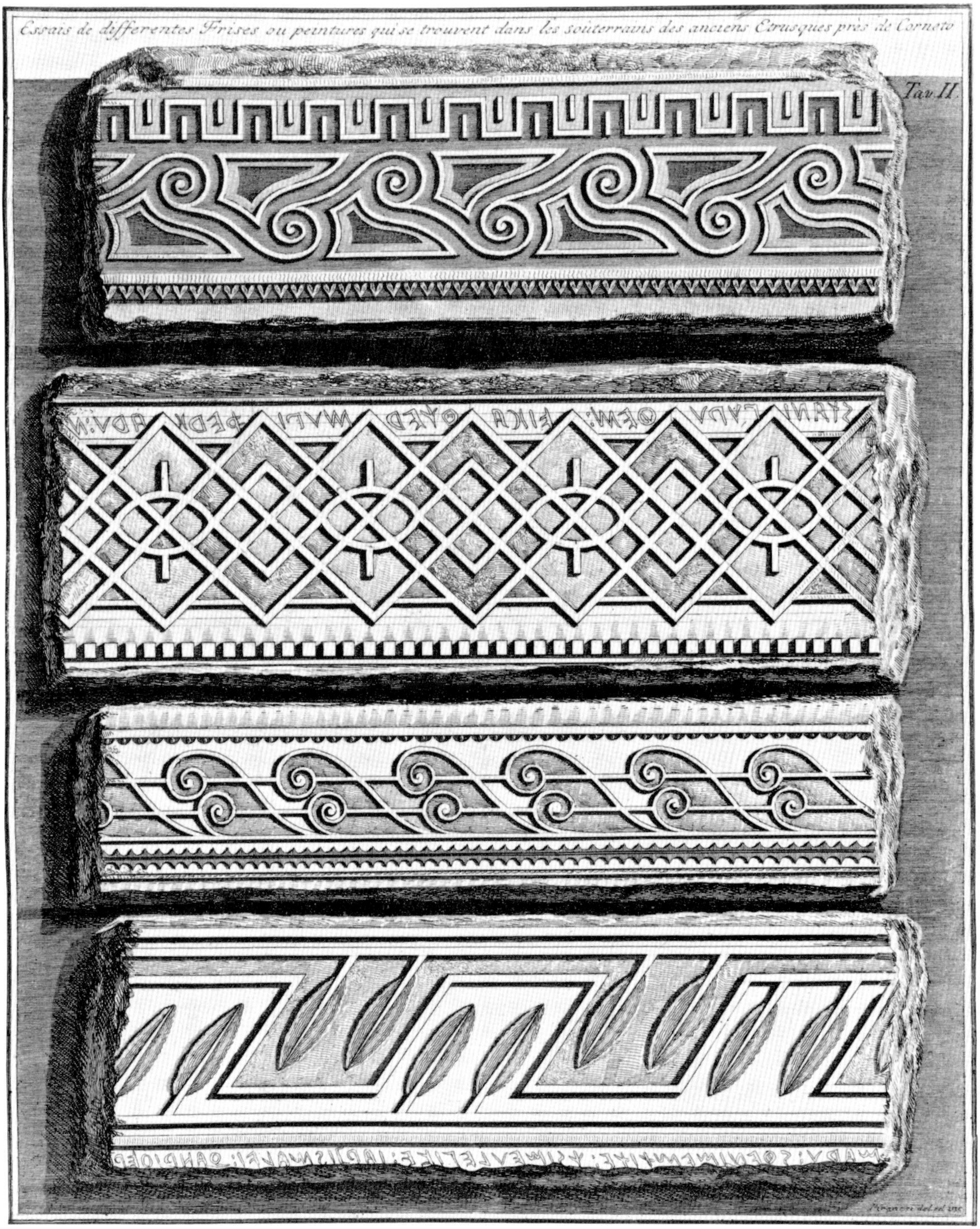

Plate II 1765, etching, 34 × 27 cm (13⅜ × 10⅝ in.)

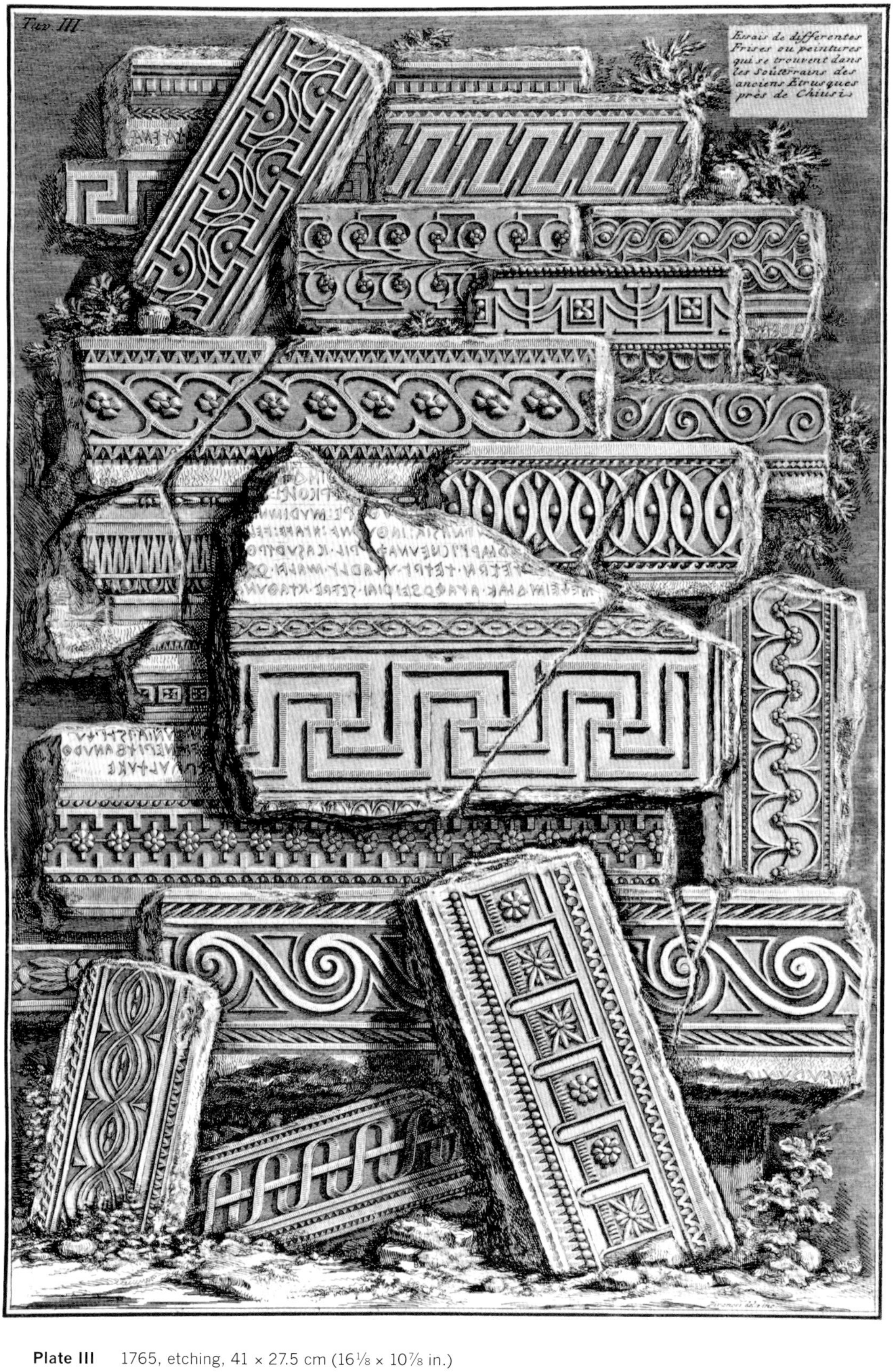

Plate III 1765, etching, 41 × 27.5 cm (16⅛ × 10⅞ in.)

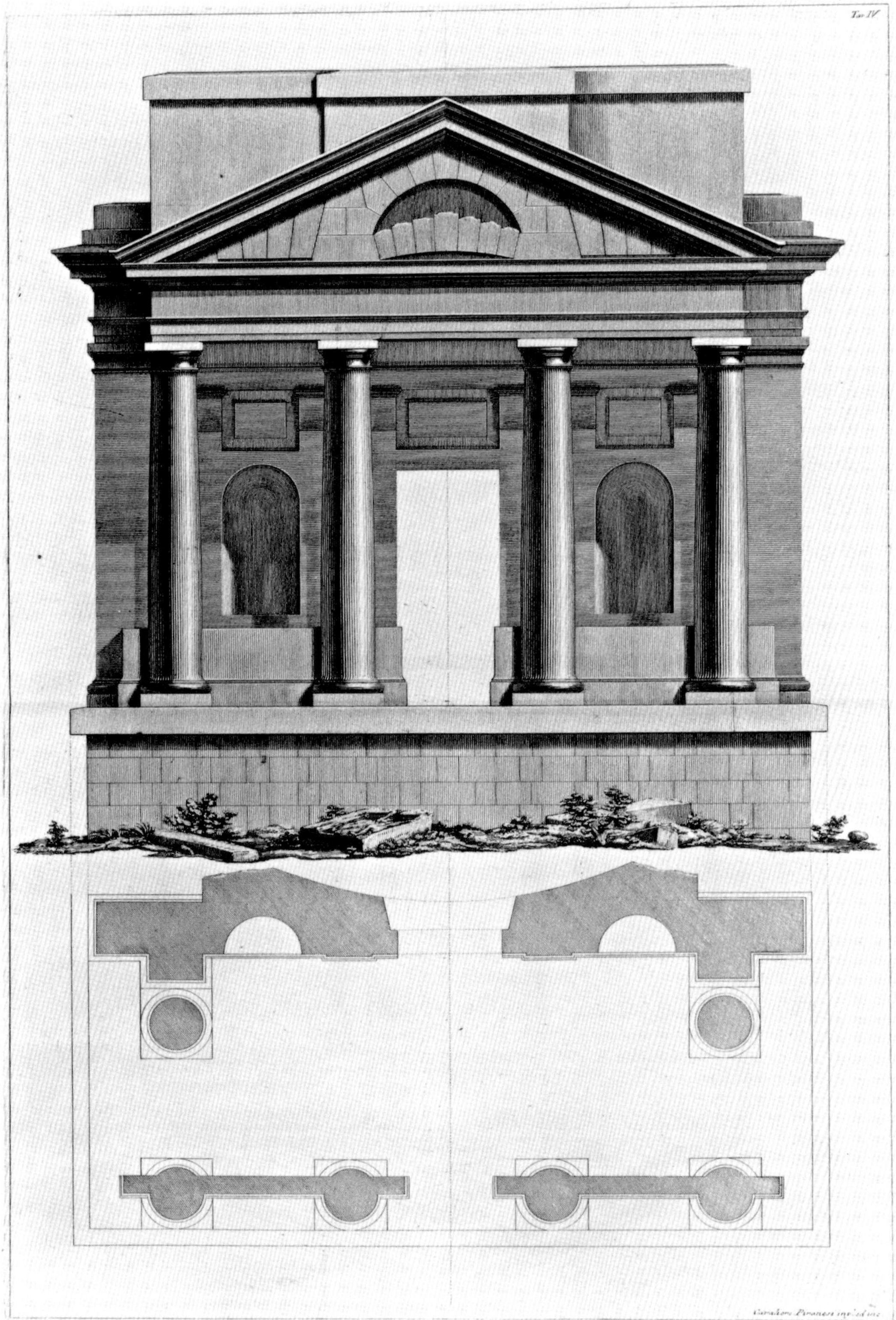

Plate IV After 1767, etching, 60 × 40 cm (23⅝ × 15¾ in.)

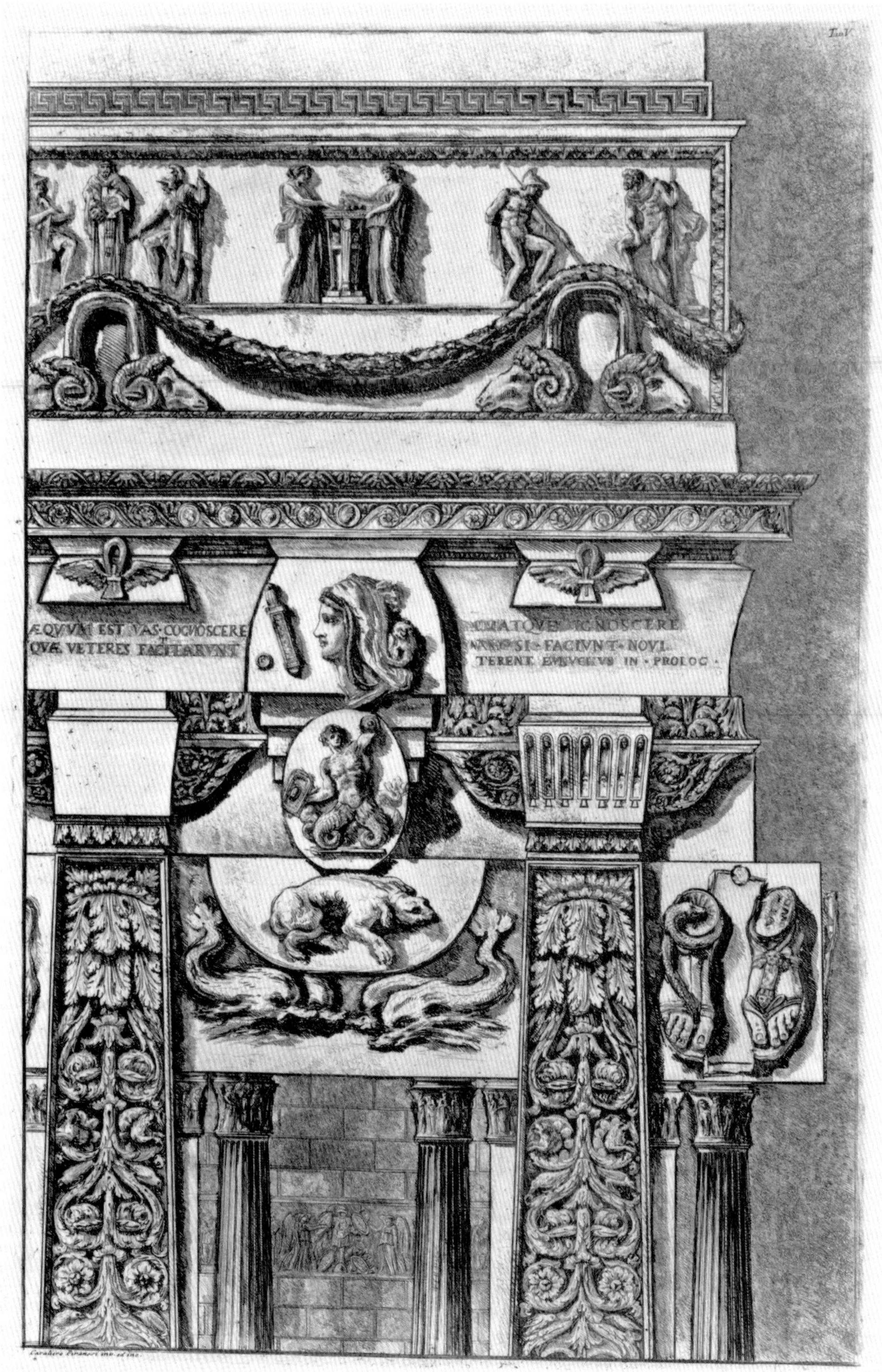

Plate V After 1767, etching, 62 × 39 cm (24⅜ × 15⅜ in.)

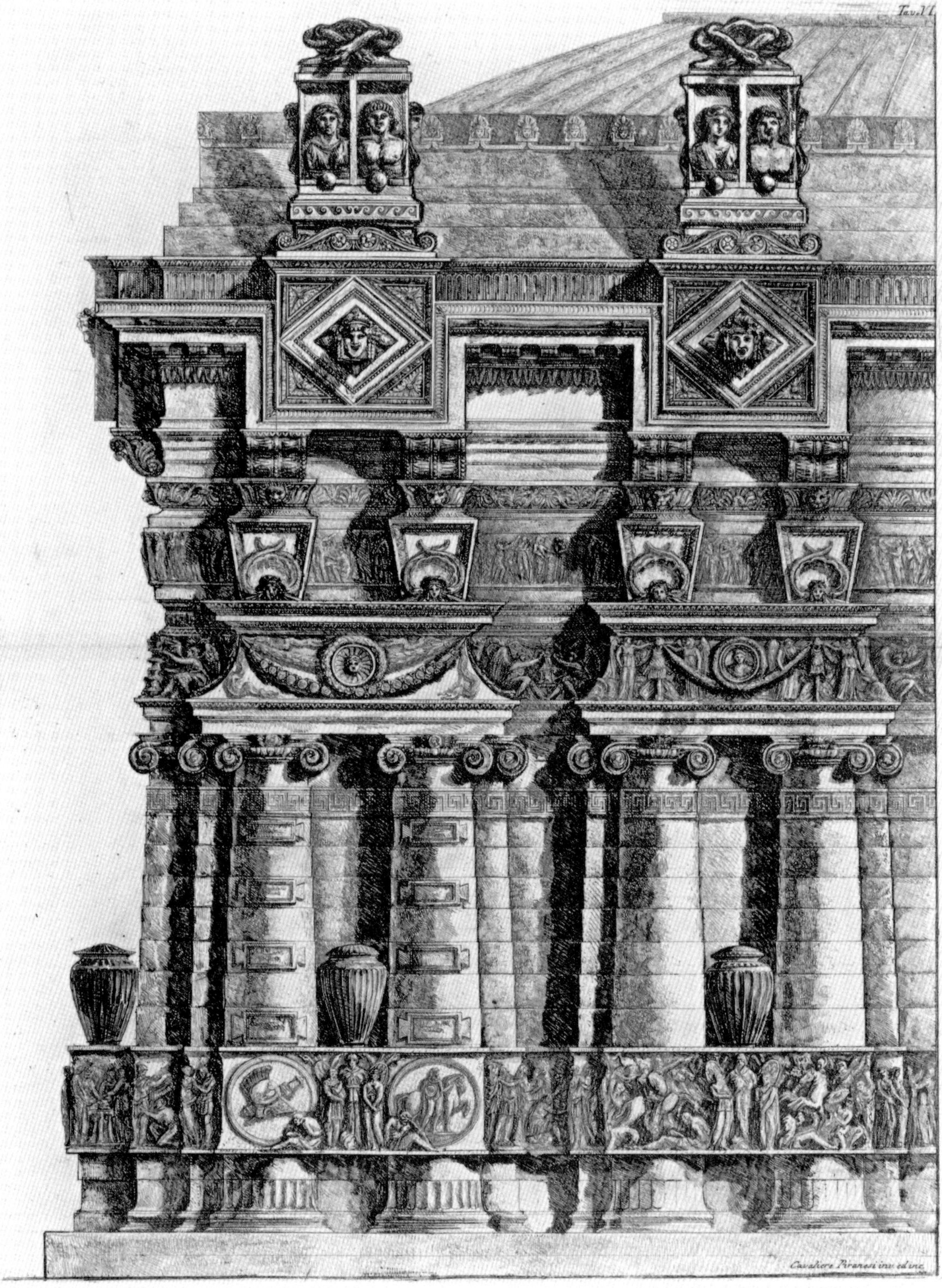

Plate VI After 1767, etching, 54 × 39 cm (21¼ × 15⅜ in.)

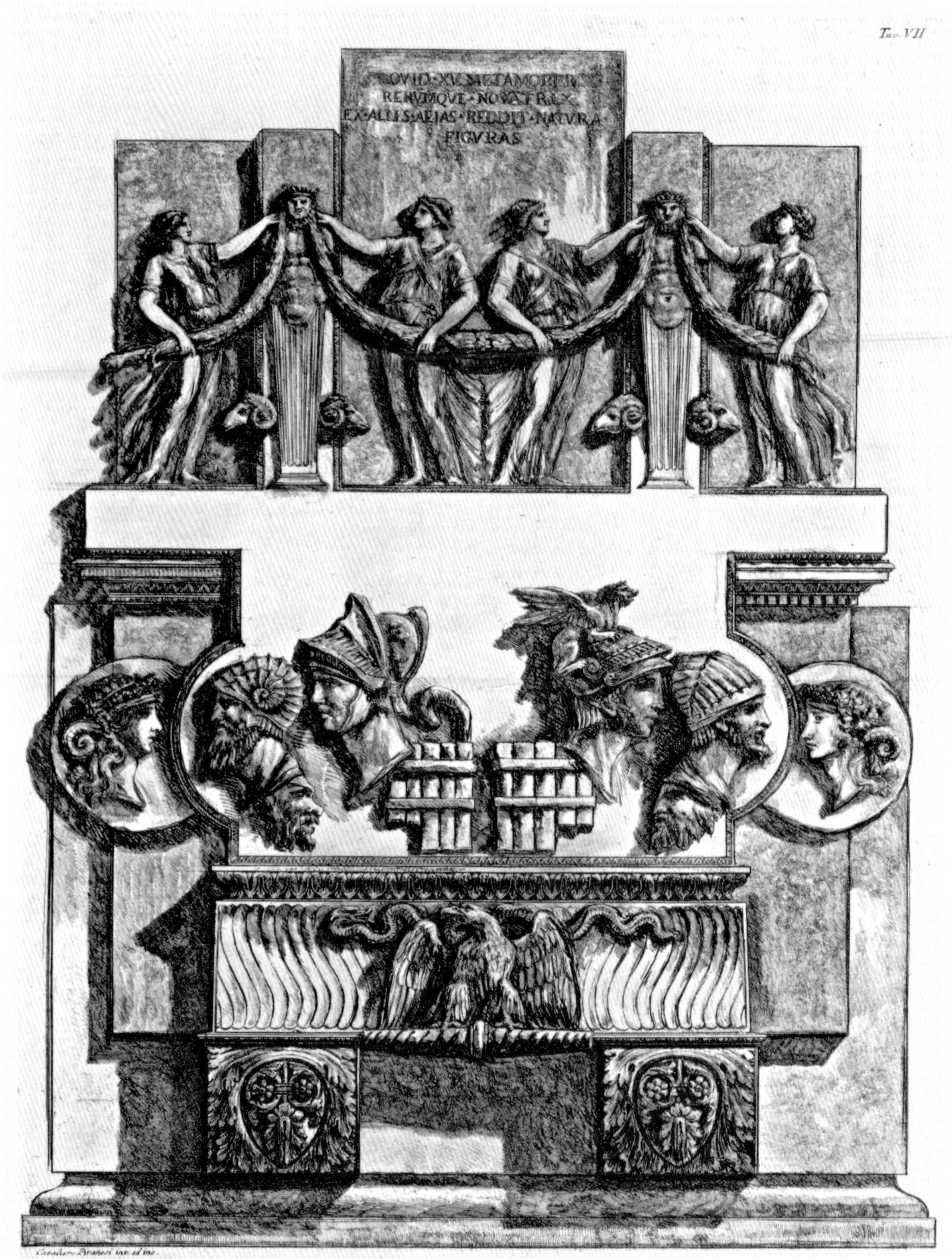

Plate VII After 1767, etching, 53 × 38.5 cm (20⅞ × 15⅛ in.)

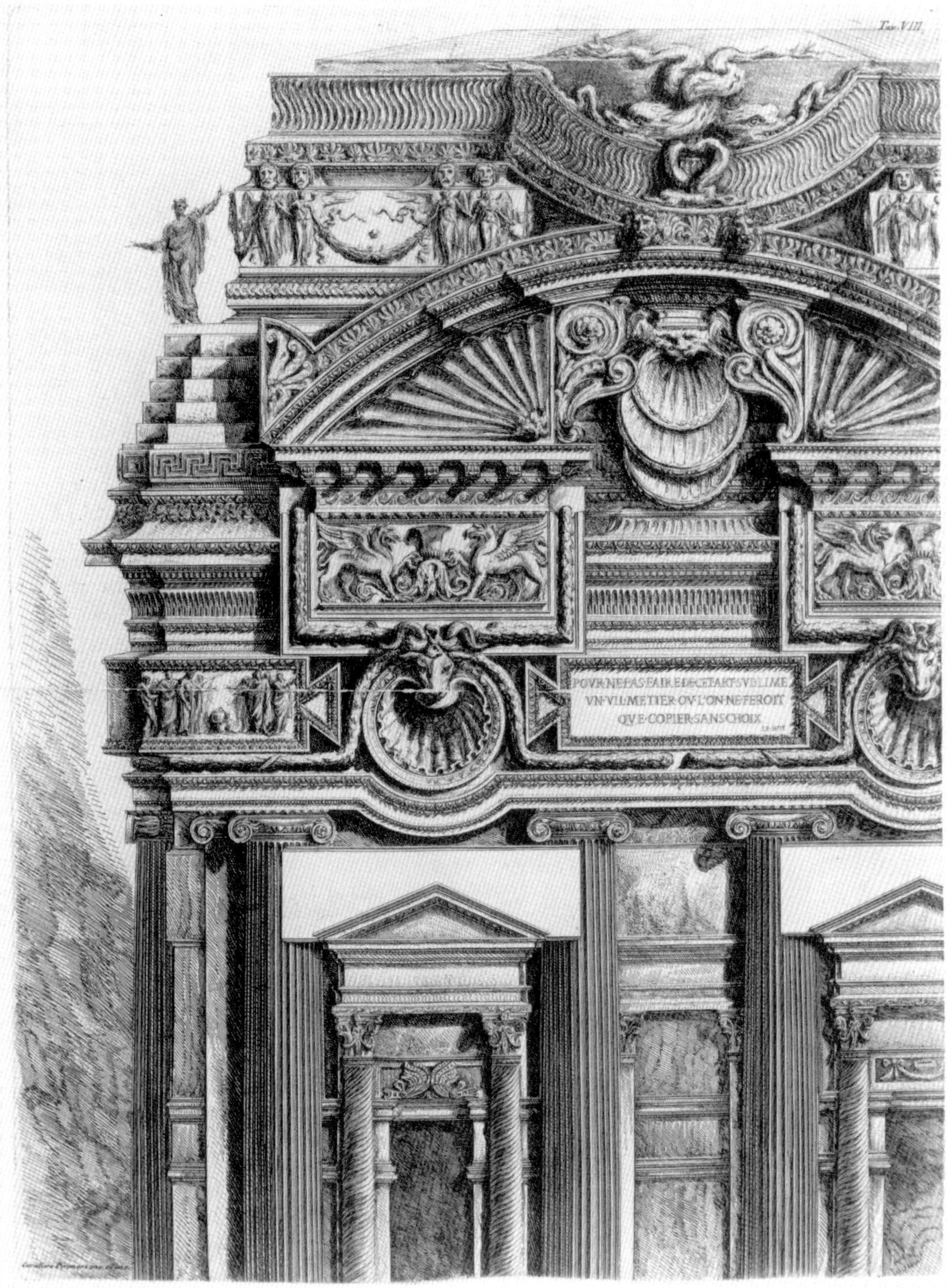

Plate VIII After 1767, etching, 54 × 39 cm (21¼ × 15⅜ in.)

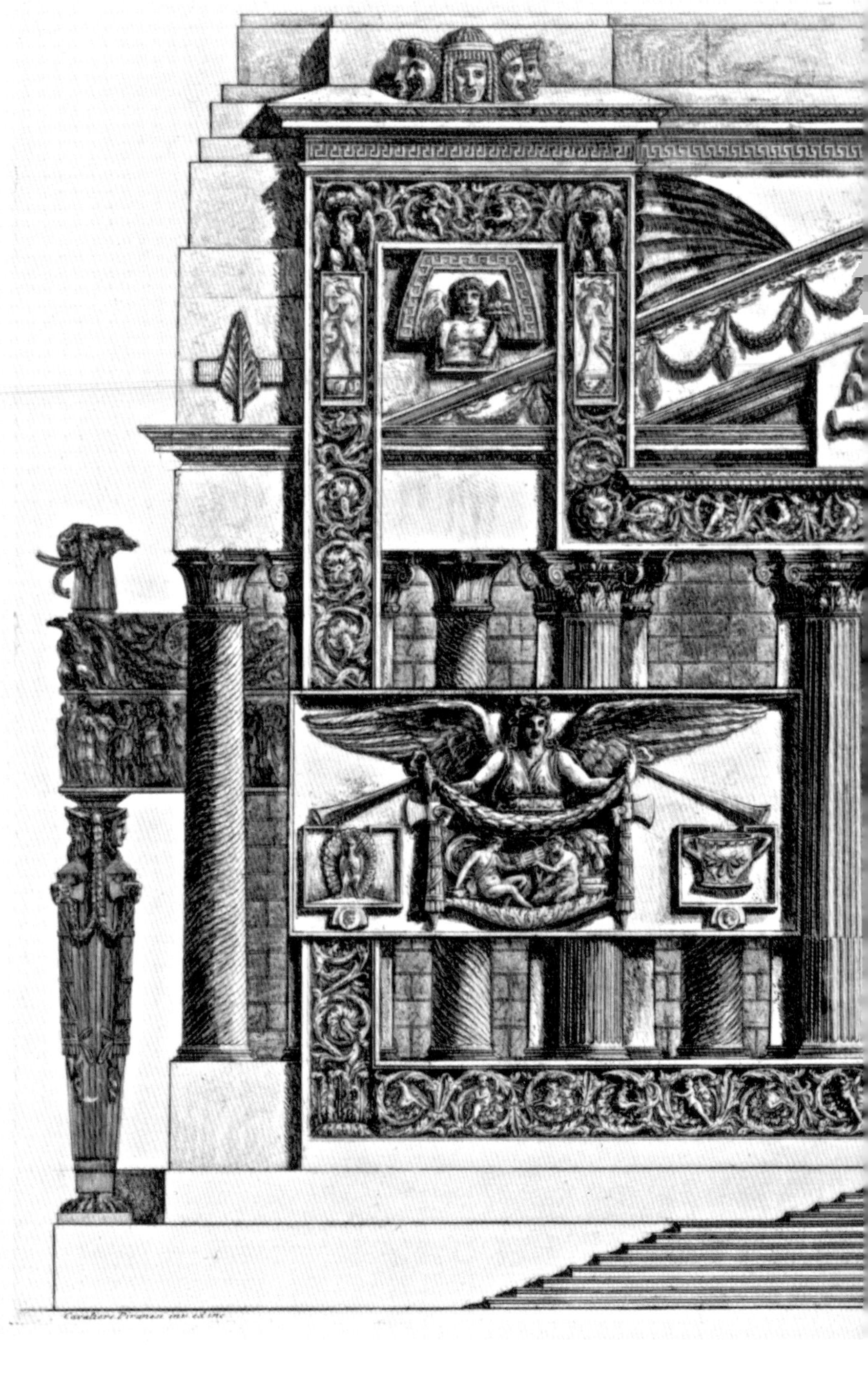

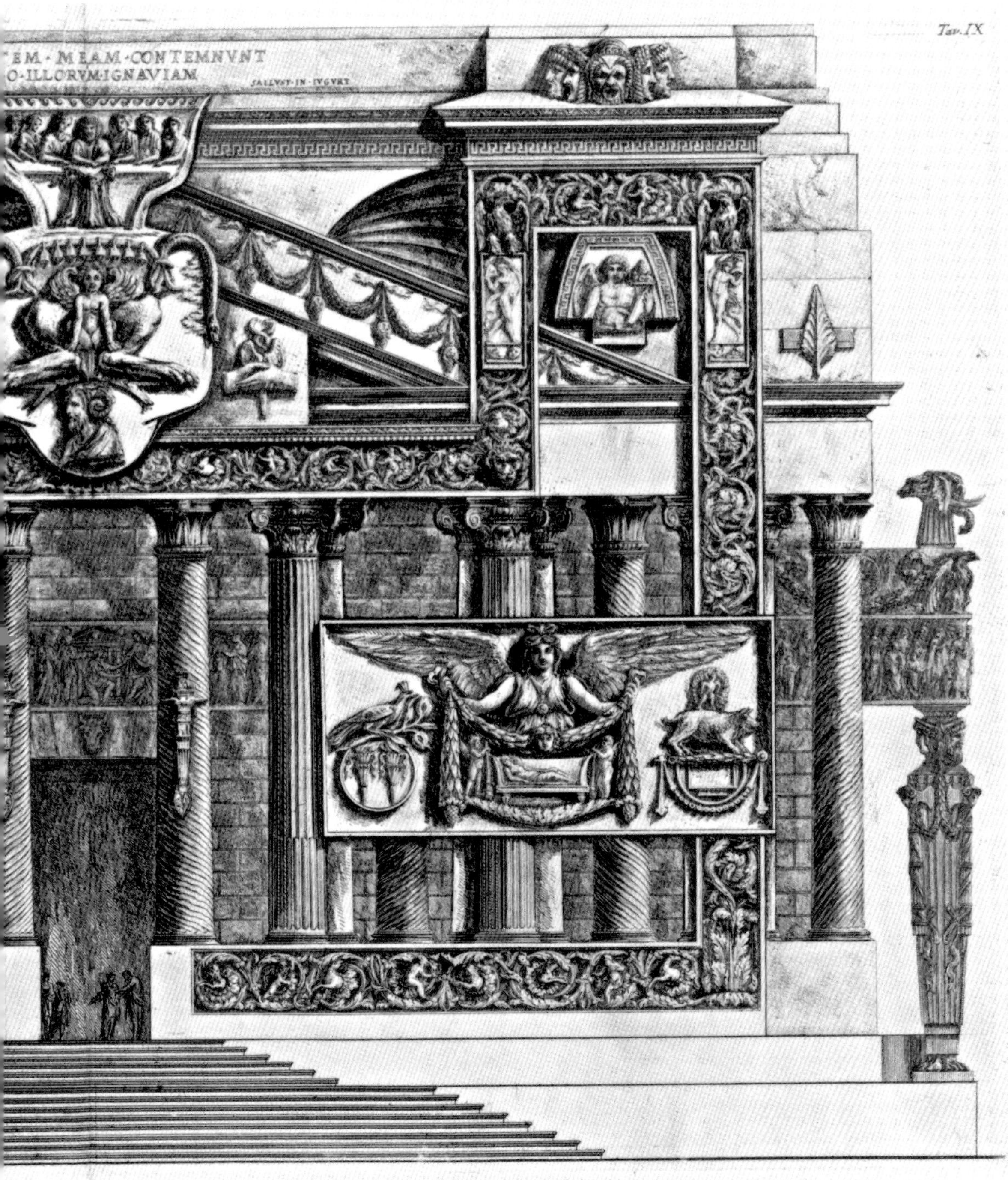

Plate IX After 1767, etching, 41 × 64.5 cm (16 1/8 × 25 3/8 in.)

Editorial Notes

Piranesi prints all quoted material in italic, without quotation marks. With the exception of quotations within quotations, this convention is retained here because Piranesi often paraphrases or adapts the original—whether in French, Italian, or Latin—rather than quoting verbatim. —TRANS.

The plates to Piranesi's *Osservazioni* do not always appear in the same order in the extant copies. Here the order is dictated by the roman numerals incised at the upper right in each plate in the edition at the Getty Research Institute. —ED.

"Observations on the Letter of Monsieur Mariette"

87 us] In Mariette's letter as printed in the *Gazette,* "nous" (us) occurs here rather than "vous" (you), and Piranesi not only reproduces this typographical error but deliberately capitalizes on it in his comment.

Livy] See Livy, *Livy* [*Ab urbe condita*], trans. B. O. Foster et al. (Cambridge: Harvard Univ. Press, 1965–83), 5.15.11–12, 5.16.8–11, 5.19.1.

90 Gori] See Antonio Francesco Gori, "Orthii Carminis Lamentabilis Etruscorum Antiquorum Dedicatio," in idem, *Museum Etruscum Exhibens Insignia Veterum Etruscorum Monumenta* (Florence: C. Albizinius, 1737–43), 1:XLV–LXVI.

Herodotus] Herodotus, *Herodotus* [*History*], trans. A. D. Godley (Cambridge: Harvard Univ. Press, 1981–87), 1.94:

> οὕτω δὴ τὸν βασιλέα αὐτῶν δύο μοίρας διελόντα Λυδῶν πάντων κληρῶσαι τὴν μὲν ἐπὶ μόνῃ τὴν δὲ ἐπὶ ἐξόδῳ ἐκ τῆς χώρης, καὶ ἐπὶ μὲν τῇ μένειν αὐτοῦ λαγχανούσῃ τῶν μοιρέων ἑωυτὸν τὸν βασιλέα προστάσσειν ἐπὶ δὲ τῇ ἀπαλλασσομένῃ τὸν ἑωυτοῦ παῖδα, τῷ οὔνομα εἶναι Τυρσηνόν. λαχόντας δὲ αὐτῶν τοὺς ἑτέρους ἐξιέναι ἐκ τῆς χώρης καταβῆναι ἐς Σμύρνην καὶ μηχανήσασθαι πλοῖα,... ἀποπλέειν κατὰ βίον τε καὶ γῆς ζήτησιν, ἐς ὃ ἔθνεα πολλὰ παραμειψαμένους ἀπικέσθαι ἐς Ὀμβρικούς, ἔνθα σφέας ἐνιδρύσασθαι πόλιας καὶ οἰκέειν τὸ μέχρι τοῦδε. ἀντὶ δὲ Λυδῶν μετονομασθῆναι αὐτοὺς ἐπὶ τοῦ βασιλέος τοῦ παιδός, ὅς σφεας ἀνήγαγε, ἐπὶ τούτου τὴν ἐπωνυμίην ποιευμένους ὀνομασθῆναι Τυρσηνούς.
>
> (At last their king divided the people into two portions, and made them draw lots, so that the one part should remain and the other leave the country; he himself was to be the head of those who drew the lot to remain there, and his son, whose name was Tyrrhenus, of those who departed. Then one part of them,

having drawn the lot, left the country and came down to Smyrna and built ships, . . . and sailed away to seek a livelihood and a country; till at last, after sojourning with many nations in turn they came to the Ombrici [in northern and central Italy], where they founded cities and have dwelt ever since. They no longer called themselves Lydians, but Tyrrhenians [that is, Etruscans], after the name of the king's son who had led them thither.)

Strabo] Strabo, *The Geography*, trans. Horace Leonard Jones (Cambridge: Harvard Univ. Press, 1923), 5.2.2: "Οἱ Τυρρηνοὶ τοίνυν παρὰ τοῖς Ῥωμαίοις Ἑτροῦσκοι καὶ Τοῦσκοι προσαγορεύονται. οἱ δ᾽ Ἕλληνες οὕτως ὠνόμασαν αὐτοὺς ἀπὸ τοῦ Τυρρηνοῦ τοῦ Ἄτους, ὥς φασι, τοῦ στείλαντος ἐκ Λυδίας ἐποίκους δεῦρο"; "The Tyrrheni, then, are called among the Romans 'Etrusci' and 'Tusci.' The Greeks, however, so the story goes, named them thus after Tyrrhenus, the son of Atys, who sent forth colonists hither from Lydia."

Patrocles] The work written by the Greek commander Patrocles (fl. 312–280 B.C.) survives only in a few fragments, and its title and scope are unknown. See Felix Jacoby, *Fragmente der griechischen Historiker*, pt. 3, *Geschichte von Städten und Völkern (Horographie und Ethnographie)*, C, *Autoren über einzelne Länder*, vol. 2, *Illyrien–Thrakien, Nr. 709–856* (Leiden: E. J. Brill, 1958), no. 712 (Patrokles).

Dionysius] Dionysius of Halicarnassus, *The Roman Antiquities*, trans. Earnest Cary (Cambridge: Harvard Univ. Press, 1937), 1.30:

> οὐ μὲν δὴ οὐδὲ Λυδῶν τοὺς Τυρρηνοὺς ἀποίκους οἶμαι γενέσθαι· οὐδὲ γὰρ ἐκείνοις ὁμόγλωσσοι εἰσιν, οὐδ᾽ ἔστιν εἰπεῖν ὡς φωνῇ μὲν οὐκέτι χρῶνται παραπλησίᾳ, ἄλλα δέ τινα διασώζουσι τῆς μητροπόλεως μηνύματα. οὔτε γὰρ θεοὺς Λυδοῖς τοὺς αὐτοὺς νομίζουσιν οὔτε νόμοις οὔτ᾽ ἐπιτηδεύμασι κέχρηνται παραπλησίοις. . . . κινδυνεύουσι γὰρ τοῖς ἀληθέσι μᾶλλον ἐοικότα λέγειν οἱ μηδαμόθεν ἀφιγμένον, ἀλλ᾽ ἐπιχώριον τὸ ἔθνος ἀποφαίνοντες, ἐπειδὴ ἀρχαῖόν τε πάνυ καὶ οὐδενὶ ἄλλῳ γένει οὔτε ὁμόγλωσσον οὔτε ὁμοδίαιτον ὂν εὑρίσκεται.
>
> (I do not believe, either, that the Tyrrhenians were a colony of the Lydians; for they do not use the same language as the latter, nor can it be alleged that, though they no longer speak a similar tongue, they still retain some other indications of their mother country. For they neither worship the same gods as the Lydians nor make use of similar laws or institutions. . . . Indeed, those probably come nearest to the truth who declare that the nation migrated from nowhere else, but was native to the country, since it is found to be a very ancient nation and to agree with no other either in its language or in its manner of living.)

92 Pliny] Pliny the Elder, *Natural History*, vol. 10, *Books XXXVI–XXXVII*, trans. D. E. Eichholz (Cambridge: Harvard Univ. Press, 1978), 34.1:

> navesque marmorum causa fiunt, ac per fluctus, saevissimam rerum naturae partem, huc illuc portantur iuga. . . . secum quisque cogitet, et quae pretia horum audiat, quas vehi trahique moles videat, et quam sine iis multorum sit beatior vita. ista facere, immo verius pati mortales quos ob usus quasve ad voluptates alias nisi ut unter maculas lapidum iaceant.

(and ships are built specially for marble. And so, over the waves of the sea, Nature's wildest element, mountain ranges are transported to and fro.... When we hear of the prices paid for these vessels, when we see the masses of marble that are being conveyed or hauled, we should each of us reflect, and at the same time think how much more happily many people live without them. That men should do such things, or rather endure them, for no purpose or pleasure except to lie amid spotted marbles.)

94 Magic Lantern] This sobriquet for the Lantern of Demosthenes, as the choregic Monument of Lysikrates in Athens was popularly known well into the nineteenth century, seems to be a rather heavy-handed joke by Piranesi at Mariette's and Julien-David Le Roy's expense.

95 Perrault] Claude Perrault, "Preface," in Vitruvius, *Les dix livres d'architecture de Vitruve,* trans. Claude Perrault (Paris: Jean Baptiste Coignard, 1673), [iii]:

> Mais l'excellence de ces sortes d'ouvrages, qui eut d'abord quelque estime, n'ayant pas continué à recevoir en France les témoignages avantageux qu'elle a dans les autres Païs, où les pesonnes de la plus haute qualité se font un honneur de la connaissance de ces belles choses, où l'on ne traite point d'Artisans et de gens méchaniques ceux qui en font profession, mais où on leur donne la qualité de Chevalier et de Comte Palatin, et enfin où l'on parle d'eux avec éloge, les mettant parmy les hommes Illustres; il ne faut pas s'étonner si l'Architecture, que la premiere faveur des Rois du siecle passé avait commencé à élever en France, est retombée dans son premier abaîssement.
>
> (But when these sorts of works, which had been lauded at the outset, did not continue to receive the favorable reception in France that they received in other countries—where persons of the best sort consider a familiarity with these beautiful things an honor, where those who make of them their profession are not treated as artisans and mechanics but rather are endowed with titles such as Chevalier and Count Palatine, and where, finally, these men are praised and placed among the illustrious—one should not be surprised to find that architecture, which had begun to be elevated in France owing to the high favor it was shown by the kings of the last century, had fallen once again to its original lowly status.)

Cossutius] See Vitruvius, *On Architecture,* trans. Frank Granger (Cambridge: Harvard Univ. Press, 1970), 7.*pref.*15, 7.*pref.*17.

97 answers] Note that Piranesi is quoting here from the comments appended to Mariette's letter by the editors of the *Gazette littéraire* in which they expand his critique of Roman architecture to encompass Roman rhetoric, poetry, and philosophy.

98 Cicero] Marcus Tullius Cicero, "The Letters to His Brother Quintus," trans. W. Glynn Williams, in idem, *The Letters to His Brother Quintus, . . . , Letter to Octavian* (Cambridge: Harvard Univ. Press, 1989), 3.1.2.

99 *Horace*] Horace, "De arte poetica," in idem, *Satires, Epistles, and Ars poetica,* trans. H. Rushton Fairclough (Cambridge: Harvard Univ. Press, 1978), 19–21: "et fortasse cupressum / scis simulare: quid hoc, si fractis enatat exspes / navibus, aere dato qui pingitur?"; "Perhaps, too, you can draw a cypress. But what of that, if you are

paid to paint a sailor swimming from his wrecked vessel in despair?"

cuccagna] Piranesi refers here to a festival contest involving foodstuffs (fruit, nuts, game, and so forth) placed on a platform (or hung from a metal hoop) attached to the top of a pole. Whichever contestant managed to climb the pole to the top could claim the prize, the *cuccagna*. Thus, a column topped with an architrave supporting a decorated frieze is like the pole topped with a platform supporting a *cuccagna*. For the elaborate Neapolitan version of this practice and an engraving by Giuseppe Vasi depicting the *cuccagna* for the birth in 1747 of Filippo, heir to the Kingdom of the Two Sicilies, see Heather Hyde Minor, "Rejecting Piranesi," *Burlington Magazine* 143 (2001): 412–19.

100 *published*] Giovanni Battista Piranesi, *Le antichità romane*, 4 vols. (Rome: Stamperia di Angelo Rotilj [etc.], 1756).

101 *artists*] See, for example, Francesco Algarotti, *Saggio sopra l'Accademia di Francia che è in Roma* (Livorno: Marco Coltelline, 1763), where in the course of praising the king for his patronage of the Académie de France à Rome, Algarotti stops to chastise its detractors: "Se non che alcuni ci furono, e massimamente al di' d'oggi alcuni ci sono in Francia, i quali pensano, ed hanno scritto in contrario; quasi adontassero di dover passare i monti per divenir buoni pittori, o architetti" (If there were not some people, and in particularly many in France today, who think, and have written to the contrary, as if they would almost be offended to have to cross the mountains to become good painters or good architects); see Francesco Algarotti, *Opere del conte Algarotti* (Cremona: per Lorenzo Manini, 1778–84), 3:12.

Algarotti] As to Algarotti on the right of the great artist to borrow from his predecessors, see Francesco Algarotti, *Saggio sopra la pittura* (Livorno: Marco Coltellini, 1763), esp. "De l'imitation."

"Opinions on Architecture"

102 *mind*] Charles de Secondat, baron de Montesquieu, "Essai sur le goût dans les choses de la nature et de l'art: Fragment": "Un bâtiment d'ordre gothique est une espece d'énigme pour l'oeil qui le voit, et l'ame est embarrassée, comme quand on lui présente un poëme obscur" (A building in the Gothic order is a sort of enigma to the eye, and the soul grows discomfited, as it does when presented with an obscure poem).

Piranesi may have read Montesquieu's essay in Denis Diderot and Jean Le Rond d'Alembert, eds., *Encyclopédie; ou, Dictionnaire raisonné des sciences, des arts et des métiers . . . par une société de gens de lettres* (Paris: Briasson, 1751–80), s.v. "goût" (quotation 7:763–64, under heading "Des plaisirs de la variété"); or in one of the many editions of Montesquieu's *Considérations sur les causes de la grandeur des Romains, et de leur décadence; nouvelle édition, à laquelle on à joint . . . l'Essai sur le goût, fragment* (Amsterdam: Arkstee & Merkus, 1759).

legge] See Emanuel Strauss, *Dictionary of European Proverbs* (New York: Routledge, 1994), no. 793.

103 *episkēnia*] A portion of a Greek theater, namely, the upper story of the *skēnē* (stage), the story above the scenery; see Vitruvius, *On Architecture*, trans. Frank Granger (Cambridge: Harvard Univ. Press, 1970), 7.5.5.

105 huts] Vitruvius, *On Architecture*, trans. Frank Granger (Cambridge: Harvard Univ.

Press, 1970), 2.1.3: "Primumque furcis erectis et virgulis interpositis luto parietes texerunt"; "And first, with upright forked props and twigs put between, they wove their walls."

Note that Vitruvius does not state directly that columns represent the forked uprights of huts. This connection was made explicitly in Marc-Antoine Laugier, *Essai sur l'architecture* (Paris: Duchesne, 1753), 12–13; *An Essay on Architecture*, trans. Wolfgang Herrmann and Anni Herrmann (Los Angeles: Hennessey & Ingalls, 1977), 12:

> La petite cabane rustique que je viens de décrire, est le modele sur lequel on a imaginé toutes les magnificences de l'Architecture, c'est en se raprochant dans l'exécution de la simplicité de ce premier modele, que l'on évite les défauts essentiels, que l'on saisit les perfections véritables. Les pieces de bois élevées perpendiculairement nous ont donné l'idée des colomnes. Les pieces horisontales qui les surmontent, nous ont donné l'idée des entablemens. Enfin les pieces inclinées qui forment le toit, nous ont donné l'idée des frontons.
> (All the splendors of architecture ever conceived have been modeled on the little rustic hut I have just described. It is by approaching the simplicity of this first model that fundamental mistakes are avoided and true perfection is achieved. The pieces of wood set upright have given us the idea of the column, the pieces placed horizontally on top of them the idea of the entablature, the inclining pieces forming the roof the idea of the pediment.)

gown] Vitruvius, *On Architecture*, trans. Frank Granger (Cambridge: Harvard Univ. Press, 1970), 4.1.7: "et cymatiis et encarpis pro crinibus dispositis frontes ornaverunt truncoque toto strias uti stolarum rugas matronali more dimiserunt"; "And arranging cymatia and festoons in place of hair, they ornamented the front, and, over all the trunk (i.e. the shaft), they let fluting fall, like the folds of matronly robes."

soffits] Vitruvius, *On Architecture*, trans. Frank Granger (Cambridge: Harvard Univ. Press, 1970), 4.2.2: "uti nunc fiunt fixerunt et eas cera caerulea depinxerunt, ut praecisiones tignorum tectae non offenderent visum"; "they fixed tablets shaped as triglyphs now are, against the cut-off beams, and painted them with blue wax, in order that the cut-off beams might be concealed so as not to offend the eyes."

manner] Vitruvius, *On Architecture*, trans. Frank Granger (Cambridge: Harvard Univ. Press, 1970), 4.3.1: "Nonnulli antiqui architecti negaverunt dorico genere aedes sacras oportere fieri, quod mendosae et disconvenientes in his symmetriae conficiebantur"; "Some ancient architects have said that temples should not be constructed in the Doric style, because faulty and unsuitable correspondences arose in them."

106 condemns] Vitruvius, *On Architecture*, trans. Frank Granger (Cambridge: Harvard Univ. Press, 1970), 7.5.5–6:

> praeterea supra ea nihilominus episcenium, in qua tholi, pronai, semifastigia omnisque tecti.... Licymnius mathematicus prodiit et ait "... Videamus item nunc, ne a picturis scaena efficiat et nos Alabandis aut Abderitas. Qui enim vestrum domos supra tegularum tecta potest habere aut columnas seu fasti-

giorum expolitionis? Haec enim supra contignationis ponuntur, non supra tegularum tecta. Si ergo, quae non possunt in veritate rationem habere facti, in picturis probaverimus, accedimus et nos his civitatibus, quae propter haec vitia insipientes sunt iudicatae."

(Besides, the story above the scenery had domes, porticoes, half pediments, and every kind of roof.... Licymnius the mathematician came forward and said, that "...Let us see to it that our stage scenery with its pictures does not make us citizens of Alabanda or of Abdera! For who of you can have above your roof tiles, buildings with columns and elaborate gables? For the latter stand upon floors, not above roof tiles. If we approve in pictures what cannot justify itself in reality, we are added to those cities which, because of such faults, are esteemed slow-witted.")

107 Horace] Horace, "Satyrarum," in idem, *Satires, Epistles, and Ars poetica,* trans. H. Rushton Fairclough (Cambridge: Harvard Univ. Press, 1978), 1.1.106: "est modus in rebus, sunt certi denique fines, / quos ultra citraque nequit consistere rectum"; "There is measure in all things. There are, in short, fixed bounds, beyond and short of which right can find no place."

108 architect] The sense of Piranesi's original, "Il più grande Architetto, che vi sia stato, voi biasimate, e che sia per esservi," is "You criticize any architect, even the greatest, whoever that may be."

110 *enough*] See Julien-David Le Roy, *Les ruines des plus beaux monuments de la Grèce,* 2 vols. (Paris: H. L. Guerin & L. F. Delatour, 1758); and James Stuart and Nicholas Revett, *The Antiquities of Athens Measured and Delineated,* 4 vols. (London: printed by J. Haberkorn, 1762–1816).

111 said] See Julien-David Le Roy, *Les ruines des plus beaux monuments de la Grèce* (Paris: H. L. Guerin & L. F. Delatour, 1758), 2:i:

> Un juste appréciation de ces principes nous feroit éviter deux inconvénients très-dangereux dans l'Architecture, celui de n'admettre aucunes regles, et de ne prendre pour guide, dans la composition des Monuments que le caprice; et celui d'en admettre un trop grand nombre; de gêner par-là l'imagination des Architectes, et de faire de ce Art sublime un espece de métier où chacun ne feroit que copier, sans choix, ce qui a été fait par quelques Architectes anciens.
>
> (A proper understanding of these principles would help us to avoid two highly dangerous pitfalls in architecture: that of accepting no rules, and taking caprice as our sole guide in the composition of monuments; and that of accepting too many, fettering the architect's imagination and reducing this noble art to a kind of craft, confined to the blind copying of a few ancient architects.)

"On the Introduction and Progress of the Fine Arts"

116 leader] Most likely Piranesi is referring to Johann Joachim Winckelmann.

117 Eusebius] Eusebius of Caesarea, *Preparation for the Gospel,* trans. Edwin Hamilton Gifford (Oxford: Clarendon, 1903; reprint, Grand Rapids: Baker Book House, 1981), 5a–c (bk. 1, chap. 2):

> And how can men fail to be in every way impious and atheistical, who have apostatized from those ancestral gods by whom every nation and every state is sustained? Or what good can they reasonably hope for, who have set themselves at enmity and at war against their preservers, and have thrust away their benefactors? For what else are they doing than fighting against the gods?
>
> And what forgiveness shall they be thought to deserve, who have turned away from those who from the earliest time, among all Greeks and Barbarians, both in cities and in the country, are recognized as gods with all kinds of sacrifices, and initiations, and mysteries by all alike, kings, law-givers and philosophers, and have chosen all that is impious and atheistical among the doctrines of men? And to what kind of punishments would they not justly be subjected, who deserting the customs of their forefathers have become zealots for the foreign mythologies of the Jews, which are of evil report among all men?
>
> And must it not be a proof of extreme wickedness and levity lightly to put aside the customs of their own kindred, and choose with unreasoning and unquestioning faith the doctrines of the impious enemies of all nations? Nay, not even to adhere to the God who is honoured among the Jews according to their customary rites, but to cut out for themselves a new kind of track in a pathless desert, that keeps neither the ways of the Greeks nor those of the Jews?

The "certain Jewish fairy tales" Piranesi mentions are, of course, the teachings of Judaism and Christianity.

119 *architecture*] "Italie," *Gazette littéraire de l'Europe* 2, no. 30 (22 August 1764): 318–19. This notice addresses Piranesi's *Le rovine del castello dell'Acqua Giulia...* (Rome: Stamperia Generoso Salomoni, 1761); and his *Descrizione e disegno dell'emissario del Lago Albano* (Rome: n.p., 1762). Piranesi mentions as well his *Antichità d'Albano e di Castel Gandolfo* (Rome: n.p., 1764). A long review of these three works, together with Piranesi's *Antichità di Cora* ([Rome: n.p., 1764]), would appear in *Supplément à la Gazette littéraire de l'Europe* 5, no. 10 (28 April 1765): 193–211.

Dio] Cassius Dio, *Dio's Roman History*, trans. Earnest Cary (Cambridge: Harvard Univ. Press, 1969–82), 67.1.2: "θεῶν μὲν γὰρ τὴν Ἀθηνᾶν ἐς τὰ μάλιστα ἤγαλλε, καὶ διὰ τοῦτο καὶ τὰ Παναθήναια μεγάλως ἑώρταζε, καὶ ἐν αὐτοῖς ἀγῶνας καὶ ποιητῶν καὶ λογογράφων μονομάχων τε κατ᾽ ἔτος ὡς εἰπεῖν ἐν τῷ Ἀλβανῷ ἐποίει·"; "The god that he revered most was Minerva, in consequence of which he was wont to celebrate the Panathenaea on a magnificent scale; on these occasions he held contests of poets and orators and gladiators almost every year at his Alban Villa."

Suetonius] Suetonius, "The Lives of the Caesars: Domitian," in idem, *Suetonius*, trans. J. C. Rolfe (Cambridge: Harvard Univ. Press, 1979), 8.4: "Celebrabat et in Albano quotannis Quinquatria Minervae"; "He celebrated the Quinquatria too every year in honour of Minerva at his Alban villa."

120 *bars*] Vitruvius, *On Architecture*, trans. Frank Granger (Cambridge: Harvard Univ. Press, 1970), 4.7.4: "Supra columnas trabes compactiles inponantur.... et ita sint conpactae subscudibus et securiclis"; "Above the columns, beams are to be placed bolted together.... and they are to be so coupled with dowels and mortices."

Vitruvius] See Vitruvius, *On Architecture*, trans. Frank Granger (Cambridge: Harvard Univ. Press, 1970), 4.4.1, 4.7.2. A *pronaos* is the inner portico in front of the *naos* or *cella*—namely, the sanctuary containing the cult statue—of a classical temple.

121 *Gori*] See Antonio Francesco Gori, *Museum Etruscum Exhibens Insignia Veterum Etruscorum Monumenta* (Florence: C. Albizinius, 1737–43), 3:63, pls. XI–XIII from class. I.

volume] Giovanni Battista Piranesi, *Descrizione e disegno dell'emissario del Lago Albano* (Rome: n.p., 1762).

122 gentleman] Pierre-Jean Mariette.

123 *strophio*] Aristophanes, *Women at the Thesmophoria*, in idem, *Birds, Lysistrata, Women at the Thesmophoria*, trans. Jeffrey Henderson (Cambridge: Harvard Univ. Press, 2000), 139: "ΚΗΔΕΣΤΗΣ: . . . τί λήκυθος καὶ στρόφιον; ὡς οὐ ξύμφορα"; "KINSMAN: . . . Here's an oil flask and a brassiere: how ill-fitting!"

Also see Desiderius Erasmus, *Adagia* 3.7.72: "Non est oleum in lecytho." Erasmus's explanation is as follows:

> Ἔλαιον οὐκ ἔνεστιν εὐ τῷ ληκύθῳ, id est *Olei liquor nequaquam inest in lecytho*, scilicet cum significamus non esse precibus locum apud inexorabilem. Refertur apud Aristophanem in Auibus [1589]. Est autem allusio ad vocem. Nam ἔλαιον, *oleum*, significat et ἔλεος, *misericordiam*, et haud scio an altera ab altera sit deriuata.
>
> (Ἔλαιον οὐκ ἔνεστιν εὐ τῷ ληκύθῳ, *There is no olive oil at all in the bottle*, which is used when we wish to indicate that there is no room for entreaties with a pitiless person. It is recorded in Aristophanes' *Birds* [line 1589]. There is, moreover, a play on the word, for ἔλαιον means *olive oil* and ἔλεος means *pity*, and I am inclined to think that the one is derived from the other.) (trans. Amir Baghdadchi)

See *Opera Omnia Desiderii Erasmi Roterodami*, vol. 6, pt. 2, *Adagiorum Chilias Tertia (pars Altera)*, ed. Felix Heinimann and Emanuel Kienzle (Amsterdam: North-Holland, 1981), 466–67; and also Aristophanes, *Birds*, in idem, *Birds, Lysistrata, Women at the Thesmophoria*, trans. Jeffrey Henderson (Cambridge: Harvard Univ. Press, 2000), 1589–90: "ΠΕΙΣΕΤΑΙΡΟΣ: ἔλαιον οὐκ ἔνεστιν ἐν τῇ ληκύθῳ. / ΗΡΑΚΛΗΣ: καὶ μὴν τά γ' ὀρνίθεια λιπάρ' εἶναι πρέπει"; "PEISETAERUS: There's no oil in the bottle. / HERACLES: And bird meat should be glistening with it."

Engravings for the Observations

125 ***Observations* title page**

AUT CUM HOC AUT IN HOC

(Either with this or in this)

This phrase occurs in an early emblem book by Paolo Giovio, *Dialogo dell'imprese militari et amorose* (Rome: Antonio Barre, 1555), 88–90, where Paolo Giovio tells Ludovico Domenichi that it was the motto carried by

> il gran Marchese di Pescara la prima volta ch'egli andò Capitano generale de tutti cavalli leggieri, la qual fu ben veduta de nemici nel fatto d'arme di

> Ravenna, nel quale esso Marchese per difendere la bandiera sua fu gravemente ferito, e poi trovato fra morti, fatto prigione de Frazesi.
>
> DOM. Dite Mons. che portava egli nella bandiere e sopravesta.
>
> GIO. Un targone Spartano col motto, AVT CVM HOC, AVT IN HOC, Quale la magnanima Donna porse al figliuolo che andava alla battaglia di Mantinea, volendo intendere ch'il figliuolo si deliberasse di combattere si valorosamente che riportasse vittoria, ò morendo come generoso e degno del nome Spartano, fosse riportato morto nel targone à casa, come era anchora antica usanza di Greci, notata etiadio da Verg. IMPOSITVM SCVTO REFERVNT PALLANTA FREQVENTES, Il che anche si coprende dalle parole di quel famoso Epaminonda Spartano, che essendo stato nella battaglia ferito à morte e riportato da suoi soldati, domandò con grande istanza s'el suo scudo era salvo; et essendogli risposto di sì, morendo dimostrò segno d'alegrezza. Fu la detta inventione del nobile Poeta M. Pietro Gravina.
>
> (the grand marchese of Pescara the first time that he was general captain of all light cavalry, which was evident to his opponents at the battle of Ravenna [in 1512], in which this marchese was gravely injured in defending his flag and then found among the dead and made prisoner by the French.
>
> DOM. Tell me, sir, what was his flag and surcoat.
>
> GIO. A Spartan shield with the motto, AVT CVM HOC, AVT IN HOC [Either with this or on this], which the noble lady gave to the son who was going to the battle of Mantinea [in Greece], wishing to make it understood that he was to fight very valiently to obtain victory or, dying with the largesse and dignity worthy of the Spartan name, come back dead on the shield, as was then the ancient custom of the Greeks, noted by Verg[il, *Aeneid* 10.506], IMPOSITVM SCVTO REFERVNT PALLANTA FREQVENTES [laying young Pallas on his shield they bore him back], and that also includes words from the famous Spartan Epaminondas, who having been mortally wounded in battle [at Mantinea in 362 B.C.] and carried to his soldiers, asked them, with great urgency, whether his shield was safe, and having been told yes, died showing signs of great joy. It was the invention of the noble poet Pietro Gravina.)

In the much abridged English version entitled *The Worthy Tract of Paulus Jovius*, trans. Samuel Daniel (London: Simon Waterson, 1585), Eviii^{r}, the motto is translated as "Either with this or on this."

This phrase also appears in Giambattista Vico, *Principj di scienza nuova d'intorno alla comune natura delle nazioni*, 3d ed. (Naples: Stamperia Muziana, a spese di Gaetano, e Steffano Elia, 1744; reprint, Florence: Leo S. Olschki, 1994), 232: "il motto della *Madre Spartana*, che consegna lo *scudo* al figliuolo, che va alla guerra, dicendo, *aut cum hoc, aut in hoc*, volendo dire, *ritorna o con questo, o sopra una bara*"; *The New Science of Giambattista Vico*, trans. Thomas Goddard Bergin and Max Harold Fisch (Ithaca: Cornell Univ. Press, 1984), 185 (§529): "the phrase of the Spartan mother, presenting the shield to her son as he goes to war, *aut cum hoc, aut in hoc*, must be understood as meaning 'Return with this or on a bier.'"

126 **"Observations" headpiece**

Capitello ornato di Sirene e delfini, e colonna di marmo a guisa d'un tronco d'albero, giacenti nel Cortile del palazzo di Sua Eccellenza il Sig. Marchese Gabrielli

(Capital ornamented with sirens and dolphins, and a marble column in the form of a tree trunk, lying in the courtyard of the palace of his excellency, the marquis Gabrielli)

127 **"Opinions" headpiece**

REI ANTIQUARIAE LONDINENSI SAC

(To the Royal Society of Antiquaries of London)

Note that Piranesi gave this organization a royal connection that it never actually had; see Joan Evans, *A History of the Society of Antiquaries* (Oxford: printed at the University Press by Charles Batey for the Society of Antiquaries, 1956).

129 **"Introduction" headpiece**

Pinna o merlo Etrusco, posseduto dal Sig. Matteo Nulty pittore Inglese in Roma (*Pinna,* or Etruscan acroterion, in the possession of Mr. Matthew Nulty, English painter in Rome)

Matthew Nulty (ca. 1716–78), an Irish artist, antiquarian, and agent, was a member of Piranesi's circle; see John Ingamells, ed., *A Dictionary of British and Irish Travellers in Italy, 1701–1800, Compiled from the Brinsley Ford Archive* (New York: Yale Univ. Press, 1997), 717–18.

132 **Plate I**

Essais de differentes Frises ou peintures qui se trouvent dans les soûterrains des anciens Etrusques près de Corneto. Le colori est sur le gout des vases Etrusques, sçavoir le noir pour le fonds, et le blanc ou le jaune pour l'oeuvre. Le blanc pour le fonds, et le rouge ou l'azur ou le noir pour l'oeuvre. Le rouge ou l'azur pour le fonds, et le blanc pour l'oeuvre.

(Studies of various friezes or paintings that are in the subterranean chambers of the ancient Etruscans near Corneto [Tarquinia]. The colors are after the taste of Etruscan vases, namely, black for the ground, and white or yellow for the design. White for the ground, and red or blue or black for the design. Red or blue for the ground, and white for the design.)

Problême historique à l'avantage des Tailleurs. Qui des Etrusques ou des Grecs a été l'inventeur de ces espèces de gallons qui out été decouvertes par Piranesi en Toscane dans les cavernes de Corneto et de Chiusi.

(A historical problem of interest to tailors/stonecutters. Were the Etruscans or the Greeks the inventors of these sorts of trimmings, which Piranesi found in Tuscany in the caves of Corneto [Tarquinia] and Chiusi.)

133 **Plate II**

Essais de differentes Frises ou peintures qui se trouvent dans les soûterrains des anciens Etrusques près de Corneto.

(Studies of various friezes or paintings that are in the subterranean chambers of the ancient Etruscans near Corneto [Tarquinia].)

134 **Plate III**

Essais de differentes Frises ou peintures qui se trouvent dans les soûterrains des anciens Etrusques près de Chiusi.

(Studies of various friezes or paintings that are in the subterranean chambers of the ancient Etruscans near Chiusi.)

136 **Plate V**

AEQUUM EST VAS COGNOSCERE ATQUE IGNOSCERE QUAE VETERES FACTITARUNT SI FACIUNT NOVI —TERENTI EUNUCHUS IN PROLOG

(You should know this and make allowances if the moderns do what the ancients used to do. —Terence's *Eunuchus* in the Prologue)

Terence, *The Eunuch*, in idem, *The Lady of Andros, The Self-Tormentor, The Eunuch*, trans. John Sargeaunt (Cambridge: Harvard Univ. Press, 1979), 40–43: "denique / nullumst iam dictum quod non sit dictum prius. / qua re aequomst vos cognoscere atque ignoscere, / quae veteres factitarunt si faciunt novi"; "In fact nothing is said that has not been said before. So you should recognize facts and pardon new playwrights if they present what their predecessors presented before them."

See also John Wilton-Ely, this volume, 77 n. 96.

138 **Plate VII**

OVID XV METAMORPH / RERUMQUE NOVATRIX EX ALIIS ALIAS REDDIT NATURA FIGURAS

(Ovid, *Metamorphoses* XV / And Nature, the great renewer, ever makes up forms from other forms)

Ovid, *Metamorphoses, Books IX–XV*, 2d ed., trans. Frank Justus Miller and G. P. Goold (Cambridge: Harvard Univ. Press, 1984), 15.252–53: "'Nec species sua cuique manet, rerumque novatrix / ex aliis alias reparat natura figuras'"; "'Nothing retains its own form; but Nature, the great renewer, ever makes up forms from other forms.'"

Note that Piranesi has substituted the verb "reddo" for the verb "reparo." See also John Wilton-Ely, this volume, 78 n. 98.

139 **Plate VIII**

POUR NE PAS FAIRE DE CET ART SUBLIME UN VIL METIER OU L'ON NE FEROIT QUE COPIER SANS CHOIX —LE ROY

(So as not to make this sublime art into a vile profession where one would only copy without choice. —Le Roy)

See Julien-David Le Roy, *Les ruines des plus beaux monuments de la Grèce* (Paris: H. L. Guerin & L. F. Delatour, 1758), 2:i:

> Un juste appréciation de ces principes nous feroit éviter deux inconvénients très-dangereux dans l'Architecture, celui de n'admettre aucunes regles, et de ne prendre pour guide, dans la composition des Monuments que le caprice; et celui d'en admettre un trop grand nombre; de gêner par-là l'imagination des Architectes, et de faire de ce Art sublime un espece de métier où chacun ne feroit que copier, sans choix, ce qui a été fait par quelques Architectes anciens.

(A proper understanding of these principles would help us to avoid two highly dangerous pitfalls in architecture: that of accepting no rules, and taking caprice as our sole guide in the composition of monuments; and that of accepting too many, fettering the architect's imagination and reducing this noble art to a kind of craft, confined to the blind copying of a few ancient architects.)

140 **Plate IX**

NOVITATEM MEAM CONTEMNUNT, EGO ILLORUM IGNAVIAM — SALLUST IN INGURT

(They despise my novelty, I their timidity. — Sallust in *Bellum Igurthinum*)

Sallust, *The War with Jugurtha,* in idem, *Sallust,* trans. J. C. Rolfe (Cambridge: Harvard Univ. Press, 1980), 85.14: "Nunc vos existumate facta an dicta pluris sint. Contemnunt novitatem meam, ego illorum ignaviam; mihi fortuna, illis probra obiectantur"; "think now for yourselves whether words or deeds are worth more. They scorn my humble birth, I their worthlessness; I am taunted with my lot in life, they with their infamies."

See also John Wilton-Ely, this volume, 48, 78 n. 99.

Selected Bibliography

Where multiple titles are listed for an author or editor, the entries are arranged chronologically by year of publication, then alphabetically by title.

Piranesi's Published Works with Significant Texts

Prima parte di architetture, e prospettive. Rome: Stamperia de' Fratelli Pagliarini, 1743.

Le antichità romane. 4 vols. Rome: Stamperia di Angelo Rotilj [etc.], 1756.

Lettere di giustificazione scritte a Milord Charlemont e à di lui agenti di Roma. Rome: n.p., 1757. Reprinted in Giovanni Battista Piranesi, *The Polemical Works, Rome 1757, 1761, 1765, 1769,* ed. John Wilton-Ely (Farnborough, England: Gregg, 1972).

Della magnificenza ed architettura de' romani = De Romanorum Magnificentia et Architectura. Rome: n.p., 1761. Reprinted in Giovanni Battista Piranesi, *The Polemical Works, Rome 1757, 1761, 1765, 1769,* ed. John Wilton-Ely (Farnborough, England: Gregg, 1972).

Le rovine del castello dell'Acqua Giulia situato in Roma presso S. Eusebio e falsamente detto dell'Acqua Marcia colla dicharazione di uno de' celebre passi del comentario Frontiniano e sposizione della maniera con cui gli antichi romani distribuiuan le acque per uso della citta. Rome: Stamperia Generoso Salomoni, 1761.

Il Campo Marzio dell'antica Roma = Campus Martius Antiquae Urbis. Rome: n.p., 1762.

Descrizione e disegno dell'emissario del Lago Albano. Rome: n.p., 1762.

I. B. Piranesii Lapides Capitolini, sive, Fasti Consulares Triumphalesq[ue] Romanorum ab Urbe Condita usque ad Tiberium Caesarem. Rome: Typis Generoso Salomoni, 1762.

Antichità d'Albano e di Castel Gandolfo. Rome: n.p., 1764.

Antichità di Cora. Rome: n.p., 1764.

Osservazioni di Gio. Battista Piranesi sopra la lettre de M. Mariette aux auteurs de la Gazette littéraire de l'Europe, *inserita nel supplemento dell'istessa gazzetta stampata dimanche 4. novembre MDCCLIV; e Parere su l'architettura, con una prefazione ad un nuovo trattato Della introduzione e del progresso delle belle arti in Europa ne' tempi antichi.* Rome: Generoso Salomoni, 1765. Reprinted in Giovanni Battista Piranesi, *The Polemical Works, Rome 1757, 1761, 1765, 1769,* ed. John Wilton-Ely (Farnborough, England: Gregg, 1972).

Diverse maniere d'adornare i cammini ed ogni altra parte degli edifizj, desunte dall'ar-

chitettura egizia, etrusca, e greca, con un ragionamento apologetico in difesa dell'architettura egizia, e toscana = Divers Manners of Ornamenting Chimneys and All Other Parts of Houses, Taken from the Egyptian, Tuscan, and Grecian Architecture, with an Apologetical Essay in Defence of the Egyptian and Tuscan Architecture = Differentes manieres d'orner les cheminées et toute autre partie des edifices, tirées de l'architecture egyptienne, etrusque, et greque, avec un discours apologetique en faveur de l'architecture egyptienne, et toscane. Rome: Stamperia Generoso Salomoni, 1769. Reprinted in Giovanni Battista Piranesi, *The Polemical Works, Rome 1757, 1761, 1765, 1769*, ed. John Wilton-Ely (Farnborough, England: Gregg, 1972).

Primary Sources and Publications before 1850

Adam, Robert, and James Adam. *The Works in Architecture of Robert and James Adam = Les ouvrages d'architecture de Robert et Jaques Adam.* 3 vols. London: vols. 1–2: printed for the authors, 1773–79; vol. 3: Priestley & Weale, 1822. Reprint, New York: Dover, 1980. Rev. ed., ed. Robert Oresko, New York: St. Martin's, 1975.

Algarotti, Francesco. *Opere del conte Algarotti.* Cremona, Italy: Lorenzo Manini, 1778–84.

Bianconi, Giovanni Lodovico. "Elogio storico del cavaliere Giambattista Piranesi." *Antologia romana,* no. 34 (1779): 265–84. Reprinted in Giovanni Lodovico Bianconi, *Opere,* vol. 2, *Lettere al marchese Filippo Hercolani* (Milan: Tipografia de' Classici Italiani, 1802), 125–40; and in "L'*Elogio* di Bianconi," *Grafica grafica* 2 (1976): 127–35.

Bottari, Giovanni, and Stefano Ticozzi. *Raccolta di lettere sulla pittura, scultura ed architettura scritte da' più celebri personaggi del secoli XV, XVI e XVII.* 8 vols. Milan: G. Silvestri, 1822–25.

Caylus, Anne Claude Philippe, comte de. *Recueil d'antiquités egyptiennes, etrusques, grecques et romaines.* 7 vols. Paris: Desaint & Saillant, 1752–67.

Chambers, Sir William. *A Treatise on Civil Architecture, in Which the Principles of That Art Are Laid Down, and Illustrated by a Great Number of Plates Accurately Designed, and Elegantly Engraved by the Best Hands.* London: printed for the author by J. Haberkorn, 1759. The third edition of this work, published in 1791, as well as various later editions, is entitled *A Treatise on the Decorative Part of Civil Architecture.*

Correspondance des directeurs de l'Académie de France à Rome avec les surintendants des bâtiments. 18 vols. Paris: Charavay frères, 1887–1912.

Gazette littéraire de l'Europe. Paris, 1764–84.

d'Hancarville, Pierre-François Hugues, called Baron. *Collection of Etruscan, Greek, and Roman Antiquities from the Cabinet of the Honble. Wm. Hamilton = Antiquités étrusques, grecques, et romaines tirées du cabinet du M. William Hamilton.* 4 vols. Naples: imprimé par François Morelli, [1767–76].

Laugier, Marc-Antoine. *Essai sur l'architecture.* Paris: Duchesne, 1753. Published in English as *An Essay on Architecture,* trans. Wolfgang Herrmann and Anni Herrmann (Los Angeles: Hennessey & Ingalls, 1977).

———. *Observations sur l'architecture.* The Hague: Desaint, 1765. Reprint, Geneva: Minkoff, 1972.

Legrand, Jacques Guillaume. "Notice historique sur la vie et les ouvrages de J. B. Piranesi. . . . Rédigée sur les notes et les pièces communiquées per ses fils, les compagnons et les continuateurs de ses nombreaux travaux [Paris, 1799]." Nouv. acq. franç. 5968, Département des Manuscrits. Bibliothèque Nationale de France, Paris. Transcribed in Gilbert Erouart and Monique Mosser, "À propos de la 'Notice historique sur la vie et les ouvrages de J.-B. Piranesi': Origine et fortune d'une biographie," in Georges Brunel, ed., *Piranèse et les Français: Colloque tenu à la Villa Médicis, 12–14 mai 1976* (Rome: Edizioni dell'Elefante, 1978), 221–52.

Le Roy, Julien-David. *Les ruines des plus beaux monuments de la Grèce.* 2 vols. Paris: H. L. Guerin & L. F. Delatour [etc.], 1758.

Memmo, Andrea. *Elementi d'architettura Lodoliana; ossia, L'arte del fabbricare con solidità scientifica e con eleganza non capricciosa.* 2 vols. Zara, Italy: Tipi dei Fratelli Battara, 1833. Reprint, Milan: G. Mazzotta, 1973.

Milizia, Francesco. *Roma, delle belle arti del disegno: Parte prima: Dell'architettura civile.* Bassano, Vicenza, Italy: [G. Remondini], 1787.

Montfaucon, Bernard de. *L'antiquité expliquée et représentée en figures.* 5 vols. in 10. Paris: Florentin Delaulne [etc.], 1719–24. Published in English as *Antiquity Explained and Represented in Sculptures,* trans. David Humphreys, 7 vols. (London: J. Jonson & J. Watts, 1721–25).

Soane, Sir John. "Lectures on Architecture [1809–36]." In David Watkin, *Sir John Soane: Enlightenment Thought and the Royal Academy Lectures,* 489–667. Cambridge: Cambridge Univ. Press, 1996.

Stuart, James, and Nicholas Revett. *The Antiquities of Athens Measured and Delineated.* 4 vols. London: printed by J. Haberkorn [etc.], 1762–1816. Reprint, New York: B. Blom, 1968.

Winckelmann, Johann Joachim. *Gedanken über die Nachahmung der griechischen Wercke in der Mahlerey und Bildhauer-Kunst.* Friedrichstadt, Germany: gedruckt bey Christian Heinrich Hagenmüller, 1755. Reprint, Nendeln, Liechtenstein: Kraus Reprint, 1968. Reprint, with English translation by Elfriede Heyer and Roger C. Norton, La Salle, Ill.: Open Court, 1987. Published in English as *Reflections on the Painting and Sculpture of the Greeks,* trans. Henry Fuseli (London: printed by A. Millar, 1765; reprint, London: Routledge/Thoemmes, 1999).

———. *Anmerkungen über die Baukunst der Alten.* Leipzig: verlegts Johann Gottfried Dyck, 1762. Reprint, Baden-Baden: Heitz, 1964.

———. *Geschichte der Kunst des Alterthums.* Dresden: aus der Breitkopfischen Buchdruckerey, 1764. Reprint, Baden-Baden: Heitz, 1966.

Secondary Sources and Publications after 1850

Articles, Books, and Papers Focused on Piranesi

Bacou, Roseline, ed. *Piranèse: Gravures et dessins.* Paris: Chêne, 1974. Published in English as *Piranesi: Etchings and Drawings* (London: Thames & Hudson, 1975).

Bertelli, Carlo, ed. *Grafica grafica* 2 (1976). Issue devoted to holdings of Piranesi's works at the Calcografia Nazionale, Rome, produced to accompany an exhibition held at the Calcografia Nazionale (includes the exhibition catalog, Teresa Villa Salamon, ed., "Catalogo," pp. 7–49).

Bettagno, Alessandro, ed. *Piranesi tra Venezia e l'Europa*. Proceedings, Fondazione Giorgio Cini, Venice, 13–15 October 1978. Florence: Leo S. Olschki, 1983.

Bloomer, Jennifer. *Architecture and the Text: The (S)crypts of Joyce and Piranesi.* New Haven: Yale Univ. Press, 1993.

Braham, Allan. "Piranesi as Archaeologist and French Architecture in the Late Eighteenth Century." In Georges Brunel, ed., *Piranèse et les Français: Colloque tenu à la Villa Médicis, 12–14 mai 1976,* 67–76. Rome: Edizioni dell'Elefante, 1978.

Brauer, Heinrich. "Gio. Batt. Piranesi verwirklicht einen Traum: Einen Zeichnung zum St. Basilius-Altar in Sta. Maria del Priorato." In *Miscellanea Bibliothecae Hertzianae zu Ehren von Leo Bruhns, Franz Graf Wolff Metternich, Ludwig Schudt,* 474–77. Munich: Verlag Anton Schroll, 1961.

Brunel, Georges, ed. *Piranèse et les Français: Colloque tenu à la Villa Médicis, 12–14 mai 1976*. Rome: Edizioni dell'Elefante, 1978.

Calvesi, Maurizio. "Saggio introduttivo." In Henri Focillon, *Giovanni Battista Piranesi,* ed. Maurizio Calvesi and Augusta Monferini, trans. Giuseppe Guglielmi, iii–xlii. Bologna: Alfa, 1967.

———. "Nota ai 'grotteschi' o capricci di Piranesi." In Anna Lo Bianco, ed., *Piranesi e la cultura antiquaria, gli antecedenti e il contesto: Atti del convegno, 14–17 novembre 1979,* 135–40. Rome: Multigrafica, 1983.

Cavicchi, Adriano, and Silla Zamboni. "Due 'taccuini' inediti di Piranesi." In Alessandro Bettagno, ed., *Piranesi tra Venezia e l'Europa,* 177–216. Proceedings, Fondazione Giorgio Cini, Venice, 13–15 October 1978. Florence: Leo S. Olschki, 1983.

Cochetti, Lorenza. "L'opera teorica di Piranesi." *Commentari* 6 (1955): 35–49.

Connors, Joseph. "Il Libro dei conti della Avery Architectural Library della Columbia University." In Barbara Jatta, ed., *Piranesi e l'Aventino,* 86–94. Exh. cat., Santa Maria del Priorato, Rome, 16 September–8 December 1998. Milan: Electa, 1998.

Contardi, Bruno. "Piranesi come architetto." In Elisa Debenedetti, ed., *Giovanni Battista Piranesi: La raccolta di stampe della Biblioteca Fardelliana,* 47–56. Exh. cat., Palazzo Milo, Trapani, 15 March–25 April 1996. Trapani, Italy: Corrao, 1996.

———. "Piranesi e la corte Rezzonico." In Barbara Jatta, ed., *Piranesi e l'Aventino,* 49–55. Exh. cat., Santa Maria del Priorato, Rome, 16 September–8 December 1998. Milan: Electa, 1998.

Conti, Vincenzo, ed. *Piranesi: Vedute e antichità di Tivoli.* Exh. cat., Palazzo di Villa d'Este, Tivoli, n.d. Rome: Vincenzo Conti, 1996.

Cristofani, Mauro. "Le opere teoriche di G. B. Piranesi e l'etruscheria." In Anna Lo Bianco, ed., *Piranesi e la cultura antiquaria, gli antecedenti e il contesto: Atti del convegno, 14–17 novembre 1979,* 211–20. Rome: Multigrafica, 1983.

Debenedetti, Elisa. "Disegni del Valadier in rapporto alle tecniche del Piranesi." In Anna Lo Bianco, ed., *Piranesi e la cultura antiquaria, gli antecedenti e il contesto:*

Atti del convegno, 14–17 novembre 1979, 385–404. Rome: Multigrafica, 1983.

———. "Piranesi teorico." In Elisa Debenedetti, ed., *Giovanni Battista Piranesi: La raccolta di stampe della Biblioteca Fardelliana,* 23–44. Exh. cat., Palazzo Milo, Trapani, 15 March–25 April 1996. Trapani, Italy: Corrao, 1996.

de Seta, Cesare. "Luigi Vanvitelli e Giovan Battista Piranesi: Un'ipotesi integrativa del ruolo sociale dell'artista a metà Settecento." In Alessandro Bettagno, ed., *Piranesi tra Venezia e l'Europa,* 103–25. Proceedings, Fondazione Giorgio Cini, Venice, 13–15 October 1978. Florence: Leo S. Olschki, 1983. Revised version published in Cesare de Seta, ed., *Luigi Vanvitelli* (Naples: Electa, 1998), 167–75.

Di Castro, Eugenio. "Giovanni Battista Piranesi e i mobili del Settecento romano." *L'urbe* 24, n.s., no. 2 (1961): 23–28.

Dixon, Susan M. "Giovanni Battista Piranesi's *Diverse maniere d'adornare i cammini* and Chimneypiece Design as a Vehicle for Polemic." *Studies in the Decorative Arts* 1, no. 1 (1993): 76–98.

Ebert, Hans, and Renate Kroll. *Rom in Ansichten von Giovanni Battista Piranesi.* Exh. cat., Kupferstichkabinett und Sammlung der Zeichnungen, Berlin, East Germany, n.d. Berlin: Staatliche Museen zu Berlin, [1972].

Eisenstein, Sergei. "Piranesi, or the Fluidity of Forms." Translated by Roberta Reeder. *Oppositions,* no. 11 (1977): 83–110. Reprinted in Manfredo Tafuri, *The Sphere and the Labyrinth: Avant-Gardes and Architecture from Piranesi to the 1970s,* trans. Pellegrino d'Acierno and Robert Connolly (Cambridge: MIT Press, 1987), 65–90.

Erichsen, Johannes. "Eine Zeichnung zu Piranesis *Prima parte.*" *Pantheon* 34 (1976): 212–16.

Fasolo, Vincenzo. "Il *Campo Marzio* di G. B. Piranesi." *Quaderni dell'Istituto di storia dell'architettura,* no. 15 (1956): 1–14.

Fischer, Manfred F. "Die Umbaupläne des Giovanni Battista Piranesi für den Chor von S. Giovanni in Laterano." *Münchner Jahrbuch der bildenden Kunst,* 3d ser., 19 (1968): 207–28.

Fischer, Marianne. "Giovanni Battista Piranesi." In Sabine Jacob, ed., *Italienische Zeichnungen der Kunstbibliothek Berlin: Architektur und Dekoration 16. bis 18. Jahrhundert,* 169–77 (cat. nos. 858–900). Berlin: Staatliche Museen Preussischer Kulturbesitz, 1975.

Focillon, Henri. *Giovanni-Battista Piranesi: Essai de catalogue raisonné de son oeuvre.* Paris: Libraire Renouard/Henri Laurens, 1918.

———. *Giovanni-Battista Piranesi, 1720–1778.* Paris: Henri Laurens, 1918.

Garms, Jörg. "Considérations sur la *Prima parte.*" In Georges Brunel, ed., *Piranèse et les Français: Colloque tenu à la Villa Médicis, 12–14 mai 1976,* 265–80. Rome: Edizioni dell'Elefante, 1978.

Gasparri, Carlo. "Piranesi a Villa Albani." In *Committenze della famiglia Albani—Note sulla Villa Albani Torlonia,* 211–19. Studi sul Settecento romano, 1/2. Rome: Multigrafica, 1985.

Gavuzzo-Stewart, Silvia. *Nelle carceri di G. B. Piranesi.* Leeds: Northern Universities Press, 1999.

González-Palacios, Alvar. "Piranesiana." In idem, *Il tempio del gusto: Roma e il Regno delle Due Sicilie: Le arti decorative in Italia fra classicismi e barocco,* 1:113–48. Milan: Longanesi, 1984.

Harris, John. "Le Geay, Piranesi and International Neo-Classicism in Rome, 1740–1750." In Douglas Fraser, Howard Hibbard, and Milton J. Lewine, eds., *Essays in the History of Architecture Presented to Rudolf Wittkower,* 189–96. London: Phaidon, 1967.

Hind, Arthur M. *Giovanni Battista Piranesi: A Critical Study with a List of His Published Works and Detailed Catalogues of the Prisons and the Views of Rome.* London: Cotswold Gallery, 1922. Reprint, London: Holland, 1978.

Höper, Corinna, Jeannette Stoschek, and Elisabeth Kieven, eds. *Giovanni Battista Piranesi—Die Wahrnehmung von Raum und Zeit.* Proceedings, Staatsgalerie Stuttgart, 25 and 26 June 1999. Marburg: Jonas, 2002.

Junod, Philippe. "Tradition et innovation dans l'esthétique de Piranèse." *Études de lettres* (Lausanne), no. 199 (1983): 3–24.

Kaufmann, Emil. "Piranesi, Algarotti and Lodoli (A Controversy in Eighteenth Century Venice)." *Gazette des beaux-arts,* 6th ser., 46 (1955): 21–28. Reprinted in Ernst Gombrich, Julius S. Held, and Otto Kurz, eds., *Essays in Honor of Hans Tietze, 1880–1954* (New York: Gazette des Beaux-Arts, 1958), 309–16.

Keller, Luzius. *Piranèse et les Romantiques français: Le mythe des escaliers en spirale.* Paris: José Corti, 1966.

Körte, Werner. "Giovanni Battista Piranesi als praktischer Architekt." *Zeitschrift für Kunstgeschichte* 2 (1933): 16–33.

Kupfer, Alexander. *Piranesis* Carceri*: Enge und Unendlichkeit in den Gefängnissen der Phantasie*. Stuttgart: Belser, 1992.

Lehmann, Karl. "Piranesi as Interpreter of Roman Architecture." In [Robert O. Parks et al.], *Piranesi,* 88–98. Exh. cat., Smith College Museum of Art, 4 April–4 May 1959. Northampton, Mass.: Smith College Museum of Art, 1961.

Lo Bianco, Anna, ed. *Piranesi e la cultura antiquaria, gli antecedenti e il contesto: Atti del convegno, 14–17 novembre 1979*. Rome: Multigrafica, 1983.

MacDonald, William L. *Piranesi's* Carceri: *Sources of Invention*. Northampton, Mass.: Smith College, 1979.

MacDonald, William L., and John A. Pinto. "Piranesi and Archaeology." In idem, *Hadrian's Villa and Its Legacy,* 246–65. New Haven: Yale Univ. Press, 1995.

Mayor, A. Hyatt. *Giovanni Battista Piranesi.* New York: H. Bittner, 1952.

McCarthy, Michael. "Documents of the Greek Revival in Architecture." *Burlington Magazine* 114 (1972): 760–69.

———. "Sir Roger Newdigate and Piranesi." *Burlington Magazine* 114 (1972): 466–72.

———. "Thomas Pitt, Piranesi and John Soane: English Architects in Italy in the 1770s." *Apollo* 134 (1991): 380–86.

———. "Andrew Lumisden and Giovanni Battista Piranesi." In Clare Hornsby, ed., *The Impact of Italy: The Grand Tour and Beyond,* 65–81. London: British School at Rome, 2000.

Melis, Paolo. "G. B. Piranesi: Un *Ampio magnifico collegio* per l'architettura: Intenzionalità iconologica in un documento storico dell'Illuminismo." *Psicon,* no. 4 (1975): 85–100.

Messina, Maria Grazia. "Teoria dell'architettura in Giovanbattista Piranesi: L'affermazione dell'eclettismo." *Controspazio* 2, nos. 8–9 (1970): 6–13; 3, no. 6 (1971): 20–28.

———. "Piranesi: L'ornato e il gusto egizio." In Anna Lo Bianco, ed., *Piranesi e la cultura antiquaria, gli antecedenti e il contesto: Atti del convegno, 14–17 novembre 1979*, 375–84. Rome: Multigrafica, 1983.

Miller, Norbert. *Archäologie des Traums: Versuch über Giovanni Battista Piranesi.* Munich: Carl Hanser, 1978. Reprint, Munich: Deutscher Taschenbuch, 1994.

Minor, Heather Hyde. "Rejecting Piranesi." *Burlington Magazine* 143 (2001): 412–19.

Molajoli, Bruno. "Piranesi architetto." *Bolletino del Centro internazionale di studi di architettura "Andrea Palladio"* 5 (1963): 212–14.

Monferini, Augusta. "Piranesi e Bottari." In Anna Lo Bianco, ed., *Piranesi e la cultura antiquaria, gli antecedenti e il contesto: Atti del convegno, 14–17 novembre 1979*, 221–29. Rome: Multigrafica, 1983.

———. "Piranesi e l'ambiente di Ridolfino Venuti." In Alessandro Bettagno, ed., *Piranesi tra Venezia e l'Europa*, 35–44. Proceedings, Fondazione Giorgio Cini, Venice, 13–15 October 1978. Florence: Leo S. Olschki, 1983.

Murray, Peter. *Piranesi and the Grandeur of Ancient Rome.* London: Thames & Hudson, 1971.

Oechslin, Werner. "Pyramide et sphère: Notes sur l'architecture révolutionnaire du XVIIIe siècle et ses sources italiennes." *Gazette des beaux-arts*, 6th ser., 77 (1971): 201–38.

———. "L'intérêt archéologique et l'expérience architecturale avant et après Piranèse." In Georges Brunel, ed., *Piranèse et les Français: Colloque tenu à la Villa Médicis, 12–14 mai 1976*, 395–418. Rome: Edizioni dell'Elefante, 1978.

Pane, Roberto. *Paestum nelle acqueforti di Piranesi.* Milan: Edizioni di Comunità, 1980.

———. "Piranesi a Paestum." In Alessandro Bettagno, ed., *Piranesi tra Venezia e l'Europa*, 377–88. Proceedings, Fondazione Giorgio Cini, Venice, 13–15 October 1978. Florence: Leo S. Olschki, 1983.

[Patzig, Eberhard, ed.] *Piranesi: Faszination und Ausstrahlung: Begleitpublikation zur Ausstellung im Grassimuseum Leipzig, Museum für Kunsthandwerk.* 2 vols. Leipzig: Grassimuseum Leipzig, 1994.

Penny, Nicholas. *Piranesi.* London: Oresko, 1978.

———. "Antique Sculpture in the Work of Piranesi." In Alessandro Bettagno, ed., *Piranesi tra Venezia e l'Europa*, 45–50. Proceedings, Fondazione Giorgio Cini, Venice, 13–15 October 1978. Florence: Leo S. Olschki, 1983.

Pérouse de Montclos, Jean-Marie. "Piranèse, les Français et le classicisme international." In Georges Brunel, ed., *Piranèse et les Français: Colloque tenu à la Villa Médicis, 12–14 mai 1976*, 419–22. Rome: Edizioni dell'Elefante, 1978.

Pietrangeli, Carlo. "La 'Sala nuova' di Don Abbondio Rezzonico." *Capitolium* 38 (1963): 244–47.

Pinto, John A. "Piranesi at Hadrian's Villa." In Russell T. Scott and Ann Reynolds Scott, eds., *Eius Virtutis Studiosi: Classical and Postclassical Studies in Memory of Frank Edward Brown (1908–1988)*, 465–77. Proceedings, Center for Advanced Study in the Visual Arts, Washington, D.C., 17 and 18 November 1989, and the

American Academy, Rome, 6 June 1989. Studies in the history of art, 43. Washington, D.C.: National Gallery of Art, 1993.

Piranesi, Giovanni Battista. *Protopiro e Didascalo; ovvero, Il confronto fra le ragioni di verità scientifica con i diritti di varietà fantastica raccontato da Giovanbattista Piranesi nel "Parere sull'architettura"; con un sunto antologico dei fatti precedenti all'opera di Piranesi ed un commento dove si ipotizza la sua continuità nell'architettura contemporanea scritto da Sandro Raffone.* Naples: CLEAN (Cooperativa Libraria Editrice Architettura Napoli), 1993.

———. *Scritti di storia e teoria dell'arte.* Edited by Pierluigi Panza. Carnago, Varese, Italy: Sugarco, 1993.

Pressouyre, Sylvia. "La poétique ornementale chez Piranèse et Delafosse." In Georges Brunel, ed., *Piranèse et les Français: Colloque tenu à la Villa Médicis, 12–14 mai 1976,* 423–42. Rome: Edizioni dell'Elefante, 1978.

Puppi, Lionello. "Appunti sulla educazione veneziana di Giambattista Piranesi." In Alessandro Bettagno, ed., *Piranesi tra Venezia e l'Europa,* 217–64. Proceedings, Fondazione Giorgio Cini, Venice, 13–15 October 1978. Florence: Leo S. Olschki, 1983.

Raffone, Sandro. *Protopiro e Didascalo; ovvero, Il confronto fra le ragioni di verità scientifica con i diritti di varieta fantastica. . . .* Naples: CLEAN (Cooperativa Libraria Editrice Architettura Napoli), 1993.

Reudenbach, Bruno. *G. B. Piranesi, Architektur als Bild: Der Wandel in der Architekturauffassung des achtzehnten Jahrhunderts.* Munich: Prestel, 1979.

Rieder, William. "Piranesi's *Diverse maniere.*" *Burlington Magazine* 115 (1973): 309–17.

———. "Piranesi at Gorhambury." *Burlington Magazine* 117 (1975): 582–91.

Robison, Andrew. *Piranesi—Early Architectural Fantasies: A Catalogue Raisonné of the Etchings.* Chicago: Univ. of Chicago Press, 1986.

———. "Giovanni Battista Piranesi." In Jane Martineau and Andrew Robison, eds., *The Glory of Venice: Art in the Eighteenth Century,* 376–405. Exh. cat., Royal Academy of Arts, London, 15 September–14 December 1994; and National Gallery of Art, Washington, D.C., 29 January–23 April 1995. New Haven: Yale Univ. Press, 1994.

Rosa, Joseph, ed. *The Imagined and Real Landscapes of Piranesi: Critical Writings in America.* Exh. cat., Rosa Architectural Gallery, Buell Hall, Columbia University, 13 October–12 December 1992. New York: Columbia Books of Architecture, 1992.

Rowan, Alistair. "Wedderburn Castle, Berwickshire." *Country Life,* 8 August 1974, 354–57.

Ruler, Dick van. *Verbeeldingen van werkelijkheid: Speurtochten vanuit de kerkers van Piranesi.* 3 vols. Rotterdam: 010 Uitgeverij, 1992.

Sambricio, Carlos. "Piranesi y el *Parere.*" *Revista de ideas estéticas* (Madrid), no. 117 (1972): 81–101.

Scarisbrick, Diana. "Piranesi and the *Dactyliotheca Zanettiana.*" *Burlington Magazine* 132 (1990): 413–14.

Scott, Jonathan. *Piranesi.* London: Academy Editions, 1975.

———. "Another Chimney Piece by Piranesi." In Alessandro Bettagno, ed., *Piranesi tra Venezia e l'Europa,* 51–57. Proceedings, Fondazione Giorgio Cini, Venice, 13–15 October 1978. Florence: Leo S. Olschki, 1983.

———. "Some Sculpture from Hadrian's Villa, Tivoli." In Anna Lo Bianco, ed., *Piranesi e la cultura antiquaria, gli antecedenti e il contesto: Atti del convegno, 14–17 novembre 1979,* 339–55. Rome: Multigrafica, 1983.

Sekler, Patricia May. "Giovanni Battista Piranesi's *Carceri* Etchings and Related Drawings." *Art Quarterly* (Detroit Institute of Arts) 25 (1962): 331–63.

Stampfle, Felice. *Giovanni Battista Piranesi: Drawings in the Pierpont Morgan Library.* New York: Dover, 1978.

Stillman, Damie. "Robert Adam and Piranesi." In Douglas Fraser, Howard Hibbard, and Milton J. Lewine, eds., *Essays in the History of Architecture Presented to Rudolf Wittkower,* 197–206. London: Phaidon, 1967.

Tafuri, Manfredo. "Giovan Battista Piranesi: L'architettura come 'utopia negativa.'" *Angelus novus: Trimestrale di estetica e critica,* no. 20 (1971): 89–127. Reprinted in *Bernardo Vittone e la disputa fra classicismo e barocco nel Settecento: Atti del convegno internazional promosso dall'Accademia delle scienze di Torino . . . , 21–24 settembre 1970* (Turin: Accademia delle Scienze, 1972), 265–319.

———. "The Dialectics of the Avant-Garde: Piranesi and Eisenstein." Translated by Marlène Barsoum and Liviu Dimitriu. *Oppositions,* no. 11 (1977): 73–80.

———. "'L'architetto scellerato': G. B. Piranesi, l'eterotopia e il vaggio" and "Storicità dell'avanguardia: Piranesi e Ejzenštein." In Manfredo Tafuri, *La sfera e il labirinto: Avanguardie e architettura da Piranesi agli anni '70,* 33–75, 77–88. Turin: Giulio Einaudi, 1980. Published in English as "'The Wicked Architect': G. B. Piranesi, Heterotopia, and the Voyage" and "The Historicity of the Avant-Garde: Piranesi and Eisenstein," in Manfredo Tafuri, *The Sphere and the Labyrinth: Avant-Gardes and Architecture from Piranesi to the 1970s,* trans. Pellegrino d'Acierno and Robert Connolly (Cambridge: MIT Press, 1987), 25–54, 55–64.

———. "Borromini e Piranesi: La città come 'ordine infranto.'" In Alessandro Bettagno, ed., *Piranesi tra Venezia e l'Europa,* 89–101. Proceedings, Fondazione Giorgio Cini, Venice, 13–15 October 1978. Florence: Leo S. Olschki, 1983.

Tait, A. A. "Reading the Ruins: Robert Adam and Piranesi in Rome." *Architectural History* 27 (1984): 524–33.

Thomas, Hylton. *The Drawings of Giovanni Battista Piranesi.* London: Faber & Faber, 1954.

Villa Salamon, Teresa. "Catalogando Piranesi." In Alessandro Bettagno, ed., *Piranesi tra Venezia e l'Europa,* 265–68. Proceedings, Fondazione Giorgio Cini, Venice, 13–15 October 1978. Florence: Leo S. Olschki, 1983.

Vogt-Göknil, Ulya. *Giovanni Battista Piranesi:* Carceri. Zurich: Origo, 1958.

———. "Piranesi als Architekturtheoretiker und Polemiker." In Alessandro Bettagno, ed., *Piranesi tra Venezia e l'Europa,* 389–95. Proceedings, Fondazione Giorgio Cini, Venice, 13–15 October 1978. Florence: Leo S. Olschki, 1983.

Volkmann, Hans. *Giovanni Battista Piranesi, Architekt und Graphiker.* Berlin: Hessling, 1965.

Wallis de Vries, Gijs. *Piranesi en het idee van de prachtige stad.* Amsterdam: Uitgeverij Duizend & Een, 1990.

Watson, Francis J. B. "A Masterpiece of Neo-Classic Furniture: A Side-Table Designed by Piranesi." *Burlington Magazine* 107 (1965): 101–2, figs. 55–57. Expanded in Francis J. B. Watson, "A Side Table by Piranesi: A Masterpiece of Neo-Classic Furniture," *Minneapolis Institute of Arts Bulletin* 54 (1965): 19–30.

Wilton-Ely, John. "A Bust of Piranesi by Nollekens." *Burlington Magazine* 118 (1976): 593–95.

———. "Piranesian Symbols on the Aventine." *Apollo* 103 (1976): 214–27. Reprinted in *Annales de l'Ordre souverain militaire de Malte* 34, nos. 1–2 (1976): 8–23.

———. "*Lettere di giustificazione scritte a Milord Charlemont*"; "Il Ponte di Blackfriars"; "*The Works in Architecture* di Robert e James Adam"; and "*Osservazioni sopra la lettre de M. Mariette. . . .*" In Alessandro Bettagno, ed., *Piranesi: Incisioni, rami, legature, architetture,* 39–40, 50, 51, 55–56. Exh. cat., Fondazione Giorgio Cini, Venice, 1978. Venice: Neri Pozza, 1978.

———. *The Mind and Art of Giovanni Battista Piranesi.* London: Thames & Hudson, 1978. Published in Dutch as *Giovanni Battista Piranesi: Zijn visie en zijn werk,* trans. Coen Pranger (Amsterdam: Meulenhoff, 1978); in German as *Giovanni Battista Piranesi: Vision und Werk,* trans. Johannes Erichsen and Margret Tipton (Munich: Hirmer, 1978); and in Italian as *Piranesi,* trans. Augusto Roca De Amicis (Milan: Electa, 1994).

———. "Piranesi at the Lateran." *Architectural Review,* May 1978, 252–53, 256.

———. "Vision and Design: Piranesi's 'Fantasia' and the Graeco-Roman Controversy." In Georges Brunel, ed., *Piranèse et les Français: Colloque tenu à la Villa Médicis, 12–14 mai 1976,* 529–52. Rome: Edizioni dell'Elefante, 1978.

———. "The Relationship between Giambattista Piranesi and Luigi Vanvitelli in Eighteenth-Century Architectural Theory and Practice." In *Luigi Vanvitelli e il '700 Europeo: Congresso internazionale di studi: Atti,* 2:83–99. Proceedings, Istituto di Storia dell'Architettura, Università di Napoli, 5–10 November 1979. Naples: Arte Tipografica, 1979.

———. "Giovanni Battista Piranesi." In Dora Wiebenson, ed., *Architectural Theory and Practice from Alberti to Ledoux,* cat. no. II-32. Exh. cat., Sterling Library, Yale University, 1 March–31 May 1982; Low Memorial Library, Columbia University, 4 November–2 December 1982; Art Library, University of California, Los Angeles, 26 May–4 August 1983; and Alderman Library, University of Virginia, 12 February–27 April 1984. Chicago: Architectural Publications, 1982.

———. "Piranesi and the Role of Archaeological Illustration." In Anna Lo Bianco, ed., *Piranesi e la cultura antiquaria, gli antecedenti e il contesto: Atti del convegno, 14–17 novembre 1979,* 317–37. Rome: Multigrafica, 1983.

———. "Utopia or Megalopolis? The *Ichnographia* of Piranesi's *Campus Martius* Reconsidered." In Alessandro Bettagno, ed., *Piranesi tra Venezia e l'Europa,* 293–304. Proceedings, Fondazione Giorgio Cini, Venice, 13–15 October 1978. Florence: Leo S. Olschki, 1983.

———. "Soane and Piranesi." In Roger White and Caroline Lightburn, eds., *Late Georgian Classicism: Papers Given at the Georgian Group Symposium 1987,* 45–57. London: Georgian Group, 1988.

———. "Giovanni Battista Piranesi." *Composición arquitectonica, Art and Architecture* (Bilbao), no. 6 (1990): 72–102.

———. "Nature and Antiquity: Reflections on Piranesi as a Furniture Designer." *Furniture History* 26 (1990): 191–97.

———. "The Art of Polemic: Piranesi and the Graeco-Roman Controversy." In Philippe Boutry et al., eds., *La Grecia antica: Mito e simbolo per l'età della grande rivoluzione: Genesi e crisi di un modello nella cultura del Settecento,* 121–30. Proceedings, Accademia Nazionale dei Lincei et al., Rome, 11–15 December 1989. Milan: Guerini, 1991.

———. "Giovanni Battista Piranesi." In Cara D. Denison, Myra Nan Rosenfeld, and Stephanie Wiles, *Exploring Rome: Piranesi and His Contemporaries,* xxv–xxxii. Exh. cat., Centre Canadien d'Architecture/Canadian Centre for Architecture, Montreal, 17 August 1993–2 January 1994. New York: Pierpont Morgan Library; Montreal: Centre Canadien d'Architecture/Canadian Centre for Architecture, 1993.

———. *Piranesi as Architect and Designer.* Franklin Jasper Walls Lectures, Series 11, Pierpont Morgan Library, New York, 1980. New York: Pierpont Morgan Library; New Haven: Yale Univ. Press, 1993.

———. *Giovanni Battista Piranesi: The Complete Etchings.* 2 vols. San Francisco: Alan Wofsy Fine Arts, 1994.

———. "Giovanni Battista Piranesi: The Fantasist as Designer." In Eunice D. Howe et al., *The Art of Exaggeration: Piranesi's Perspectives on Rome,* 12–21. Exh. cat., Fisher Gallery, University of Southern California, 22 February–15 April 1995. Los Angeles: Fisher Gallery, 1995.

———. "The Voices of the Imagination: Creative and Critical Responses to Piranesi from His Contemporaries and from Posterity." Getty Lecture Series in Art and Art History, University of Southern California, Los Angeles, 1, 2, and 7 March 1995.

———. "Antiquity Applied: Piranesi, Clérisseau and the Adam Brothers." *Bulletin de l'Association des historiens de l'art italien* (Paris), no. 2 (1995–96): 15–24.

———. "El diseño a través de la fantasía: Los dibujos 'Capricci' de Piranesi." In Mariano J. Ruiz de Ael, ed., *Arquitecturas dibujadas: I jornadas internacionales sobre el estudio y conservación de las fuentes de arquitectura, Vitoria-Gasteiz, mayo 1994,* 81–92. Vitoria-Gasteiz, Spain: Centro Vasco de Arquitectura, 1996.

———. "Piranesi architetto" and "Piranesi: Designer e antiquario." In Barbara Jatta, ed., *Piranesi e l'Aventino,* 63–78, 95–104. Exh. cat., Santa Maria del Priorato, Rome, 16 September–8 December 1998. Milan: Electa, 1998.

———. "Design through Fantasy: Piranesi as Architect." In Corinna Höper, Jeannette Stoschek, and Elisabeth Kieven, eds., *Giovanni Battista Piranesi—Die Wahrnehmung von Raum und Zeit,* 65–88. Proceedings, Staatsgalerie Stuttgart, 25 and 26 June 1999. Marburg: Jonas, 2002.

———. "'Amazing and Ingenious Fancies': Piranesi and Robert Adam." Paper presented at the conference "Piranesi: Nuovi contributi," American Academy in Rome, Centro di Studi sulla Cultura e l'Immagine di Roma, Bibliotheca Hertziana, and Accademia Nazionale dei Lincei, Rome, 6 April 2001.

———. "'Sognare il sublime': L'influenza di Piranesi e della sua scuola sul Grand

Tour." In Cesare de Seta, ed., *Grand Tour: Viaggi narrati e dipinti,* 106–18. Proceedings, Palazzo delle Esposizioni, Rome, 20 and 21 March 1997. Naples: Electa Napoli, 2001.

———. *Piranesi, Paestum and Soane.* London: Sir John Soane's Museum, 2002.

Wittkower, Rudolf. "Piranesi's *Parere su l'architettura.*" *Journal of the Warburg Institute* 2 (1938–39): 147–58. Republished as "Piranesi's Architectural Creed," in Rudolf Wittkower, *Studies in the Italian Baroque* (London: Thames & Hudson, 1975), 235–46.

———. "Piranesi as Architect." In [Robert O. Parks et al.], *Piranesi,* 99–109. Exh. cat., Smith College Museum of Art, 4 April–4 May 1959. Northampton, Mass.: Smith College Museum of Art, 1961. Republished in Rudolf Wittkower, *Studies in the Italian Baroque* (London: Thames & Hudson, 1975), 247–58.

———. "Piranesi e il gusto egiziano." In Vittore Branca, ed., *Sensibilità e razionalità nel Settecento,* 659–74. Conference papers, VII Corso internazionale di alta cultura, Fondazione Giorgio Cini, Venice, 1965. Florence: Sansoni, 1967.

———. "Piranesi and Eighteenth-Century Egyptomania." In idem, *Studies in the Italian Baroque,* 258–73. London: Thames & Hudson, 1975.

Wunder, Richard P. "The Spread of 'Piranesism' to France through Legeay and Challe." In Georges Brunel, ed., *Piranèse et les Français: Colloque tenu à la Villa Médicis, 12–14 mai 1976,* 553–66. Rome: Edizioni dell'Elefante, 1978.

Yourcenar, Marguerite. "Le cerveau noir de Piranèse." In Marguerite Yourcenar, *Sous bénéfice d'inventaire,* 116–69. Paris: Gallimard, 1962. Published in English as "The Dark Brain of Piranesi," in Margueritte Yourcenar, *The Dark Brain of Piranesi and Other Essays,* trans. Richard Howard (Henley-on-Thames, England: Aidan Ellis, 1985), 88–128.

Zamboni, Silla. "Il percorso di Giovanni Battista Piranesi." *Arte antica e moderna,* no. 25 (1964): 66–85.

———. "Due quaderni di Piranesi scoperti nella Biblioteca Estense di Modena." *Studi romani: Rivista trimestrale dell'Istituto di studi romani* 27 (1979): 332–34.

Exhibition Catalogs Focused on Piranesi

Bettagno, Alessandro, ed. *Disegni di Giambattista Piranesi.* Exh. cat., Fondazione Giorgio Cini, Venice, 1978. Venice: Neri Pozza, 1978.

———. *Piranesi: Incisioni, rami, legature, architetture.* Exh. cat., Fondazione Giorgio Cini, Venice, 1978. Venice: Neri Pozza, 1978.

[Brunel, Georges, and Pierre Arizzoli, eds.] *Piranèse et les Français, 1740–1790.* Exh. cat., Villa Medici, Rome; Palais des États de Bourgogne, Dijon; and Hôtel de Sully, Paris, May–November 1976. Rome: Edizioni dell'Elefante, 1976.

[Calvesi, Maurizio.] *Giovanni Battista e Francesco Piranesi.* Exh. cat., Calcografia Nazionale, Rome, 1967–68. Rome: De Luca, 1967.

[Campbell, Malcolm, ed.] *Piranesi: Rome Recorded: A Complete Edition of Giovanni Battista Piranesi's* Vedute di Roma *from the Collection of the Arthur Ross Foundation.* Exh. cat., Arthur Ross Gallery, University of Pennsylvania, 5 May–14 June 1989. New York: Arthur Ross Foundation, 1989.

Catelli Isola, Maria, Amalia Mezzetti, and Silla Zamboni, eds. *Mostra di incisioni di*

G. B. Piranesi. Exh. cat., Palazzo di Re Enzo, Bologna, 27 January–24 February 1963. Bologna: Edizioni Alfa, 1963.

[Croft-Murray, Edward.] *Giovanni Battista Piranesi: His Predecessors and His Heritage.* Exh. cat., British Museum, London, n.d. London: Trustees of the British Museum, 1968.

Debenedetti, Elisa, ed. *Giovanni Battista Piranesi: La raccolta di stampe della Biblioteca Fardelliana.* Exh. cat., Palazzo Milo, Trapani, 15 March–25 April 1996. Trapani, Italy: Corrao, 1996.

Denison, Cara D., Myra Nan Rosenfeld, and Stephanie Wiles. *Exploring Rome: Piranesi and His Contemporaries.* Exh. cat., Centre Canadien d'Architecture/ Canadian Centre for Architecture, Montreal, 17 August 1993–2 January 1994. New York: Pierpont Morgan Library; Montreal: Centre Canadien d'Architecture/Canadian Centre for Architecture, 1993.

Höper, Corinna, with Jeannette Stoschek and Stefan Heinlein. *Giovanni Battista Piranesi: Die poetische Wahrheit: Radierungen.* Exh. cat., Graphische Sammlung, Staatsgalerie Stuttgart, 27 March–27 June 1999. Ostfildern-Ruit: Verlag Gerd Hatje, 1999.

Howe, Eunice D., et al. *The Art of Exaggeration: Piranesi's Perspectives on Rome.* Exh. cat., Fisher Gallery, University of Southern California, 22 February–15 April 1995. Los Angeles: Fisher Gallery, 1995.

Jatta, Barbara, ed. *Piranesi e l'Aventino.* Exh. cat., Santa Maria del Priorato, Rome, 16 September–8 December 1998. Milan: Electa, 1998.

Kieven, Elisabeth, ed. *Von Bernini bis Piranesi: Römische Architekturzeichnungen des Barock.* Exh. cat., Graphische Sammlung, Staatsgalerie Stuttgart, 1993. Stuttgart: Verlag Gerd Hatje, 1993.

Lütgens, Annelie. *Giovanni Battista Piranesi: Bilder von Orten und Räumen.* Exh. cat., Hamburger Kunsthalle, 19 May–17 July 1994. Stuttgart: Verlag Gerd Hatje, 1994.

[Nyberg, Dorothea, ed.] *Giovanni Battista Piranesi: Drawings and Etchings at Columbia University.* Exh. cat., Low Memorial Library, Columbia University, 21 March–14 April 1972. New York: Avery Architectural Library/Department of Art History & Archaeology, Columbia University, 1972.

[Nyberg, Dorothea, and Herbert Mitchell.] *Piranesi: Drawings and Etchings at the Avery Architectural Library, Columbia University, New York: The Arthur M. Sackler Collection.* Exh. cat., traveling exhibition, October 1975–December 1978. New York: Arthur M. Sackler Foundation, 1975.

[Parks, Robert O., et al.] *Piranesi.* Exh. cat., Smith College Museum of Art, 4 April–4 May 1959. Northampton, Mass.: Smith College Museum of Art, 1961.

Robison, Andrew. *Giovanni Battista Piranesi: The Early Architectural Fantasies: A Guide to the Exhibition.* Exh. cat., National Gallery of Art, Washington, D.C., 1 June–1 October 1978. Washington, D.C.: National Gallery of Art, 1978.

Salamon, Fernando, ed. *G. B. Piranesi: Acqueforti e disegni.* Exh. cat., Galleria Civica d'Arte Moderna, Turin, 1 December 1961–21 January 1962. Turin: Galleria Civica d'Arte Moderna, 1961.

[Santoro, Pasquale, Renato Flenghi, Giovanna Martinelli, and Cecilia Valli, eds.] *Piranesi nei luoghi di Piranesi.* 5 vols. in 1. Exh. cat., five-part exhibition held simultaneously in Rome at the Orti Farnesiani, Castel Sant'Angelo, Istituto Nazionale per la Grafica-Calcografia, and Santa Maria del Priorato, and in Cori at the Palazzetto Luciani, 1979. Rome: Multigrafica/Fratelli Palombi, 1979.

Wilton-Ely, John. *Piranesi.* Exh. cat., Hayward Gallery, London, 27 April–11 June 1978. London: Arts Council of Great Britain, 1978.

Wilton-Ely, John, with Joseph Connors. *Piranesi architetto.* Exh. cat., American Academy in Rome, 15 May–4 July 1992. Rome: Edizioni dell'Elefante, 1992.

Piranesi's Artistic, Intellectual, and Historical Context

The Age of Neo-Classicism. Exh. cat., Royal Academy, London, and Victoria and Albert Museum, London, 9 September–19 November 1972. London: Arts Council of Great Britain, 1972.

Bassi, Elena. *Architettura del Sei e Settecento a Venezia.* Naples: Edizioni Scientifiche Italiane, 1962.

Borsi, Franco, ed. *Fortuna degli etruschi.* Exh. cat., Sotterranei dello Spedale degli Innocenti, Florence, 16 May–20 October 1985. Milan: Electa, 1985.

Boutry, Philippe, et al., eds. *La Grecia antica: Mito e simbolo per l'età della grande rivoluzione: Genesi e crisi di un modello nella cultura del Settecento.* Proceedings, Accademia Nazionale dei Lincei and Istituto Svizzero di Roma, Rome; and Università di Salerno, Fisciano, 11–15 December 1989. Milan: Guerini, 1991.

Bowron, Edgar Peters, and Joseph J. Rishel, eds. *Art in Rome in the Eighteenth Century.* Exh. cat., Philadelphia Museum of Art, 16 March–28 May 2000; and Museum of Fine Arts, Houston, 25 June–17 September 2000. London: Merrell, 2000.

Braham, Allan. *The Architecture of the French Enlightenment.* London: Thames & Hudson, 1980.

Brusatin, Manlio, ed. *Illuminismo e architettura del '700 Veneto.* Exh. cat., Palazzo del Monte, Castelfranco Veneto, 31 August–9 November 1969. Resina, Treviso, Italy: Grafiche Giorgio Paroni, 1969.

Collins, Peter. *Changing Ideals in Modern Architecture, 1750–1950.* 2d ed. Montreal: McGill-Queen's Univ. Press, 1998.

Colvin, Howard. *A Biographical Dictionary of British Architects, 1660–1840.* 3d ed. New Haven: Yale Univ. Press, 1995.

Contardi, Bruno, and Giovanna Curcio, eds. *In Urbe Architectus: Modelli, disegni, misure: La professione dell'architetto Roma 1680–1750.* Exh. cat., Museo Nazionale di Castel Sant'Angelo, Rome, 12 December–29 February 1992. Rome: Àrgos, 1991.

Cristofani, Mauro. *La scoperta degli etruschi: Archeologia e antiquaria nel '700.* Rome: Consiglio Nazionale delle Ricerche, 1983.

Crook, J. Mordaunt. *The Greek Revival: Neo-Classical Attitudes in British Architecture, 1760–1870.* Rev. ed. London: John Murray, 1995.

De Grummond, Nancy Thomson, ed. *An Encyclopedia of the History of Classical Archaeology.* 2 vols. Westport, Conn.: Greenwood, 1996.

Den Broeder, Frederick. *The Academy of Europe: Rome in the Eighteenth Century.* Exh. cat., William Benton Museum of Art, University of Connecticut, Storrs, 13 October–21 November 1973. Storrs: University of Connecticut Foundation, 1973.

de Seta, Cesare, ed. *Grand Tour: Viaggi narrati e dipinti.* Proceedings, Palazzo delle Esposizioni, Rome, 20 and 21 March 1997. Naples: Electa Napoli, 2001.

Eriksen, Svend. *Early Neo-Classicism in France: The Creation of the Louis Seize Style . . . in the Mid-Eighteenth Century.* Translated and edited by Peter Thornton. London: Faber & Faber, 1974.

Evans, Joan. *A History of the Society of Antiquaries.* Oxford: printed at the University Press by Charles Batey for the Society of Antiquaries, 1956.

Fleming, John. *Robert Adam and His Circle in Edinburgh and Rome.* London: John Murray, 1962.

González-Palacios, Alvar. *Il tempio del gusto: Roma e il Regno delle Due Sicilie: Le arti decorative in Italia fra classicismi e barocco.* 2 vols. Milan: Longanesi, 1984.

Harris, Eileen. *The Genius of Robert Adam: His Interiors.* New Haven: Yale Univ. Press, 2001.

Harris, Eileen, with Nicholas Savage. *British Architectural Books and Writers, 1556–1785.* Cambridge: Cambridge Univ. Press, 1990.

Harris, John. *Sir William Chambers: Knight of the Polar Star.* London: A. Zwemmer, 1970.

Harris, John, and Michael Snodin, eds. *Sir William Chambers: Architect to George III.* Exh. cat., Courtauld Gallery, London, 10 October–5 January 1997; and Nationalmuseum, Stockholm, 20 February–20 April 1997. New Haven: Yale Univ. Press, 1996.

Haskell, Francis. *Patrons and Painters: A Study in the Relations between Italian Art and Society in the Age of the Baroque.* Rev. ed. New Haven: Yale Univ. Press, 1980.

Haskell, Francis, and Nicholas Penny. *Taste and the Antique: The Lure of Classical Sculpture, 1500–1900.* New Haven: Yale Univ. Press, 1981.

Herrmann, Wolfgang. *Laugier and Eighteenth Century French Theory.* London: A. Zwemmer, 1962.

Honour, Hugh. *Neo-Classicism.* Rev. ed. Harmondsworth, England: Penguin, 1977.

Hornsby, Clare, ed. *The Impact of Italy: The Grand Tour and Beyond.* London: British School at Rome, 2000.

Howard, Seymour. *Antiquity Restored: Essays on the Afterlife of the Antique.* Vienna: IRSA, 1990.

Humbert, Jean-Marcel, Michael Pantazzi, and Christiane Ziegler. *Egyptomania: Egypt in Western Art, 1730–1930.* Exh. cat., Musée du Louvre, Paris, 20 January–18 April 1994; National Gallery of Canada, Ottawa, 17 June–18 September 1994; and Kunsthistorisches Museum, Vienna, 16 October 1994–29 January 1995. Paris: Réunion des Musées Nationaux; Ottawa: National Gallery of Canada, 1994. Published in French by the same copublishers as *Egyptomania: L'Egypte dans l'art occidental, 1730–1930. Ägyptomanie: Ägypten in der europäischen Kunst, 1730–1930,* the catalog for this exhibition issued in German, has fewer entries.

Ingamells, John, ed. *A Dictionary of British and Irish Travellers in Italy, 1701–1800, Compiled from the Brinsley Ford Archive*. New Haven: Yale Univ. Press, 1997.

Irwin, David. *Neoclassicism*. London: Phaidon, 1997.

Jenkins, Ian, and Kim Sloan. *Vases and Volcanoes: Sir William Hamilton and His Collection*. Exh. cat., British Museum, London, n.d. London: British Museum Press, 1996.

Kaufmann, Edgar, Jr. "Memmo's Lodoli." *Art Bulletin* 46 (1964): 159–75.

Kaufmann, Emil. *Architecture in the Age of Reason: Baroque and Post-Baroque in England, Italy, and France*. Cambridge: Harvard Univ. Press, 1955.

Kieven, Elisabeth. "Roman Architecture in the Time of Piranesi, 1740–1776." In Cara D. Denison, Myra Nan Rosenfeld, and Stephanie Wiles, *Exploring Rome: Piranesi and His Contemporaries*, xv–xxiv. Exh. cat., Centre Canadien d'Architecture/Canadian Centre for Architecture, Montreal, 17 August 1993–2 January 1994. New York: Pierpont Morgan Library; Montreal: Centre Canadien d'Architecture/Canadian Centre for Architecture, 1993.

[Lavagnino, Emilio, et al.] *Il Settecento a Roma*. Exh. cat., Palazzo delle Esposizioni, Rome, 19 March–31 May 1959. Rome: De Luca, 1959.

Lewis, Lesley. *Connoisseurs and Secret Agents in Eighteenth-Century Rome*. London: Chatto & Windus, 1961.

MacDonald, William L., and John A. Pinto. *Hadrian's Villa and Its Legacy*. New Haven: Yale Univ. Press, 1995.

Middleton, Robin, and David Watkin. *Architettura moderna*. Venice: Electa, 1977. Published in English as *Neoclassical and Nineteenth Century Architecture* (New York: Abrams, 1980).

Pevsner, Nikolaus, and Susanne Lang. "The Doric Revival" and "The Egyptian Revival." In Nikolaus Pevsner, *Studies in Art, Architecture and Design*, vol. 1, *From Mannerism to Romanticism*, 197–211, 213–35. London: Thames & Hudson, 1968.

Potts, Alex. *Flesh and the Ideal: Winckelmann and the Origins of Art History*. New Haven: Yale Univ. Press, 1994.

Richardson, Margaret, and MaryAnne Stevens, eds. *John Soane, Architect: Master of Space and Light*. Exh. cat., Royal Academy of Arts, London, 11 September–3 December 1999. London: Royal Academy of Arts, 1999.

Rosenblum, Robert. *Transformations in Late Eighteenth Century Art*. Princeton: Princeton Univ. Press, 1967.

Rykwert, Joseph. "Lodoli on Function and Representation." *Architectural Review*, July 1976, 21–26.

———. *The First Moderns: The Architects of the Eighteenth Century*. Cambridge: MIT Press, 1980.

———. *On Adam's House in Paradise: The Idea of the Primitive Hut in Architectural History*. 2d ed. Cambridge: MIT Press, 1981.

Salmon, Frank. *Building on Ruins: The Rediscovery of Rome and English Architecture*. Burlington, Vt.: Ashgate, 2000.

Serra, Joselita Raspi, ed. *La fortuna di Paestum e la memoria moderna del dorico, 1750–1830*. 2 vols. Exh. cat., Certosa di San Lorenzo a Padula, Salerno, June 1986. Florence: Centro Di, 1986.

———. *Paestum, idea e immagine: Antologia di testi critici e di immagini di Paestum, 1750–1836.* Modena: Franco Cosimo Panini, 1990.

Stillman, Damie. "Chimney-Pieces for the English Market: A Thriving Business in Late Eighteenth-Century Rome." *Art Bulletin* 59 (1977): 85–94.

———. *English Neo-Classical Architecture.* 2 vols. London: A. Zwemmer, 1988.

Summerson, John. *Architecture in Britain, 1530 to 1830.* 9th ed. New Haven: Yale Univ. Press, 1993.

Tafuri, Manfredo. *Teorie e storia dell'architettura.* Bari, Italy: Laterza, 1968. Published in English as *Theories and History of Architecture,* trans. Giorgio Verrecchia (New York: Granada, 1980).

———. *La sfera e il labirinto: Avanguardie e architettura da Piranesi agli anni '70.* Turin: Giulio Einaudi, 1980. Published in English as *The Sphere and the Labyrinth: Avant-Gardes and Architecture from Piranesi to the 1970s,* trans. Pellegrino d'Acierno and Robert Connolly (Cambridge: MIT Press, 1987).

Venturi, Robert. *Complexity and Contradiction in Architecture.* New York: Museum of Modern Art, 1966.

Watkin, David. *Thomas Hope (1769–1831) and the Neo-Classical Idea.* London: John Murray, 1968.

———. *Athenian Stuart: Pioneer of the Greek Revival.* London: George Allen & Unwin, 1982.

———. *Sir John Soane: Enlightenment Thought and the Royal Academy Lectures.* Cambridge: Cambridge Univ. Press, 1996.

Watkin, David, and Tilman Mellinghoff. *German Architecture and the Classical Ideal, 1740–1840.* London: Thames & Hudson, 1987.

Wilton, Andrew, and Ilaria Bignamini, eds. *Grand Tour: The Lure of Italy in the Eighteenth Century.* Exh. cat., Tate Gallery, London, 10 October 1996–5 January 1997; and Palazzo delle Esposizioni, Rome, 5 February–7 April 1997. London: Tate Gallery Publishing, 1996.

Winckelmann, Johann Joachim. *Writings on Art.* Selected and edited by David Irwin. London: Phaidon, 1972.

Wittkower, Rudolf. *Art and Architecture in Italy, 1600 to 1750.* 3d rev. ed., corrected. Harmondsworth, England: Penguin, 1986.

Illustration Credits

Unless otherwise specified, photographs of works by Giovanni Battista Piranesi are courtesy the Getty Research Institute, Research Library, ID no. 90-B18303 (vols. 1–3, 7, 8, 10). © 2002 The J. Paul Getty Trust. The following other sources have granted permission to reproduce illustrations in this book:

Fig. 1 Private collection, England

Fig. 5 © The British Museum, London

Fig. 6 By courtesy of the Trustees of Sir John Soane's Museum. Adam 26/163. Photo: © The Trustees of Sir John Soane's Museum; Geremy Butler Photography, London

Fig. 14 Biblioteca Comunale dell'Archiginnasio, Bologna. GDS, Disegni Autori Vari, cart. 7, n. 1190

Fig. 16 Collection Frits Lugt, Institut Néerlandais, Paris. Inv. no. 1975-P.14

Fig. 17 Avery Architectural and Fine Arts Library, Columbia University in the City of New York

Fig. 18 Fototeca Nazionale, Istituto Centrale per il Catalogo e la Documentazione, Ministero per i Beni e le Attività Culturali, Rome

Fig. 19 The Pierpont Morgan Library, New York. 1966.11:51

Fig. 20 Avery Architectural and Fine Arts Library, Columbia University in the City of New York

Fig. 22 Staatliche Museen zu Berlin. Kunstbibliothek, Preussischer Kulturbesitz, Hdz 134r. Photo: Dietmar Katz, Berlin

Fig. 23 © The British Museum, London. Prints and Drawings Collection, inv. no. 1908-6-16-44

Fig. 25 Photo: Bibliothèque Nationale de France, Paris

Fig. 26 Photo: © A. F. Kersting, London. G.16445

Index

Page references to illustrations are in italic.

Académie de France à Rome, 3, 5, 16
Accademia Colombaria (Florence), 17
Accademia dell'Arcadia (Rome), 5
Accademia Etrusca (Cortona), 17
Adam, James, British order of, 41, *42*, 75n.86, 109
Adam, Robert, 14, 41, 63n.28; Etruscan dressing room by, *55*, *56*; and Piranesi's *Il Campo Marzio*, 25, 27; Piranesi's influence on designs of, 51, *55*, 79n.107; tomb in Via Appia fantasy, *12–13*, 16, 64n.33; on Tuscan order, 40
Albani, Alessandro, Cardinal, 30, 70n.61
Albano, Lago. *See* Lago Albano
Algarotti, Francesco, 101, 145
Le antichità romane (Piranesi), 9–10, 14–16, 145; influence on British architects, 14; plates in, *12–13*, *14*
The Antiquities of Athens (Stuart and Revett), 16, 147
Antiquus Bivii Viarum Appiae (Piranesi), *12–13*, 14, 16
"An Apologetical Essay in Defense of the Egyptian and Tuscan Architecture" (Piranesi). See *Diverse maniere d'adornare i cammini, ed ogni altra parte degli edifizj*
Appartenenze d'antiche terme con scale che conducono alla palestra, e al teatro (Piranesi), *28–29*, 33
Aqua Julia (Rome), castellum of, 123–24
aqueducts, Roman, Piranesi on, 119–23
archaeology: and challenges to classical design, 1; at Etruscan sites, 17–21; impact on Piranesi, 2, 9; Piranesi's fantasies based on, *12–13*, 14; Piranesi's treatises on, 24
architraves: debate on, in "Parere su l'architettura," 105; in Tuscan architecture, 120
Aristophanes, 149
Aventine church. *See* Santa Maria del Priorato
Avery Architectural and Fine Arts Library (New York), Piranesi's drawings for the Lateran Basilica at, 35, *36*

Bank of England (London), Soane's designs for, *58*
Barry, James, *55–57*
Bélanger, François-Joseph, 51, *53*
Benedict XIV, 78n.100
Bernini, Gian Lorenzo, 40, 107
Bianchi, Giuseppe Antonio, 72n.70
Bianconi, Giovanni Lodovico, 57, 65n.41
Biblioteca Comunale dell'Archiginnasio (Bologna), Piranesi's drawing at, *31*, 33
Blackfriars Bridge (London), 14
Blondel, Jacques-François, 14, 40
La Bocca della Verità (Rome), *22–23*, 24
Borromini, Francesco, 35, 40, 72n.68; critique of, 107; design for Lateran Basilica, 72n.70; influence on Piranesi, 37, 44
Bottari, Giovanni Gaetano, 5
British architects, Piranesi's influence on, 14, 27, 51, 79n.107
British Museum (London), Piranesi's drawing at, 48, *50*, 51
British order (James Adam), 41, *42*, 109
Buonarotti, Filippo, 21
Burke, Edmund, 55
Byres, James, 21, 51, 66n.46

Caffè degli Inglesi (Rome), Piranesi's decorations for, 37, 74n.78
Calvesi, Maurizio, 58, 78n.100, 82n.125
Il Campo Marzio della Roma antica (Piranesi), 25–33; aerial reconstructions in, *26*, 33; dedication of, 27–30
Campus Martius (Rome), Piranesi's speculative reconstruction of, 25–33, *26*

capital(s): debate on, in "Parere su l'architettura," 105; Ionic, *22–23,* 24; Sphinx, *50,* 51, 78n.103. *See also* order(s)
Capitolium (Rome), 87
capriccio (fantasy), Piranesi's use of, 9, 33. *See also* fantasies
Carceri (Piranesi), 9, 61n.18, 82n.124; "The Drawbridge," *8;* "The Man on the Rack," *32,* 33
Carceri d'invenzione (Piranesi). See *Carceri*
Casino di Pio IV (Vatican), 40
Castel Gandolfo: aqueduct at, 119; papal residence at, 37
Caylus, Anne Claude Philippe de Tubières, comte de, 35
Challe, Charles Michel-Ange, 5
Chambers, William, 14; on Piranesi, 63n.25
Charlemont, James Caulfeild, Earl of, 10
chimneypieces: Bélanger's design for, *53;* Piranesi's designs for, 51, *52*
Chiusi, Etruscan tombs at, 21, 51, 152
Cicero, Marcus Tullius, 98, 144
Circus Maximus (Rome), Piranesi's archaeological fantasy of, 14
Clement XII, 78n.100
Clement XIII, 16, 35, 37, 45, 71n.66
Cloaca Maxima (Rome), 87
Coke, Thomas, First Earl of Leicester, 17
Collegio plan (Piranesi), 5, *7,* 27
column(s): debate on, in "Parere su l'architettura," 105; Marcus Aurelius's, 113; Trajan's, *43,* 44, 113
Comédie-Française (Paris), 9
Cordemoy, Jean-Louis, abbé de, 16
Corinth, sack of, 93
Corneto (Tarquinia), Etruscan tombs at, 21, 51, 151
Correggio, 100
cuccagna (festival contest), 99, 145

Dance, George, the Younger, 14, 63n.27; Piranesi's influence on, 51, 79n.107
Dawkins, James, 70n.59
De architectura (Vitruvius), 1, 16, 95, 104–5, 120–21, 144, 145, 146–47, 148–49
"Della introduzione e del progresso delle belle arti in Europa ne' tempi antichi" (Piranesi), 40, 51; chapter opening of, *129;* text of, 115–24
Della magnificenza ed architettura de' romani (Piranesi), 16–24; discussed in "Parere su l'architettura," 103, 106; plates in, *18–19, 20, 22–23;* references to Etruscan architecture in, 21
Dempster, Thomas, 17
Descrizione e disegno dell'emissario del Lago Albano (Piranesi), 24, 149; critique of, 119; excerpts from, 119–23
de Wailly, Charles, 5, 9, 68n.55
Dio, Cassius, 119, 148
Dionysius of Halicarnassus, on Etruscans, 90, 143
Diverse maniere d'adornare i cammini, ed ogni altra parte degli edifizj (Piranesi), 51–55, *52;* dedication of, 73n.73; influence of, 79n.107
Domitian, 119
Doric order: in Graeco-Roman debate, 105, 116; Lodoli on, 21; Piranesi's diagrams of, *20;* Tuscan order compared with, 40
"The Drawbridge" (Piranesi), *8*

Egyptian art, and Piranesi's designs, 51, 54, 79n.108
emissarium. *See* Lago Albano
Encyclopédie (Diderot and d'Alembert), 145
Enlightenment: neoclassical movement in, 1; Rome as major center of, 3
Erasmus, Desiderius, 149
Essai sur l'architecture (Laugier), 16, 146
Etruscans: Adam's designs inspired by, 55, *56;* archaeological discoveries and, 17–21; earliest discussions of, 17; Lodoli's advocacy for, 2; Mariette's claims regarding, 35, 90–91; Piranesi's defense of, 54, 88; Piranesi's interest in, 21; relief patterns invented by, Piranesi on, 45, 51, 76n.91, *132–34;* Roman civilization, origins of, and, 17, 90–91, 115–24
Eusebius of Caesarea, 117, 147–48
evolutionary theory of architecture, 30
experimental design, Piranesi's, 2, 3, 9

fantasies, Piranesi's: archaeological, *12–13,* 14; architectural, 2, 3, 9, *11,* 14, *31,* 33, *49, 50, 127, 128, 131, 135–41*
Freemasonry, Piranesi and, 48, 78n.100
Frémin, Michel de, 16
French architects, Piranesi's influence on, 5–9, 27, 51, 79n.107
furniture, Piranesi's designs for, *52,* 54, 80n.111

Gazette littéraire de l'Europe: on Adam's design, 109; Mariette's letter in, 33, 35, 40, 87–101; Piranesi's attacks on, 109, 118–24
Giobbe, Nicola, 3–5
Giovio, Paolo: *Dialogo dell'imprese militari et amorose,* 149–50
Gori, Antonio Francesco, 21, 46, 90, 121, 142, 149
Graeco-Roman debate, 1; "Della introduzione e del progresso delle belle arti in Europa" and, 115–24; *Della magnificenza ed architettura de' romani* and, 16; "Osservazioni sopra la lettre de Monsieur Mariette" and, 87–101; "Parere su l'architettura" and, 102–14; Piranesi's introduction to, 2; questions of aesthetics and style in, 30
Grand Tour, 3, 9, 41
Greek art, simplicity as virtue in, 30, 35. *See also* Graeco-Roman debate
Greek Revival: restraint in taste associated with, 35; supporters of, 16–17; Winckelmann's writings and, 30
Gualtieri, Niccolo, 54
Guarnacci, Mario, 21

Hadrian, 95; villa of, and Piranesi, 27, 69n.57
Hamilton, Sir William, 21
Herodotus, on Etruscans, 90, 142–43
Hollis, Thomas, 54, 80n.109
Horace, 90, 92, 97, 99, 107, 144, 147

***Ichnographiam Campi Martii Antiquae Urbis* (Piranesi),** 25–27, *26*
Invenzioni capric di carceri (Piranesi). See *Carceri*
The Investigator, Number 332 (Ramsay), 16, 65n.38
Ionic capitals, Piranesi's comparison of Roman and Greek, *22–23,* 24
Italy: contemporary design in, Piranesi's influence on, 79n.107; fine arts in, Piranesi on, 115; patriotic movement in, 17. *See also* Roman civilization; Rome; Venice

Jenkins, Thomas, 21, 51, 66n.45
Jones, Thomas, 74n.78

Körte, Werner, 59n.1
Kunstbibliothek (Berlin), Piranesi's drawing at, 48, *49*

Lago Albano, emissarium of: Piranesi's discussion of, 24, 87, 119–23; Piranesi's image of, *18–19,* 21
Lantern of Demosthenes. *See* Monument of Lysikrates
Lateran Basilica (Rome), 3; Borromini's designs for, 72nn.68, 70; Piranesi's designs for, 35–37, *36,* 72n.67
Latin, Piranesi's knowledge of, 77n.96
Laugier, Marc-Antoine, 16, 30, 146
Ledoux, Claude-Nicolas, ix, 27
Legrand, Jacques Guillaume, 71n.66
Le Lorrain, Louis-Joseph, 5
Le Roy, Julien-David: Piranesi's quotations from, 21, *22–23,* 47, 67n.50, 152–53; *Les ruines des plus beaux monuments de la Grèce,* ix, 16–17, 147, 152–53; on Tuscan order, 40
Ligorio, Pirro, 27, 40, 45
literature: ornament in, compared with architecture, 112; Piranesi's influence on, 58, 82n.124
Livy, 87, 142
Lodoli, Carlo, 2, 25, 67n.48; influence on Piranesi, 21; and Vico, 68n.53
Lucchesi, Matteo, 2
Lumisden, Andrew, 68n.56

Maffei, Scipione, 2, 17
Magic Lantern, 94, 144
Magistrato delle Acque (Venice), 2
"The Man on the Rack" (Piranesi), *32,* 33
Marcus Aurelius, column of, 113
Mariette, Pierre-Jean, 33, *34,* 71n.64; letter in *Gazette littéraire de l'Europe,* 33–35, 71n.64, 87–101; Piranesi's response to, 40, 87–101, 113–14, 118–24
Masonic symbols, in Piranesi's etchings, 48, 78n.100
Mausoleo antico eretto per le ceneri d'un imperadore romano (Piranesi), *4,* 5
Memmo, Andrea, 67n.48
Michelangelo, 100
Milizia, Francesco, 57
Montesquieu, Charles de Secondat, baron de, 102, 112, 145
Monument of Lysikrates (Lantern of Demosthenes) (Athens), *22,* 94, 144
Mummius, Lucius, 93
Mylne, Robert, 14, 33, 63n.26, 70n.59

Natoire, Charles-Joseph, 72n.67
neoclassicism, 1; French, Piranesi's influence on, 5–9, 27, 55

Nero, 95; so-called Nymphaeum of, *15*, 16, 27
Newgate Prison (London), 14
Nulty, Matthew, 44, 76n.89, 151
Nymphaeum of Nero (Rome), Piranesi's reconstructed plan of, *15*, 16, 27

***Observations on the Letter of Monsieur Mariette* (Piranesi).** See *Osservazioni sopra la lettre de Monsieur Mariette*
"On the Introduction and Progress of the Fine Arts in Europe in Ancient Times" (Piranesi). *See* "Della introduzione e del progresso delle belle arti in Europa ne' tempi antichi"
Opere varie di architettura (Piranesi), 5; plates in, *6, 7, 28–29*
"Opinions on Architecture" (Piranesi). *See* "Parere su l'architettura"
order(s), architectural: British, 41, *42*, 109; discussion of, in "Parere su l'architettura," 108–10. *See also* capital(s); Doric order; Tuscan order
ornament, role in architecture, debate concerning, 40; in "Osservazioni sopra la lettre de Monsieur Mariette," 98–100; in "Parere su l'architettura," 102–14
Osservazioni sopra la lettre de Monsieur Mariette (Piranesi), 40–51, 76n.93; colophon of, 44, *130;* plates of Etruscan friezes in, 51, *132–34;* plates of imaginary compositions in, 45–48, *135–41;* text of, 87–124; title page of, 40, *125;* unexecuted compositions for, 48–51, *49, 50,* 77n.94; vignettes in, 44–45, *126–31*
Osterley Park House (Middlesex, London), Robert Adam's designs for, 55, *56*
Ovid: *Metamorphoses,* 47, 78n.98, 152

Palazzo Branconio dell'Aquila (Rome), 45
Palazzo Senatorio (Rome), Piranesi's decorative schemes for, 37, 73n.73
Palladio, Andrea, 3, 57; Palladian design, 14, 27, 45, 104
"Parere su l'architettura" (Piranesi), 2, 40–44; chapter opening of, 45, *127;* chapter tailpiece of, 45, *128;* plates of imaginary compositions for, 45–48, *135–41;* text of, 102–14; unexecuted compositions for, 48–51, *49, 50*
Parte di ampio magnifico porto (Piranesi), 5, *6, 57*
Passeri, Giovanni Battista, 21
Patrocles, on Etruscans, 90, 143
pensionnaires, at Académie de France à Rome, 3, 5, 16
Perrault, Claude, 95, 144
Peruzzi, Baldassare, 40, 45
Peyre, Marie-Joseph, 5, 9, 68n.55
Pianta di ampio magnifico collegio (Piranesi), 5, *7*, 27
Pierpont Morgan Library (New York), Piranesi's drawing at, 37, *39*
Piranesi, Giovanni Battista, *xii,* 1–2; archaeological fantasies of, *12–13,* 14; archaeological investigation and, 2, 9; architectural fantasies of, 2, 3, *9, 11,* 14, *31,* 33; Etruscan designs and, 21, 45, 51, 54, 76n.91, 88, *132–34;* first polemical activity of, 10; formative years of, 2–9, 25; furniture designs of, *52,* 54, 80n.111; and Graeco-Roman debate, 2, 16; influence on British and French architects, 5–9, 14, 27, 51, 79n.107; legacy and reception of, 55–59; obituary of, 57, 65n.41; pseudonym of, 5; *veduta,* development of, and, 2, 3, 24. *See also specific works*
Pliny the Elder, 92–93, 143–44
Polanzani, Felice: *Jo. Bap. Piranesi Venet. Architectus, xii*
Portici tirati d'intorno ad un foro con palazzo regio (Piranesi), 33
Prima parte di architetture, e prospettive (Piranesi), 3–5, *4,* 35
Principj di una scienza nuova (Vico), 25, 150
prisons. See *Carceri*

Quatremère de Quincy, Antoine-Chrysostome, 57–58
Quirinal Palace (Rome), Piranesi's decorative schemes for, 37

Ramsay, Allan: influence on Piranesi, 40; *The Investigator, Number 332*, 16, 65n.38; tomb in Via Appia fantasy, *12–13,* 16, 64n.33
Raphael, 45, 100
Rappresentasi nella figura I il Ninfeo, di Nerone (Piranesi), *15,* 16
rationalist viewpoint: in Graeco-Roman debate, 1, 30; in "Parere su l'architettura," 102–14; Piranesi's ridicule of, 41, 44
Revett, Nicholas, 16, 147
Rezzonico, Abbondio, 37, 73n.73

Rezzonico, Carlo. *See* Clement XIII
Rezzonico, Giovanni Battista, Cardinal, 35, 37, 54, 73n.73
Roman civilization, Etruscan roots of, 17, 90–91, 115–24
Romanticism, Piranesi's influence on, 82n.124
Rome: Piranesi's formative years in, 3–9. *See also* Graeco-Roman debate; Roman civilization; *specific architectural landmarks*
Rovine del Castello dell'Acqua Giulia (Piranesi), 24
Les ruines des plus beaux monuments de la Grèce (Le Roy), ix, 16–17, 147, 152–53
Ryckius, Theodore, 90
Rykwert, Joseph, 47, 58, 77n.93

Sade, Donatien Alphonse François, marquis de, 57
Saint-Aubin, Augustin de: *P. J. Mariette,* 34
Sallust: *Bellum Igurthinum,* 47–48, 78n.99, 153
Salvi, Nicola, 3, 5
Santa Maria del Priorato (Rome), Piranesi's designs for, 37, *38, 39,* 44, 45; criticism of, 57
Scalfurotto, Giovanni, 2
Schemata Emissarii Lacus Albani (Piranesi), *18–19,* 21
Septimius Severus, Lucius, 68n.54
Severan Marble Plan (Rome), 25, 68n.54
Severus Alexander, 95
simplicity, as virtue: in Greek art, 30, 35; Piranesi's ridicule of, 41, 44
Sir John Soane's Museum (London), Piranesi's drawings at, *11,* 14
slaves, Greek, and Roman art, 95–97, 98
Smuglewicz, Franciszek, 21
Soane, Sir John, and Piranesi, 27, 58, 82n.123. *See also* Sir John Soane's Museum
Society of Antiquaries (London), 45, 54, 76n.90, 151
Somerset House (London), 14
Sphinx capital, *50,* 51, 78n.103
Stevens, Edward, 63n.25
Strabo, 90, 143
Stuart, James, 16, 147
Suetonius, 119, 148

Tafuri, Manfredo, 9, 40, 58, 82n.125
Tarquinia. *See* Corneto
Tarquinius Superbus, Lucius, 121
Temanza, Tommaso, 2
Temple of Divus Claudius (Rome). *See* Nymphaeum of Nero
Templum Pacis (Rome), 68n.54
Terence: *Eunuchus,* 46, 77n.96, 152
Tiseio, Salcindio (Piranesi's pseudonym), 5
topographical view. See *veduta*
Trajan's Column (Rome), 44; discussed in "Parere su l'architettura," 113; Piranesi's engraving of, *43,* 76n.88
triglyphs, debate on, in "Parere su l'architettura," 105
Trofei di Ottaviano Augusto (Piranesi), 9
Trofeo o sia magnifica colonna coclide di marmo (Piranesi), *43,* 44
Tuscan order: debate on, 40; Piranesi on, 21
Tuscans: architecture of, 120–21; impact on Romans, 95. *See also* Etruscans

Valentinian, 95
Vanvitelli, Luigi, 5, 37
Vasari, Giorgio, 17
Vasi, Giuseppe, 3, 145
veduta (topographical view), Piranesi's development of, 2, 3, 24
Veduta del prospetto principale della Colonna Trajana (Piranesi), *43,* 44, 76n.88
Vedute di Roma (Piranesi), 9
Venice, Piranesi's formative years in, 2, 25
Via Appia (Rome), Piranesi's archaeological fantasy of, *12–13,* 14, 16
Vico, Giambattista, 17, 68n.53; influence on Piranesi, 25, 150–51
Villa Borghese (Rome), 78n.103
Virgil: *Aeneid,* 96–97
Vitruvius: *De architectura,* 1, 16, 95, 104–5, 120–21, 144, 145, 146–47, 148–49; violations of conventions of, 33
Vogt-Göknil, Ulya, 61n.18
Volterra, reservoir at, 121

Walpole, Horace, 57
Winckelmann, Johann Joachim, ix, 5, 30, 35, 57, 147
Wittkower, Rudolf, 59n.1, 77n.96
Wood, Robert, 70n.59
Wyatt, James, 55

Zanetti, Anton Maria, 46

Observations on the Letter of Monsieur Mariette; with Opinions on Architecture, and a Preface to a New Treatise on the Introduction and Progress of the Fine Arts in Europe in Ancient Times
Giovanni Battista Piranesi
Introduction by John Wilton-Ely
Translation by Caroline Beamish and David Britt

John Wilton-Ely was educated at Cambridge University and the Courtauld Institute of Art, and is Professor Emeritus in the History of Art at the University of Hull, England. His teaching and research focus on the visual arts of eighteenth-century Europe, with particular emphasis on the Anglo-Italian world of the Grand Tour. He has curated several international exhibitions, and he is the author of the definitive works on Piranesi, including *Giovanni Battista Piranesi* (1978), *The Mind and Art of Giovanni Battista Piranesi* (1978), *Piranesi Architetto* (with Joseph Connors, 1992), *Piranesi as Architect and Designer* (1993), *Giovanni Battista Piranesi: The Complete Etchings* (1995), and *Piranesi, Paestum and Soane* (2002). He was elected a Fellow of the Society of Antiquaries of London in 1976.

Caroline Beamish has translated an array of essays, exhibition catalogs, and books from French and Italian. Among her published translations are *Le Corbusier: Architect, Painter, Poet* by Jean Jenger (1996), *Dress in France in the Eighteenth Century* by Madeleine Delpierre (1997), and *Europe and Islam* by Franco Cardini (2001).

David Britt graduated from Cambridge University with a degree in French and German in 1961. He was an editor of art books at Thames and Hudson in London for more than twenty years and a full-time freelance translator from 1987 until his death in January 2002. His translations in the Getty Research Institute's Texts & Documents series include volumes by Friedrich Gilly, Jean-Nicolas-Louis Durand, and Aby Warburg.

Texts & Documents
A Series of the Getty Research Institute Publications Program

In Print

Otto Wagner, *Modern Architecture: A Guidebook for His Students to This Field of Art* (1902)
Introduction by Harry Francis Mallgrave
ISBN 0-226-86938-5 (hardcover), ISBN 0-226-86939-3 (paper)

Heinrich Hübsch, Rudolf Wiegmann, Carl Albert Rosenthal, Johann Heinrich Wolff, and Carl Gottlieb Wilhelm Bötticher, *In What Style Should We Build? The German Debate on Architectural Style* (1828–47)
Introduction by Wolfgang Herrmann
ISBN 0-89236-199-9 (hardcover), ISBN 0-89236-198-0 (paper)

Nicolas Le Camus de Mézières, *The Genius of Architecture; or, The Analogy of That Art with Our Sensations* (1780)
Introduction by Robin Middleton
ISBN 0-89236-234-0 (hardcover), ISBN 0-89236-235-9 (paper)

Claude Perrault, *Ordonnance for the Five Kinds of Columns after the Method of the Ancients* (1683)
Introduction by Alberto Pérez-Gómez
ISBN 0-89236-232-4 (hardcover), ISBN 0-89236-233-2 (paper)

Robert Vischer, Conrad Fiedler, Heinrich Wölfflin, Adolf Göller, Adolf Hildebrand, and August Schmarsow, *Empathy, Form, and Space: Problems in German Aesthetics, 1873–1893*
Introduction by Harry Francis Mallgrave and Eleftherios Ikonomou
ISBN 0-89236-260-X (hardcover), ISBN 0-89236-259-6 (paper)

Friedrich Gilly: Essays on Architecture, 1796–1799
Introduction by Fritz Neumeyer
ISBN 0-89236-280-4 (hardcover), ISBN 0-89236-281-2 (paper)

Hermann Muthesius, *Style-Architecture and Building-Art: Transformations of Architecture in the Nineteenth Century and Its Present Condition* (1902)
Introduction by Stanford Anderson
ISBN 0-89236-282-0 (hardcover), ISBN 0-89236-283-9 (paper)

Sigfried Giedion, *Building in France, Building in Iron, Building in Ferroconcrete* (1928)
Introduction by Sokratis Georgiadis
ISBN 0-89236-319-3 (hardcover), ISBN 0-89236-320-7 (paper)

Hendrik Petrus Berlage, *Thoughts on Style, 1886–1909*
Introduction by Iain Boyd Whyte
ISBN 0-89236-334-7 (paper)

Adolf Behne, *The Modern Functional Building* (1926)
Introduction by Rosemarie Haag Bletter
ISBN 0-89236-364-9 (paper)

Aby Warburg, *The Renewal of Pagan Antiquity: Contributions to the Cultural History of the European Renaissance* (1932)
Introduction by Kurt W. Forster
ISBN 0-89236-537-4 (hardcover)

Alois Riegl, *The Group Portraiture of Holland* (1902)
Introduction by Wolfgang Kemp
ISBN 0-89236-548-X (paper)

Walter Curt Behrendt, *The Victory of the New Building Style* (1927)
Introduction by Detlef Mertins
ISBN 0-89236-563-3 (paper)

Jean-Nicolas-Louis Durand, *Précis of the Lectures on Architecture* (1802–5) with *Graphic Portion of the Lectures on Architecture* (1821)
Introduction by Antoine Picon
ISBN 0-89236-580-3 (paper)

Karel Teige, *Modern Architecture in Czechoslovakia and Other Writings* (1923–30)
Introduction by Jean-Louis Cohen
ISBN 0-89236-596-X (paper)

In Preparation

Carl Gustav Carus, *Nine Letters on Landscape Painting, Written in the Years 1815–1824; with a Letter from Goethe by Way of Introduction* (1831)
Introduction by Oskar Bätschmann
ISBN 0-89236-674-5 (paper)

Gottfried Semper, *Style in the Technical and Tectonic Arts; or, Practical Aesthetics: A Handbook for Technicians, Artists, and Friends of the Arts* (1860–63)
Introduction by Harry Francis Mallgrave
ISBN 0-89236-597-8 (hardcover)

Johann Joachim Winckelmann, *The History of the Art of Antiquity* (1764)
Introduction by Alex Potts
ISBN 0-89236-668-0 (paper)

Julien-David Le Roy, *The Ruins of the Most Beautiful Monuments of Greece* (1770)
Introduction by Robin Middleton
ISBN 0-89236-669-9 (paper)

Designed by Bruce Mau Design Inc.,
Bruce Mau with Chris Rowat and Daiva Villa
Coordinated by Suzanne Watson and Stacy Miyagawa
Type composed by Archetype in Sabon and News Gothic
Printed by Southern California Graphics on Centura Matte
Bound by Roswell Bookbinding

Texts & Documents
Series designed by Bruce Mau Design Inc., Toronto, Canada